MW01233763

Skip E. Lowe at home.

HOLLYWOOD GOMMORAH

Skip E. Lowe

Foreword by
Jacqueline Stallone

ISBN: 1497307260
ISBN 13: 9781497307261

For Mother, Aunt Sadie and Sam Silvers, my first agent
Special thanks to Harold and Jan Katz and Jacqueline Stallone

CONTENTS

FOREWORD

Don't Call Him Skippy

I've known Skip for over 30 years, ever since I moved from Las Vegas to Los Angeles around the time my son starred in a low-budget movie you may remember, Rocky. Skip, who hates being called "Skippy," has invited me to appear on his long-running talk show many times, and we always have a ball!

So when my dear friend asked me to write the Foreword to *Hollywood Gommorah*, I was happy to oblige even before I read the delightful and disturbing prepublication manuscript.

His mordant wit and knowledgeable references to Macbeth, James Joyce and Dorothy Parker surprised and impressed me. A real-life Zelig, Skip has known major icons of the 20th century. Salvador Dali, Tennessee "call me Tom, Skip" Williams, Paul Robeson, James Dean, numbered among his friends and intimate acquaintances.

I'd kill to get my hands on Skip's Rolodex! His eyewitness accounts are often hilarious, sometimes bittersweet, a few tragic. Eddie Fischer forlornly hanging out on the set of Cleopatra in Rome while his wife,

Elizabeth Taylor, ignores him and openly carries on with Richard Burton. When Skip asks the former Top Ten pop star, "What are you up to these days?", Fischer says, "I used to be a singer."

Among these pages you'll also find Paul Bowles and other glitterati smoking a hookah pipe at the author-composer's home in Tangier in the late '50s. James Dean taking a literally cheesy shower with Skip. If Psycho's shower scene terrified you, Skip's real life version will also haunt you – or at the very least, leave a bad taste in your mouth. Then there's a blind-drunk Montgomery Cliff sharing quality time with the author. David Carradine using his Kung Fu skills on Skip and a trans-vestite streetwalker. It's Hollywood Grand Guignol- style. *The Enquirer* wouldn't touch this scorcher with oven mitts.

His encounters of the lurid kind with A-Z list celebrities struck me as unlikely, to be polite. Incredulous, I almost stopped reading *Hollywood Gommorah* when I got to Skip's account of his two-year relationship with Barbara Hutton, America's Ur-poor little rich girl

But a 10-second Internet search confirmed in G-rated language Skip's NC-17 involvement with the doomed Woolworth heiress, although my friend prefers to characterize his memoir as erotica.

Intrigued, I read on. Skip's La Dolce Vita among the upper crust and not so dolce underbelly of Hollywood and international café society also checked out.

Except for his gravelly voice, Skip has always reminded me of another elfin character, Truman Capote. But unlike Skip's similar tales, Capote's alleged trysts with matinee idols were questioned in print by Capote and Skip's nemesis, Gore Vidal, and other critics. Vidal has a nasty cameo in the sulfurous first chapter.

Dead men don't wear plaid, and they can't sue, Skip said with his usual panache before I dug into this dishy buffet. *Hollywood Gommorah* exhumes dead bodies and is libel-proof. If any ambulance chasers see billable-hour dollar signs as they read, Skip has this message for them: "I'm 83, honey, and I don't care."

As a good citizen, I have to add this caveat: Adult Material. Parental discretion is advised. As a devoted grandmother, don't let your kids read this until they're 18.

Skip, I love you dearly. And I loved your 50-year stroll down memory lane and nightmare alley.

Live long and prosper, my friend, with what I'm sure will become a bestseller!

— Jacqueline Stallone, April 2014

CHAPTER ONE

La Dolce Vita, Skip E. Lowe-Style

The sad, morbidly obese old man walking his dog on Sunset Boulevard in Beverly Hills in the 1980s was not my first sighting of Marlon Brando. In the late 1940s while he was starring in *A Streetcar Named Desire*, we both happened to be living at the Park Savoy Hotel on 58th Street in Manhattan. The Savoy had seen better days – better decades in fact. When Brando and I lived there, it had become a dilapidated relic of its former grandeur.

I only used the hotel as a pied-à-terre while traveling the world for the U.S. Army U.S. Army's Special Services, entertaining our boys in (and out of) uniform. Many of the Savoy's long-term guests were struggling artists who could afford the relatively cheap hotel in pricy Manhattan.

One of my friends at The Savoy was Leonard Bernstein who was just on the cusp of becoming "Leonard Bernstein." The composer/conductor kept the door to his room at The Savoy open, and I often heard him playing the piano beautifully and loud enough to puncture an eardrum. Brando frequently visited Bernstein's room to hear him play.

The Savoy also served as a last resting place for old-time female movie stars as well as lesser knowns like comedian Wally Cox, who had

1

yet to achieve fame as the star of the hit '50s sitcom, *Mr. Peepers*. I was surprised that Wally, whom I always presumed was gay, hung out so much with the Über macho Marlon.

I suspect Marlon was bisexual and, as unlikely as it sounds, the masculine actor and the effeminate Mr. Peepers were lovers. The two of them frequented a bar on 28th Street where a Turkish belly dancer by the name of Samia performed. She was a beautiful redhead who reminded me of Rhonda Fleming. Samia and I soon became good friends, while Marlon enjoyed a different sort of relationship with the exotic dancer.

After Brando invited her up to his room at the Savoy, she later told me what happened next. "Oh, Skippy! He was so powerful...and he has a beautiful, fat cock," although Samia added that it was rather stubby. She was telling the truth because years later I saw for myself.

Brando gave her a rave review, she continued, telling her, "You're the best fuck I ever had." I didn't want to puncture my dear friend's fantasy and tell her the actor probably said that to all the girls and possibly some of the boys. But after she related a few more details of their encounter, I bet Samia had been the best. Or at least the most cooperative.

From then on, Samia and Marlon were inseparable. He went to see her perform at the club all the time. One afternoon around three, she called and asked me to go to the market and buy a cucumber, "the biggest cucumber you can find."

Before returning to the Savoy, I made sure to wash the cucumber in case it had germs. I didn't want to poison my best friend. It turned out it was lucky that I had disinfected the cucumber. When I handed it over to Samia and said goodbye, she stopped me. "Don't leave," and I didn't.

It turned out that Samia loved to "perform" on and off stage and liked an audience for both kinds of performances. Marlon didn't object to my presence either. I guess he bought into Shakespeare's belief that all the world's a stage. I'm an unapologetic voyeur, so I made the perfect audience for this very off-off-off-Broadway production in Marlon's hotel room.

I wasn't prepared for what happened after I produced the cucumber. Samia gave it to Marlon, I presumed, so he could use it on her. Instead, he got down on his hands and knees and said, "Fuck me!"

I'm glad I only washed and hadn't julienned the cucumber.

Samia was anything if not accommodating. But before following Marlon's orders, she thoughtfully lubricated the organic dildo with K-Y Jelly, a water-soluble lubricant that doesn't shred latex condoms, unlike petroleum-based products. Gay men who enjoy anal intercourse and practice safer sex rediscovered K-Y at the beginning of the AIDS epidemic. Properly lubricated condoms provide an effective barrier against HIV and other sexually-transmitted diseases, although it's not a spermicide. Unknowingly, Samia was way ahead of her time in choosing K-Y.

When she shoved the dildo in with surprising ease, it looked as though twenty cucumbers would have fit. I thought to myself, "Oh, please. You've been fucked so many times who do you think you're kidding?"

Marlon reminded me of all the Marines I had met while touring with the U.S. Army's Full Services troupe. I never met a Marine, no matter how macho and allegedly straight, who didn't enjoy being on the receiving end of anal intercourse. I know from personal experience. I loathe anal, but I've seen a lot of "straight guys" who love doing it with other straight guys. I always wondered why heterosexual men enjoyed anal until I realized it had nothing do with being gay and everything to do with getting an intensely pleasurable prostate massage. Anyone who's even been to a proctologist knows what I'm talking about. Or anyone who's had carnal knowledge of a penis or a vegetable.

Marlon evidently found the experience extremely pleasurable because he kept asking helpful Samia to use more force while penetrating him. Or as Marlon put it, "Harder, baby, harder!" After a while, I got bored with this live porn film and left while an impatient Marlon continued to demand more vigorous effort from Samia.

After allowing me to witness such a private act, Marlon trusted me and became yet another confidant. His life, he told me, had been troubled since childhood, poisoned by his alcoholic mother and others.

So it was with surprise and regret that 30 years later the patriarch of a severely dysfunctional family became one of my worst enemies and put me in fear of my life.

ॐ

In the early 1960s, Rome was known as "Hollywood on the Tiber" because so many American films were shot at the city's famous film studio, Cinecittà ("Cinema City" in Italian). Fellini did his best work during this period, classics like *La Dolce Vita* and *8 1/2*. It seemed to me that the city was populated with Fellini-esque types. A friend said I looked like someone from the director's films. Since Fellini cast so many misfits, freaks and clowns, I didn't consider the analogy a compliment.

Elizabeth Taylor and Richard Burton were shooting *Cleopatra* in Rome, and almost bankrupted 20th Century Fox with their booze and drug-fueled behavior that delayed production and sent the budget soaring. There wouldn't be a Century City today if Fox hadn't been forced to sell off its back lot as *Cleopatra*'s runaway budget threatened to shutter the studio gates.

I was in my early 20s in Rome during this vibrant time making a few bucks from voiceover work and dubbing while staying at a *pensione* to save money. During her starving writer years, Dorothy Parker, one of the few famous people I haven't known, described a spartan existence similar to mine: "All I need is a place to lay my hat and coat and a few friends."

Like a lot of Americans visiting the Eternal City, I couldn't resist checking out the set of *Cleopatra* at Cinecittà. I met pop star Eddie Fischer there through a mutual friend and returned to the set many times at Eddie's invitation.

Married to Elizabeth Taylor, he hung out on the set while his wife made love to Richard Burton on camera. (And later, as the rest of the world and I found out, off camera.) The first time I met Eddie, he was sitting on a tall stool at Cinecittà, reading *The New York Times*.

To break the ice, I said, "What's in the paper today?" Eddie was so disconsolate he ignored my question and said, "I'm lost!" He reminded me of a lost puppy waiting for his mistress to reclaim him. Eddie was kind enough to introduce me to Taylor, who spent most of her time between takes chatting and laughing with Burton. At dinner, they sat next to each other while Eddie remained alone at the other end of a long table. He seemed like he was about to cry.

When Eddie did see his wife in Rome, they argued incessantly. I didn't know the source of their disagreement until I read about it in the papers later.

"What do you do all day?" I asked him when Taylor, as usual, wasn't around.

"I used to be a singer..." Eddie was being modest. In the 1950s, he had been a teen idol with 17 Top Ten hits and a successful variety show on NBC.

Then he met and fell in love with Taylor when they co-starred in 1960's *Butterfield 8*. Taylor won the Oscar for her role as a high-end call girl. Eddie won Liz, if that's the right word. Their affair and eventual marriage ruined his career and possibly his life. Before the sexual revolution of the late 1960s, divorce was considered a major moral failure. When Eddie fell in love with Taylor on the set of *Butterfield 8*, he was married to "America's sweetheart," Debbie Reynolds. The ensuing scandal led the network to cancel Fischer's show in 1959.

A year later, after making RCA Victor millions, the record label also dropped him.

By the time I caught up with Eddie at Cinecittà, the former teen idol was 40, unemployed and had nothing to occupy himself with other than waiting forlornly for his wife to acknowledge him.

After several visits to the set, I never saw Eddie or Taylor again.

The mutual friend who introduced us was the legendary singer/ dancer Bricktop, a native of West Virginia who owned night clubs in Paris, Rome and Mexico City.

Born Ada Beatrice Queen Victoria Louise Virginia Smith in West Virginia, she inherited her fire engine red hair from her Irish father and her magnificent sultry voice from her African- American mother.

In the early 1960s, Bricktop's eponymous nightclub in Rome was the place to be. The hostess was colorful and a lot of fun. Life was a banquet for Bricktop, and everyone was invited to join the feast, including an unknown aspiring comedian like me.

She made people feel comfortable. The word was if you're sad, go to Bricktop's; she'll make you feel good.

There must have been a lot of sad people in the city – other than my friend Eddie Fischer – because everyone who was anyone eventually turned up at Bricktop's. I met Salvador Dali there; Tennessee Williams, who insisted I call him "Tom"; Paul Newman; Gregory Peck; Jayne Mansfield; the former Mrs. Tyrone Power, Linda Christian; and the odious Gore Vidal, who snubbed me after learning I was "just a comic," a profession the author despised.

Bricktop didn't care what I did for a living, and we became great friends. She was in her mid-60s and overweight by then. Like many lonely people, she had an entourage. Most of these hangers-on were handsome young Italian or black men. Others were bit actors in spaghetti Westerns.

I don't know if she had sex with any of her entourage because all I ever saw her do was give one of them an innocent kiss. I got a lot more than that from her boy toys. We used to disappear into a stall in the ladies room at Bricktop's club, where they fucked me and I sucked them off.

Bricktop may have been popular with the boys because she introduced them to beautiful women closer to their age. A pro bono pimp, as a friend fondly described her.

She loved to play the grand dame and her speaking voice was as elegant and polished as her singing. Her speech was punctuated with pet terms of endearment like, "Oh, you are definitely beautiful, darling!" The word "definitely" accompanied most of her comments.

Bricktop often hosted parties for troubled Woolworth heiress, Barbara Hutton, and invited me many times. At one dinner party, I happened to be seated next to a black woman, a jazz singer whose name I've forgotten.

Out of the blue, she interrupted the lively table conversation by saying loud enough for all the other guests to hear, "Skip, I want you to eat Bricktop's pussy..."

"Now!"

Although that was definitely not my thing, I didn't want to embarrass myself by admitting I hate pussy. And I wanted to prove that I could do it despite myself.

Someone produced a flashlight, and I crawled under the table. Except for our hostess, everyone watched as I used the flashlight to locate Bricktop's lap. Before I began to chow down, the nauseating odor of rotten fish overwhelmed me. But I persisted until I got so sick I excused myself and went to the bathroom to throw up.

The bathroom attendant gave me a tube of toothpaste but didn't have a toothbrush. I rubbed the goo on my tongue and scrubbed vigorously – to no avail. The taste of fish lingered in my mouth for weeks afterwards.

03

In the late '50s, I hung out an artists' colony in Tangier, where I met poets, novelists, composers and other artists who lived there, including the great American novelist, Paul Bowles.

A compulsive traveler like myself, Paul had left New York in the 1940's and settled in Morocco. After studying with Aaron Copland, Paul became a successful composer. Eventually, he traded in his piano for a typewriter and penned his masterpiece, *The Sheltering Sky*, and other classics.

Once in Tangier, Paul knew he'd found his inspiration. He'd tell me, "Skip, you don't have to live in the New York jungles to find stories. Tangiers is a bustling port city, and there's as much intrigue here as you could want. Besides everybody writes about New York."

Paul hosted a literary and musical salon Madame de Stäel might have envied. Poetry readings and lectures followed by heated discussions of current events and dead writers attracted luminaries like Tennessee Williams, who insisted I call him "Tom," Salvador Dali, Paul Robeson and Jean-Paul Belmondo, one of the most beautiful men I've ever known. Unfortunately, not in the Biblical sense.

I didn't have the courage or credentials to argue with our host, a who died in 1999. Paul was a philosophical and genial soul. He didn't have a telephone in his home and was a happier person for it. A rugged man and a hero for our times or any other.

He invited me to his "at homes" many times, and I became friends with the other guests, mostly writers and composers, all of them admirers of our host. The author of *The Sheltering Sky* was an intellectual snob, but he never snubbed me, unlike that minor genius, Gore Vidal. I enjoyed Paul's company and so did the rest of the devotees who turned up chez Bowles. I still laugh when I think about the most vivid image from those gatherings – Paul and friends sitting in a circle, smoking a hookah pipe filled with a substance I didn't recognize or imbibe.

Paul Robeson was my personal hero and something of a tragic figure. Black-listed because of his Soviet-affiliations, the actor/singer/athlete/law school graduate was not only an early advocate of black civil rights but gay rights as well. And he never hid in the closet.

At Bowles's soirées, Robeson, then in his early 60s, often appeared with a Swedish youth named Victor on his arm. Victor was drop-dead gorgeous and not a hustler by any means. Intent on becoming a writer himself, Paul's young Viking listened intently to the lectures and respectfully interrogated the speakers afterwards. I got the impression that

Victor also wanted to learn about life in general, and Robeson was happy to mentor his protégé.

Both men were always beautifully dressed. Robeson, of course, spoke with his *signature basso* profondo that mesmerized me. Style really mattered to the great Shakespearean actor whose Othello in London's West End in 1959, around the time I knew him, is still considered the best portrayal of the Moor of Venice in the 20th century.

Paul was not only Victor's lover but also his mentor. Robeson liked 'em young and tall, while Scandinavians, in my experience, believe "the darker the berry, the sweeter the juice."

❦

Although few remember her today, my friend Barbara Payton had lead roles in several films, most notably 1950's *Kiss Tomorrow Goodbye*, opposite James Cagney. One critic wrote that the newcomer managed to hold her own against the veteran actor.

Barbara had such striking looks she reminded me of the woman a private eye in some film noir said was so gorgeous that if you'd just been shot in the chest, you'd still turn to look at her.

But alcohol and drugs ruined Barbara's career and ravaged her supernal beauty. Only a year after working with Cagney, her time in Hollywood began its precipitous descent with *Bride of the Gorilla*, a low-budget horror movie opposite Perry Mason's Raymond Burr.

But in 1950, the 23-year-old starlet still had her looks and talent when she auditioned for the role of the dim-bulb gangster's moll in *The Asphalt Jungle*, but Marilyn Monroe landed the career-making part.

In her (brief) heyday, Barbara had affairs with Howard Hughes (who didn't?), Bob Hope and George Raft, and was married to actor Franchot Tone, among others.

By the time I met Barbara in the early 1960s, she had lost everything. And I do mean everything. In *Barbara Payton: A Memoir*, published by the prestigious University of Chicago Press in 2009, Robert Polito describes her appearance in 1962, shortly before we met. She was only 35 at the time:

Barbara Payton

"Barbara Payton oozed alcohol even before she ordered a drink" at Ye Coach & Horses, a restaurant on the Sunset Strip where the author's father tended bar.

"[She had] brassy hair; her face displayed a perpetual sunburn, a map of veins by her nose...she carried an old man's potbelly...her gowns and dresses [were] creased and spotted...She must have weighed two hundred pounds."

The author was right about the brassy hair because I dyed it platinum many times at my apartment – the same shade my hairdresser dyes mine.

Polito omitted one unlikely detail from his verbal portrait. Barbara had not only lost her looks and career, but also her teeth and didn't bother to wear dentures. Like Martha Raye, she gave great, toothless blowjobs.

"I gum 'em to death, honey," she'd tell me during one of our marathon drinking bouts.

Despite her appearance, Barbara turned tricks at Ye Coach & Horses, but she was homeless, often sleeping on park benches johns often beat her. She had no place to take her pickups, so they often ended up at my place. I didn't realize at the time that her "dates" were paying customers. Some of the clients didn't like the mattress on my bed, so I laid out a blanket on the floor where they could couple.

When I eventually discovered that she was getting paid, I felt like a madame and jokingly said to her, "I want a percentage."

On one occasion, Barbara screamed more than usual while having sex, and I was afraid a john was hurting her. So I walked into my bedroom and discovered that she was screaming in ecstasy, not terror.

I said, "You guys are having all the fun, and I'm not having any. Can I join in?"

I was wearing Chinese silk pajamas and took them off in the dark, which made it impossible for her john to realize another man was joining them. But even with the lights on, her trick probably never realized that I wasn't a woman. I don't know how many times I've gone into public restrooms, and some guy says, "Ma'am, I think you're in the wrong room."

After I'd undressed, Barbara paused and took the client's penis out of her mouth and said, "Here, kiss it." She didn't have to ask twice, or once for that matter. Like many other johns, he didn't realize I was a man and I went straight to work pro bono.

In fact, I shared many of her tricks but never charged them. That was one of the reasons I enjoyed hanging out with Barbara despite her drunken tantrums in public and at my apartment. I don't feel like I'm betraying a friend's confidences because in her ghost-written 1963 autobiography, I

Am Not Ashamed, for which she was paid a measly thousand bucks, she revealed her life as a homeless prostitute.

Barbara's brief marriage to Franchot Tone was a nightmare. The actor came from an aristocratic family in New York. An ancestor, Wolf Tone, is considered that father of the Irish Republican Army. Franchot was a classic codependent who liked trashy, abusive women.

He met his future wife in 1950 when she won first prize in a Charleston dance contest at Ciro's on the Sunset Strip. Tone fell in love with the beautiful actress on sight.

A year later, they became engaged. This infuriated her boyfriend, B-movie actor Tom Neal (*Detour*, 1945). A former amateur boxer with a frightening record of 44 wins, 41 of them by knockout, Neal assaulted Tone at Barbara's apartment and put the actor in an 18-hour coma. Tone also suffered a crushed cheekbone, a broken nose and a concussion. Plastic surgery was required to restore Tone's matinee idol looks.

Nevertheless, the classy actor honored his commitment and married Barbara. But she left him only 53 days later and returned to Neal.

I once asked her why she preferred an abusive creep like Neal instead of such a nice guy like Tone. "That fucker [Tone] had more class in his baby finger than anyone I know. I wanted to have all his babies," she said.

That didn't answer my question, and I persisted.

She finally explained that they came from different backgrounds, or as she put it, "different worlds." Tone was a socialite. Barbara grew up with alcoholic parents in Odessa, Texas, where her father's motel failed despite the influx of workers to the oil boom town.

"I'm not a great actress. Franchot was." Although he was always the perfect gentlemen, Barbara was intimidated by Tone's background and

13

achievements. "I didn't have enough class or acting talent. You had to be 'real' with Franchot," she told me.

Tom Neal offered a different kind of reality. She said she returned to Neal after leaving Tone because "he was a real man in bed...rough." Neal would slap her around while having sex. "He made me feel like a real whore," she told me, "and that's why I became one. The French got it right: men make you feel like whores."

Weeping disconsolately (and loudly) at Ye Coach & Horses, Barbara poured out her life story as she became progressively more intoxicated.

In the last year of her life, Barbara went back home and stayed with her alcoholic, abusive parents in San Diego. She died there of cardiac arrest and liver failure on May 8, 1967. A relative said that she succumbed while cradled in the arms of the mother who had mistreated her since youth.

CƷ

Dan Dailey was one of my favorite movie musical stars in the 1940s and 50s. So you can imagine my excitement when I spotted him at a grocery store on Santa Monica Boulevard right around the corner from my apartment in West Hollywood.

We were both regulars at the market, but I didn't dare approach the ruggedly handsome actor. But one day out of the blue, he introduced himself and invited me over to his home for a drink.

The very next day, Dan phoned and casually asked what I was doing. I had a lot of things to do, but I wasn't about to brush off this handsome hunk. So I said, "Nothing much. How 'bout you?"

Then Dan surprised me by saying, "I'd love to see you."

I stuttered something profound like, "Uh, uh, me too!" But instead of inviting me back to his place again, Dan asked if he could drop by mine. Trying to conceal my excitement, I said, "Sure, c'mon over!"

Within minutes he was at my door holding a large paper sack. When he opened the sack...surprise! It was filled with women's clothing! Not, as I expected, elegant designer gowns but used dresses,

Dan Dailey

nylons, and blouses he had picked up at the Army Surplus store on Santa Monica Boulevard in Hollywood.

As he admired his tawdry apparel, he asked nonchalantly, "Mind if I try these on?" I said, "Go ahead. I don't mind. Have a ball!"

He went into my bedroom and came out wearing the entire contents of his paper sack. "Tell me what you think, Skip. Be honest!"

"You look great, Dan!" I lied. Oblivious to my insincere flattery, he laughed and said, "I knew you'd like it!" But Dan was such a nice, trusting gentleman, I couldn't keep up the deception for long.

After a while I confessed that drag didn't do anything for me. I like men, I told him, and I don't like to look like a woman." Instead of being insulted by my opinion of his unlikely fetish, he laughed good-naturedly.

I laughed too, but not for the same reason. Dan was a macho guy, muscular, around six- feet three-inches tall. With the shoulders of a full-back, he looked ridiculous wearing clothes a bag lady would be embarrassed to be seen in. But Dan loved putting on a show, and I had to endure many performances at my place.

His favorite costume was a classic French maid's uniform, black stockings and shoes with heels high enough to give you a nosebleed. "I'm going to dust your apartment," he announced without waiting for an invitation.

While he dusted and mopped, he danced around and sang songs made popular by his frequent co-star, Betty Grable. I was in another room most of the time, trying to stifle a giggle about a famous male movie star cleaning my apartment. I couldn't resist asking him if he ever wore his glamorous leading lady's designer gowns when she wasn't looking. He laughed and said never. But he did admit slipping into his wife's closet and trying on a few of her things while she was away from home.

I passed the time by getting him to talk about his work with Grable while he played for a one-man audience, me.

After breaking the ice and realizing I wouldn't criticize him about his wardrobe or housekeeping, he began showing up twice a week for a couple of hours a time. After a while, my apartment was immaculate. Cheaper than a maid, I thought, although after a while his frequent visits and performances became tiresome. I've been around too many drag queens in my life professionally and didn't want one in my home, however nice this particular drag queen happened to be.

Once I got up the nerve to ask him if he were gay. "Do you like guys, Dan?" I asked tentatively. Sweet-tempered, he wasn't offended by my question the way a closeted gay man might have been. Without sound the least bit defensive, he said nonchalantly, "Oh, no! I'm not gay. I just like to dress up," like a homeless woman, I thought but didn't say out loud.

Actually, Dan wasn't a drag queen, most of whom are gay and love to dress up in public. He always wore macho attire, except at my place or his when the missus was absent. Only then, did he allow his "inner female" to emerge.

Dan and I bonded during these private modeling/cleaning appearances and became great friends. Except for inquiring about his sexual orientation, I never discussed homosexuality with him. When he brought the subject up, which was often, he would say over and over again that he was straight to prove, in his words, that he was a "real man," whatever that is, considering this particular "real man" was a real lady while he did his one-man (woman?) drag show and apartment cleaning. Although it did seem like a case of "the lady doth protest too much," I'm certain that Dan was being truthful when he insisted he was just a heterosexual male who loved women's wear.

I didn't, and after a while, despite our friendship, I thought, "I've got to stop seeing this guy!" I've met some dizzy queens in my day, but Dan was the dizziest.

We had a terrific mutual friend, Martha Raye. The three of us used to talk about the bad old days entertaining "the boys" in more ways than one in Vietnam and other armpits in Southeast Asia.

Unlike most movie stars, who are only interested in talking about themselves, Dan showed a genuine interest in my career. He used to show up at Ye Little Club in Beverly Hills when I hosted talent show cases and also at the Continental Hyatt Hotel on the Sunset Strip.

He was always beautifully dressed...like a man. ** *

David Carradine appeared on my TV talks show about a dozen times in the 1980s, and we became great friends off-camera. He often turned up at my Monday night talent showcase at Café Roma in Beverly Hills. One night, Liddy Murphy, an aspiring country western singer and standup comic from Mississippi, performed at the showcase, and David was smitten.

The secret of Liddy's success, if that's the right term, was a great sense of humor and a great set of boobs. She would come on stage, take her shoes off, then walk around, boobs flying in all directions, while the audience screamed its approval. Her jiggle act was more popular, I think, than her jokes or vocals.

After one T&A set, David invited Liddy and me (!) to a room he had rented at a Best Western Hotel. We stayed all night, drinking and talking. David loved to tell stories and so did Liddy. For a change, the evening didn't turn into an orgy. All we did was yak until David passed out and Liddy and I fell asleep.

The next morning after Liddy left, I said to David, "You didn't fuck. Why in the hell did you rent a hotel room?" David answered with a non-sequitur, or maybe not. "Do you know any trannies, Skip?"

I knew several pre-op transsexuals, and David drove me to the inter-section of Santa Monica Boulevard and Highland Avenue in Hollywood, an infamous red-light district at the time.

Today, Santa Monica Boulevard is no longer a work site for street-walkers. Typically prostitutes don't carry ID, and it used to be impos-sible to arrest multiple offenders until area merchants chipped in and bought a new, expensive software program that kept track of prostitutes' fingerprints.

Not long after that, Santa Monica Boulevard was cleared of the gay/

transvestite sex trade. Female hookers who catered to heterosexual clients on the Sunset Strip, a few blocks north of Santa Monica Boulevard, were also "sexually cleansed" by the computer program.

At Highland and Santa Monica there's a terrific donut shop where streetwalkers took coffee breaks. While David remained in the car, I went into the shop and saw a tiny Vietnamese transvestite. "Mickey" was absolutely gorgeous and well known among her peers. You never would have guessed Mickey was actually Mike. I can usually spot a guy in a dress a mile away, but Mickey could have fooled me.

I negotiated her fee, the standard $100 at the time, then took her out to meet David. Since he hadn't checked out of the room at Best Western, we all returned there.

David immediately removed his clothes but had trouble taking off his huge cowboy boots. Liddy helped him, then took a deep whiff of the boots. She wore almost nothing – a micro-miniskirt and a silk blouse with an Oriental pattern, very slutty.

Mickey giggled a lot and repeatedly applied more makeup and lipstick at the hotel. David told her to get undressed but keep her stiletto heels on. Then he removed a short rope from a bag and told her to hit him with it while she paraded around the room, nude except for her footwear.

Mickey was nearly anorexic and not very strong. While I watched but didn't participate, David kept yelling at her, "Hit me hard! C'mon, HARDER, you little bitch. You know you fuckin' like it! C'mon, hit me!"

The strangest things pop into your mind when you witness strange things. I remember thinking, "I'm glad David doesn't write his own dialogue."

Mickey eventually got into David's scene. I suspect she liked smacking around the macho star of TV's *Kung Fu*. When he grew tired of this flagellation lite, David had vanilla intercourse with her.

Out of the bedroom, David was a gentlemen. After Mickey and he finished up, David drove her back to the workplace and me to my apartment.

Some time later, David married Gail Jensen, who became his manager and my good friend. I went to their wedding at the Hollywood Roosevelt Hotel.

I didn't see David for two years after that. He turned up at my birthday party at Café Roma, where I introduced him to the audience, and he sang a couple of songs. That was his birthday present to me. I told David, "It's strange. Your father used to come to my showcases at the Hyatt all the time, and now his son is a second generation fan!"

I also thanked him for performing and said in front of the audience, "I love you, David." I don't think I would have said that if I'd known what happened after the party.

Although I had a ride home, David insisted on driving me. He carried all my birthday loot up to my apartment on the second floor and invited himself in. We opened a bottle of champagne and talked for a long time.

Finally, David loosened up enough to say, "Skip, I like you very much. You're a friend of mine. And I know you're discreet." Long pause. "Do you have any women's clothes?" I happened to have a drawer full of trashy women's clothing, and David asked me to put them on and parade around the room like the trannie two years earlier, but I didn't remove my clothes.

"God! You're perfect, Skip! You should do drag more often!"

"People automatically think I'm a woman. I don't have to do drag." He laughed when I told him about my adventures in the men's room. "It never stops," I said about people telling me

I was in the wrong restroom. "It's tiresome. I usually have a day's growth of beard. Are people blind?"

David asked me if I enjoyed dressing up. "Yes, it makes me feel like a real woman. You make me feel like a real woman, David."

"I didn't realize how beautiful you are, Skip." David must have been as blind as my restroom tormentors because I was in my 60s at the time! He was also extremely drunk by then.

Dr. Jekyll suddenly morphed into Mr. Hyde when David grabbed and shoved me up against a door. The look in his eyes terrified me.

"David, what's wrong?" "Don't worry about it..." "Why shouldn't I, David? I want you to stop this now!" "You're not stopping anything. You're going to do what I tell you." David grabbed me by the neck and began choking me. "David! I can't breathe!" "Shut up, bitch!" Ways of escape filled my mind, but I was too frightened and weak to act on them. Eventually David tired of choking and began to rape me. Although he had a long, thin, beautiful cock, it hurt like hell. After that, David mumbled something incoherent, and I finally managed to push him away. It was around 11 p.m., and I told David I had to be somewhere and fled the apartment. When I returned around 3 a.m., David was still there, passed out. The next morning we showered separately and nothing was said of the previous night's encounter.

Variations of that scene occurred several times after that at my place and at Best Western with Mickey joining us.

Years later, just before he left for Thailand to shoot a film, we had lunch at Café Roma. I read in the papers that he died in his hotel room in Bangkok. There were conflicting reports about the cause of death. After the authorities said David had been found naked, hanging from a rope in his closet, people presumed he had committed suicide. But two autopsies determined David had actually died of accidental autoerotic asphyxiation.

After his death, David's ex-wife, Marina Anderson, appeared on my talk show and insisted he had been murdered. I disagreed. Transvestite streetwalkers are practically a tourist attraction in Bangkok. I believe David hired one to choke him to intensify his orgasm. Unlike 90- pound Mickey, another trannie apparently got carried away and choked him to death. Panicking, she stole his $10,000 Rolex and other valuables. Prostitutes all over the world are notorious for ripping off their johns.

I love Gail Jensen, another ex-wife, but didn't speak to her after the accident. Marina insisted he had been murdered, then robbed.

No matter how he died, I'll always have a special place in my heart for David – and a lingering pain in my neck.

** * By now you may be wondering why I let people abuse me. Am I just some poor schmuck who thinks he deserves what he gets? Yes.

Over the years, I must have seen half a dozen therapists to cope with my freeway phobia – to no avail. I don't drive, but even when I ride in a speeding car on a freeway, I still have panic attacks that feel like my heart has exploded.

One of these therapists did help me with another problem that has followed me ever since I was gang-raped at the age of nine. (See Chapter Two, "From Hell to Hollywood.")

The psychologist told me that adult survivors of emotional or sexual abuse during childhood often suffer from a condition called codependency. After the doctor explained the term, I told him that if you look up "codependent" in a medical dictionary, you'll find a picture of me.

Survivors tend to internalize the victimizers' low opinion of their victims. We accept and even seek out abusive partners who confirm our sense of worthlessness. If people think I'm a willing or guilty participant in relationships I had with David Carradine and others, they exhibit the same cruel philosophy of "blame the victim" my father did when I was a child.

CHAPTER TWO

From Hell to Hollywood

The boy with the Betty Grable legs...

When I was six years old, clunking around in Mother's high heels, I discovered her pearls. Scads of them. I wrapped myself around and around, greased my lips with her fiery red gloss, blackened my lashes, roughed my cheeks and dove into her basket of sweet perfumes.

I looked like a bargain-basement floozy who'd been through the spin cycle, but I didn't care. While the other boys were playing football and beating the crap out of each other, I dressed up in Mother's clothes, lost in my fantasy world.

I was born Sammy Labella in Greenville, Mississippi. (In the time it takes to spell it, you could walk clear around the place and still have time to throw flapjacks on the griddle and fill you mouth with chew.) Mother, due to deliver at any moment, had decided it was the perfect time to visit her relatives down South. And I, knowing there'd be a captive audience, hatched, spit, pooped and bawled... Greenville was my first one-night stand.

Rockford, Illinois is my hometown, but it wasn't a happy start. Kids come in two styles. Boys or girls. I was somewhere in between and became the brunt of terrible jokes and worse.

Mother was Jewish. Father was born in Palermo, Sicily. His brothers owned a chain of funeral parlors in a really rough area of Brooklyn. The motto of the family business was, "You stab 'em, we slab 'em." Pop owned a prosperous fruit and vegetable market in Greenwich Village and had unbreakable rules about how a "real boy" should behave. I wouldn't and couldn't follow his rules.

A workaholic, he had no time to spare for a son who never lived up to his impossible expectations. Even before he realized what kind of child I'd turn out to be, a nurturing black lady was hired to take care of me. After the woman forgot to close the cellar door, curiosity led me, still an infant, to peek into the dark room. Then I fell down the steep flight of stairs leading to the cellar and broke my arm. After the doctor put a splint on the fracture, no one understood why I wouldn't stop screaming. Years later another doctor discovered the source of my hysteria. Untended fractures in my vertebrae had caused the scoliosis that stunted my growth, not my sexual leanings and the neighborhood's contempt.

Occasionally Mother and I'd go to New York City's Bowery to stay with Sadie Cohn, my wonderful freight-train of an aunt. A seasoned vaudevillian and hefty belter, when Sadie let loose, you could hear clear through to Brooklyn. Bigger than life, Aunt Sadie's arms and lap were my haven.

When her apartment door creaked at 4:00 A.M., I knew Uncle Louie, Aunt Sadie's squeeze, was back from his taxi route. He'd sleep a few hours, then drive me all over Manhattan, teaching me to curse the "goddamned morons" who had the effrontery to drive around in the other cars.

When Mother had determined I'd had enough fun and was shoveling down way too much of Sadie's pot roast and kugel, home we'd go.

It was painful being different, so I played by myself. In dress-up heaven, I ruled over my very own kingdom. Some days I was fiery Carmen Miranda. On others, Betty Grable with her gorgeous gams. First I'd see the stars at the movie house, then fun home and make them appear in my mirror. A failed actress, herself, Mother delighted in my shenanigans.

The day I decided to take my routines into the great open spaces of my backyard, my career as a performer was launched.

Giving shows in back of our house, the ham in me reared its curly little tail. Sammy Goldwyn of the tinker set toy set, I pitched a show tent and took on every role. I was the ticket taker, the star, and the concessionaire who sold fresh lemonade. The entry fee for my glitzy theatrical was one penny – no IOUs please, but I'd accept a movie magazine in lieu of cash.

When the show was ready to begin, I'd announce from behind a tablecloth that served as a curtain, "Ladeeeees and Gennntlemen, please take your seats and give a warm welcome for everybody's favorite, Miss Carmen Miranda!"

Then I'd wind up the Victrola and sashay out in Mother's tropical dress and a headdress of fruit, flowers and scarves. As the phonograph chimed in "I-I-I-I-I-I," the kids would shriek, and I'd begin my crazy dance and lip synch. Dancing around, I'd remember Aunt Sadie's philosophy – "Hook 'em with the first laugh, and they're yours for the rest of the show."

Jimmy Durante was also on the payroll – and aided by my emerging Jewish-Italian schnoz, he was always raring to inka dinka do. As was Mae West. I could out-boob any bosomy babe with expert bra stuffing. From flat-chested to triple D, I was a certified pro at mammary deception.

Thanks to hammy Sammy many a Hollywood hotshot appeared at my backyard big top. At nine, my contract in show business was permanently inked in the greasepaint and spotlights (the brightest 60-watt flashlights I could get my hands on) that covered my sweet baby face.

I loved performing. Free as a little cuckoo bird, fluttering all over that rickety stage, I could be whoever I wanted. If only I could have spent every hour of my childhood up on stage...

The neighborhood kids loved watching me perform. But once the show was over, they turned their backs. They had a name for me, and it wasn't the "great junior vaudevillian." It's a sad, lonely world for a kid when no one wants to come out and play because you're "peculiar." It hurt, but I pushed it down and played with the girls. Marbles, hopscotch, jump rope. I even wore short pants, while the boys were wearing knickers. I had cute little legs, and loved showing them off.

After all, you could hardly do a respectable Betty Grable if you didn't have the gams.

One day I was walking through a park when four Italian boys at least three years older than I, ran in my direction, shouting, "Come on, Sammy. Sammy, come here."

I asked what they wanted, and one of them repeated, "Come, come.

We've got something for you."

I couldn't imagine what they could have. They never gave me the time of day. Now all of a sudden they wanted to be chums? Candy? Cookies? Maybe they wanted to trade baseball cards... My innocent little thoughts went on a detour when the boys, standing under a huge looming tree, started pulling down their pants, pointing their boy-dicks at me, and shaking them wildly.

"Look, look, Sammy. It's for you. All for you. Come and get it." I stood there frozen as they walked closer... and closer. One of them grabbed me and dragged me behind the tree. Shaking and crying, I stood there as he bent me over and yanked down my pants, screaming, "Now I'm gonna give it to you good!"

"What do you mean?" I cried.

But he ignored me, spitting on his hands and spreading the spit on his organ...then working up more spit and rubbing it into his big, mean hands.

I had no idea what to expect, as he smiled down at me and slowly, powerfully, spread the saliva all over my backside and up into my anus. Then he shoved his organ between my tender back cheeks and thrust into my tiny bottom.

Over and over and over... I felt as though I were being ripped apart. I screamed, "Please don't! It hurts! It hurts bad!!!" But all he did was laugh and shove harder, faster. Brutal, savage, angry. When he was finally done, I fell in a heap, relieved that they would finally leave. But another boy came up behind him, grabbed me by the waist and raped me again from behind. While the third stood in front of my face and pulled on his penis, back and forth, until a white greasy liquid I never saw before spurted all over my face. In my eyes. In my mouth.

Finally, unable to stand on my own, I felt them drag me back up and push me around and around. And then they were gone.

I ended up in the bushes – cut, bleeding, naked, and ashamed, feeling as though my entire body had been sliced up with a butcher's cleaver.

Filled with shame, I assaulted myself: "Why did they do this? What have I done? Am I a bad person?" Catholic sin and Jewish guilt stood, one over each shoulder, glaring down at me.

As I crawled around on my hands and knees, too petrified to lift myself up, I looked down at my brand new, freshly ripped pants, feeling that I too had been tattered to shreds.

And then...I ran all the way home, raced through the screen door, into Mother's arms and broke down in tears. As details of the rape spilled out of my mouth, Mother was shocked and furious that such a thing could happen to her sweet little boy.

As she held me, sponging my shaking body, she said we'd have to see the doctor...

All I remember is a cold white office and a wrinkled old man, probing me with a plastic glove and cold stainless steel, demanding, "Now Sonny, tell me when it-"

"It hurts!" I screamed.

I was so embarrassed showing a stranger the lacerations on my "private parts." Private? They were public by now.

First the rape, then the steel probe, and then the cops, probing with their barely disguised accusations. Questions, questions, questions. I wanted to keep the mess to myself, lock it up and forget it.

No self-respecting kid wants to squeal on the neighborhood gang and "sing for the coppers." But finally, I told, and the cops threw the boys in jail.

At first, I was relieved, thinking it would disappear forever. But suddenly, everyone knew what happened to me.

"Oh, did you hear about queer little Sammy?"

I was so ashamed. The kids teased and razzed me even worse than before. Everything was my fault – I caused the rape, I threw those "sweet boys" in jail.

"Hey sissy puss. You loved it, didn't you? You know you did, little girl." And their dreadful warnings were the worst of all. "You'll never grow another inch, Sammy. Your butthole'll shrink, and you'll never be able to crap again... One day you'll let out a giant fart, and you body will explode. Boom! No more sissy Sammy!"

I started believing all the horrible things the kids were saying.

"Oh God, what if I do stop growing? Maybe they knocked my grow-button out of whack when they were shoving inside me."

I didn't know what to believe. Every day to took out my ruler to measure my height. I pleaded, "Please God, let me grow! I don't want to be a midget and end up a circus freak."

I felt so hurt and unwanted. Even the friendly nun at my school treated me with disdain. I was tainted and nothing I could do would redeem me.

Mother tried to keep the news from Daddy, but Rockford's grapevine circulated more gossip than the local paper. Pop, who played cards with the fathers of the "Park Four," decided I was entirely to blame. Calling me "Mommy's little girl" and "Sissy," he found a heavy strap and beat my bottom or, as the spirit moved him, electrical wire. Once he tied me up and smacked me with his hands "to teach you a lesson, you fairy."

When he died in 1972, Dad left me something besides physical and emotional scars – a $200,000+ inheritance. I quickly blew my entire legacy on the ponies, ponies, ponies. I rarely went to the track and placed my bets with a bookie on Santa Monica Boulevard near my apartment in West Hollywood. I still wonder if I squandered the money because I didn't want to keep anything that had once belonged to my father.

At the time I was gang-raped, it seemed there was no way to escape the continuing aftershocks of the original nightmare. Why couldn't I have just died from embarrassment and shame? I thought about running away and joining the circus. But clown routines were too much for me, and I was too tall to pass for a midget.

Just when I thought I must be forever cursed, Mother came up with the perfect solution. "Let's move, Sammy."

I was elated! Running away! And Mother running with me. I kissed her. I cried. I was done being the "park fairy."

Mother didn't want to live in Rockford anymore. Not if her "little man" wasn't happy. So we packed up everything, sneaked out in the middle of the night and caught the bus for Hollywood, California.

In 1941, Los Angeles contained acres of orange groves – and movie stars. Heaven for a Hollywood-crazy youngster like me.

It was no accident Mother chose the city of angels for her little angel heart to start over again. It was all part of Mother's plan...

Once we left Rockford, Mama started changing. No longer the kind, caring, protective comforter – suddenly a stage mother-monster took over, right there in the bus.

Cloaked in endearments, her messages began, "Sammy, dear, you've got something special, and now we're going to Hollywood to prove it." I would be Gypsy to Mother's Madame Rose. Strong-willed and bossy, like all those power-hungry women Rosalind Russell used to play, Mama was hell-bent on making her kid a star.

And me? I couldn't have loved her more.

All her life, Mother was in love with the movies, but when her career went bust before it began, she held onto the dream. When I came along, the baby of her bunch, she was a spark of talent, and decided I'd have the brightly lit career she let lapse.

Rockford's hell became Mama's excuse to move to the land where dreams came true.

My future was mapped out. There was no stopping this whirlwind from following through on her grand design...

The one thing that made the long, weary bus trip to Hollywood bearable was the thought of actually standing at the corner of Hollywood and Vine. I pictured the pavement lined, end to end with stars. Bogies and Bettys. No extras or bit players – just A list luminaries lighting the way.

One exhausting week after we'd boarded the bus, we arrived in Hollywood. Row upon row of trees – tall, skinny and topped with green bushes. Could this be paradise? Another planet?

When our rooming house turned out to be owned by Mrs. Mars, I wasn't surprised. Hollywood was its own galaxy, ruled by the plants and its very own stars.

Determined to turn me into her own little star, Mother insisted, "Sammy, you're special. You have a talent. God made you different so you could share the talent with the world."

I asked Mama if we'd get to see any stars.

"See them? Oh, Sammy, you'll be working with them. You'll touch them, smell them, become one yourself!"

This was a lot for a skinny ten year-old to swallow. But Mother taught me not to be afraid to take chances.

"You're never too small to take big, giant leaps. Sammy." Corny, but practical – that was her specialty.

When Mama finally called Dad, he was delighted she'd taken the little prissy off his hands. Not about to close up hiss profitable Italian deli, he promised to wing it to Hollywood if he got lonesome, but otherwise, he'd stay in Rockford and we had his blessing.

At first, I couldn't understand why Mother wanted everybody to have my photo. Every day we went out with my precious eight by tens.

"What are auditions?" I'd lament. "Nothing, Honey. You just stand in front of some nice people and make friends."

But every time I went on an audition, Mother stood, coaxing me from a few feet away, "Come on, Sammy. We need this part."

I didn't care about being a star, but I wanted to make Mama proud. So I pushed and pushed and gave it my all. Sometimes I felt like the most special kid on Earth. Other times I just longed to be normal.

"Okay, Kid, show us what you got. Sing for us, Sonny. Dance for us, Kid. Recite this, whistle that."

"Tap. Spin. Jump. Climb. Move stop breathe cry... soonerfastersmoother better...nownownownowowNOW!!!"

I felt like a crazy critter from the Hollywood funny farm.

Auditions uptown. Downtown. The Valley. The beach. At first it seemed all I ever did was audition. I was starting to wonder, "What exactly is the point?"

But Mama always reminded me, "You're the most special little boy in Hollywood, but those producers don't know that unless you're out there strutting your stuff."

"Well maybe they need thicker glasses, because they'd have to be blind not to see how talented I am." I always knew what Mama wanted to hear, and I gave it to her in big doses.

"That's the spirit, Honey. Don't worry, we'll knock 'em dead."

Then one day the dam burst, and suddenly I was getting movie roles. I'll never forget the thrill of finally working in a Hollywood movie. I'd seen statues at the Wax Museum, but know I'd get to work with stars that wouldn't melt in the hot lights.

In 1943's Best Foot Forward, I won my first (uncredited) role as a tap-dancing cadet, along with Tommy Dix, the film's co-star who had everyone in America cheering and singing,

"Buckle Down, Winsocki, Buckle Down." Best Foot Forward was one of Lucille Ball's first big-budget pictures after a decade as the "Queen of the B's" – as in B-movies.

I'll never forget Lucy's loopy kindness. Walking around the lot, she'd go out of her way to stop and ask me how I was doing, whether I needed any help.

After the nightmare in Rockford, her sweetness was curative, although one encounter with Miss Ball, as I always called her, was more embarrassing than flattering.

Long before her ground-breaking 1950's sitcom, everyone already loved Lucy...and Lucy loved her grappa. Polite and kind to everyone, she was also nervous about starring in a big- budget and surreptitiously took swigs from a flask concealed in her purse. The director ended up confiscating her booze because the musical was being shot on the campus of a boys' military school where alcohol was verboten.

Before she got busted by the director, she spotted me on the set and kissed my hand. It was obvious even to a thirteen-year-old like me that Lucy was high. The director had to inform his star that the she was confusing a bit player with her co-star, Tommy Dix.

In retrospect, Lucy must have been really tipsy. Tommy and I had similar facial features, but he was 19 and I was 13. He was small for his age, but I was smaller, pre-pubescent. Unless Tommy had a hormonal deficiency, he was post-pubescent by then.

Despite the case of mistaken identity, I loved the attention and told anyone who would listen, "I got kissed by a real movie star!"

A year later, in Jane Powell's first picture, Song of the Open Road, I finally snagged a role I was born to play – a fruit picker. I stood on a stepladder in my little shorts, picking those sunny fruits. The skinniest, giddiest, singing orange picker around. Hollywood called

Sam age 12

for children who were beyond cheery and could carry a tune. The harder we worked, the louder we warbled. Never complaining, content to whistle and sing till the "massuh" came home.

Talk about misguided white bread fantasies.

One sunny day in 1944, Mama and I were having lunch in the Beverly Hills Hotel's polo lounge, waiting to meet a prospective agent. I was all of 12 years old, and the lavish hotel was the place for cutting deals between sips of martinis and bites of crust-free club sandwiches.

Mother and I were sitting at a table out on the patio near the tennis courts. As I looked around, I paid little mind to the tall fellow, courtside with Katharine Hepburn, giving her pointers on her backhand.

The agent was late and I excused myself to the bathroom. Standing at a urinal, I heard a low wolf-whistle, and looked up into a familiar face. The tall tennis player was hovering over me.

His pleasantness guided me into friendly patter, "Hello little boy, how are you?" "Fine, sir," I responded, without a second thought. "What a polite young man. Your mommy must be proud of you." Just as I was about to answer, he pulled me toward him, and suddenly, I was nine again. I wanted to scream, but I couldn't even clear my throat. "Can I help you with that?" the words oozed from his leer as it devoured my penis. "No. I'm okay," I responded, backing up. And then this man with a smile glued to his face, reached out and squeezed my exposed genitals. "W-w-what are you doing?" I managed. "Oh, isn't that nice. Look at that, so pretty."

I couldn't believe how he fawned over my bite sized boyhood. I tried to pull away, but the forceful tennis player just dropped to his knees and stuffed my penis in his mouth.

"Stop that! Please stop that!!!" But he just continued. During this entire time I was staring at his hands. He was missing his right middle finger.

The thought that some little boy bit it off overwhelmed me. And suddenly I was laughing. And then, terrified, all I could do was cry.

"Ssssh!... be quiet, damnit!" I couldn't stop laughing and crying, louder and louder. "Be a good boy now. Just forget about this. You hear me? This never happened!

Understand?" And then he was gone.

I couldn't believe it. He was nearly as scared as I. Quickly I tucked myself back into my pants and ran back to Mother.

When Mama saw her hysterical baby, she wanted to know what was wrong. But I couldn't speak, so she took me in her arms and planted a clean, lovely kiss on my forehead.

Trying to act as if nothing had happened, I joined her courtside, sitting in quiet agony.

Moments later several of the perfect lovely people called out, "Bill! Bill, how nice to see you!"

That man. The man with the glued-on smile strode back among the diners to the tennis courts.

I thought, "Bill, gee that's such a normal name..."

They were whispering something..."Bill Tilden, a Wimbledon champion...many times over...tennis pro to the stars."

But the agent, Sam Silvers, had arrived, so I stood up and shook hands and resumed our lunch with all the happy, smiling people. I was quiet for the rest of the afternoon. Again I was feeling like a very odd little boy.

I wanted to tell someone, but I was frightened and ashamed. Look what had happened in Rockford. How could I talk about a man the community held in such high regard.

So, it became my secret. One of many. Working in movies was fun because it was all about make believe. The movie sets were a big playground. Instead of swings and slides. There were klieg lights and props, costumes and makeup. Everything a kid could ever want. All the actors on the set were my playmates, but make believe was also hard work, with long hours.

There was a lot of work for child actors in the '40s, and Mother made sure I tried out for all of it. I didn't have to act, just be a kid. I was short and cute, so I could play as young as necessary. I was never too proud to lick a lollipop or throw a tantrum. Knee pants and knickers were my typical wardrobe.

Monogram Pictures kept me busy, playing wrong-side-of-the-tracks hoodlums in Maurice Duke's Dead End Kids' films. A tough Brooklyn accent, and I was all set.

I can't even recall many of the movies. But I certainly remember all the Donald O'Connor ones.

Donald and Peggy Ryan were two of my classmates at the Hollywood Professional School. HPS, as we lovingly called it, was a theatrical school for you, working actors. After school, I walked down the street to Falcon's Dance Studio to study tap and fencing. Little guys like me were never up for the swashbuckling roles, but clanking around with swords trying to avoid becoming shish kebab made for an exciting workout. The Hollywood Musical College was a hoof beat away, where Professor Lungen kept our vocal cords limber. The education was fun, but it seems I was always in a classroom or a studio, with little time for plain kid stuff.

On the studio lot, everyone met in the commissary. The movie stars sat with the rest of us hoi polio, stuffing in the roast beef, pork loin, mashed potatoes and apple pie. But God forbid you should catch a star with food stuck between his caps. What lengths they'd go to hide the offending bit.

Unlike many of her counterparts, Paramount star, Betty Hutton, paid no mind to any of this. Down to earth and accessible, she was a wacky presence onscreen and off. A big contract star for many years, Betty suddenly disappeared. She'd never hidden how she hated the movie star game, and, in the end, followed the old adage that the best way to stay sane in Hollywood was to get the hell out. So when she'd had enough, live wire Betty Hutton went to live in a nunnery. Reports were that she couldn't have been happier.

No matter how many stars I worked with, I always got goose bumps meeting them in person. I had a major crush on Peggy Cummings, a beautiful young English actress. She was riding her bicycle on the back lot one day, and I managed to get up the nerve to say hello and tell her I was just starting out. She stunned my by stopping to chat with me, again and again, letting me know what a difference we all made.

It always sent me soaring when an actor I admired spoke to me. But simply peeking on the set of Forever Amber when my favorites, Linda Darnell and Cornel Wilde had their lusty passionate scenes, overwhelmed me.

For the hopelessly star struck, every day in movie land was like being on a big star safari, hunting down favorites and getting their autographs. Some days I bagged the big game. Occasionally I'd shoot myself in the foot.

Over at MGM, I loved listening to Judy Garland. If anything came from heaven, it was her angelic voice. During lunch breaks I'd sit on the sound stage, captivated. Who needed food? Her voice charged me up for days.

One evening, walking around Beverly Hills with Mother I spied Judy walking with her husband, Vincente Minnelli. All excited, I felt the ferocious-fan in me taking over.

"There's Judy, Mama! Look, look! It's Judy." I ran up, convinced she knew how much she meant to me. But before I could say anything, she started screaming hysterically, "Get out of here! Get away from me, you... you...you..!"

You'd have thought I was trying to assault her. Boy, did she scare the hell out of me. "But, I only wanted an autograph, Miss Garland." "I said get out of here...NOW!!!" she growled, shoving me, nearly knocking me over. Indeed, Judy was temperamental, but as I got older, I understood the star's need for privacy, even if it meant being rude. Since then, whenever I'd see a star coming in my direction, I'd turn away so as not to let them know I was within firing range.

Working on the Paramount lot during the filming of Unconquered, with Gary Cooper and Paulette Goddard, I watched this tantrum thrower chew out every cast and crew member in range of her spiteful barbs. I was a little pilgrim with a couple of lines, and nothing was scarier than this Hollywood queen bee, screaming and carrying on.

Miraculously, director-tyrant Cecil B. DeMille declawed Goddard, ramming her stinger right down her throat. As I watched him, I fantasized how wonderful it must feel to have that kind of control. Some called DeMille a dictator, but I admired his even-handed discipline.

Gary Cooper watched me watching, and patted me on the head. As I looked up at this towering man – so clean, straight, lean and strong, he seemed a god. But when my vision came back to eye level, I was in line with his pant zipper. He was a manly guy, but strangely, his strong self-assurance, with no interest in me, was exciting.

Still a boy, still curious, and dying to explore, I said yes when the horror film director, James Whale invited me to his home on Beverly Glen.

I can still see the mansion approaching and his hand inching toward my crotch as we rolled into the driveway. I was excited and loved the attention, but once we got inside, fear overcame my excitement. Still curious, but more scared, I sneaked out and caught a bus home. That was my closest call to a casting couch.

It was tough being a homosexual boy, back then. I had no role models, no mentoring, no gay lib. The word "gay" hadn't been coined yet. All I'd ever heard was queer, homo, fag and cocksucker.

Once, working on the set with my idol, Betty Grable, I overheard her call out, "Oh, Mommy, Mommy. Look! Here comes another little Hollywood queen-boy."

I just smiled, too mortified to say anything. When I got older, anger would overwhelm me and I spoke out. But then I mollified myself, "How can I be mad? After all, I'm not just a fan, I want to be Betty Grable – all decked out in those million dollar legs!"

Mother was close at hand on all the shoots. Even if child labor laws hadn't required it, she still would have been just a breath away. The directors weren't crazy about the "pushy dame" who was always making life difficult for them, but it was comforting for me to look out beyond the cameras and see her nearby, ready to protect her baby chick.

But Mother couldn't be my shadow all the time, and she wasn't able to shelter me from the big mean world that lurked just outside the studio gates. Bill Tilden might have given me a bitter taste of that seamy side, but I wasn't about to let one deranged tennis pro stop me from roaming around Hollywood and exploring.

One day, after a heavy studio schedule, I walked to the Hollywood Theater to catch a movie. I'd headed upstairs to the bathroom, when I sensed someone trailing me. As I stepped up to the urinal, an older guy moved to the one adjacent and began masturbating. As my startled eyes wandered in his direction, he slapped me with handcuffs.

"I'm taking you to jail, you little queer." "Jail!!?" I couldn't believe I was being arrested by a masturbating cop. "You liked looking at my pee-pee didn't you, girlie?" the guy snorted. "Are you crazy? You were showing it off to me!!" The bastard just grinned, "It doesn't matter, Missy. You're a fucking fairy, and it's my job to put a net over you sickos." I was scared to death as he slammed me into the squad car, and hauled me into the precinct. How naïve I was. I didn't know anything about vice cops.

That was standard procedure in those days.

When we got to the station, I was on the verge of angry tears. But I held it all in and yelled to everyone, "He tricked me. He shook his thing at me. It was hard not to look, the way he was wiggling himself!"

The cops just laughed and called me "queer" and "faggot," and the more derisive they got, the angrier I became.

Finally Mother came running in. I blurted out what had happened and she was furious. The arresting officer knew better than to fight this irate woman.

"OK, young man," he sneered ironically. "just go home and we'll forget everything." Mother hauled me out of there, figuring anything was liable to pop out of my mouth. The cops were like a jovial lynching party and she wasn't taking any chances.

A half century later I was interviewing Fred Otash on my television show. A retired Hollywood cop, he'd just written a book bout his famous cases, like Lana Turner and John Belushi. When he laughed that he first joined the force as a vice cop, "hauling in fairies from the Hollywood Theater," I was incredulous.

Shaking all over, I asked, "You ever haul in Sammy Labella, a skinny little kid who yelled at the cops till they sent him home with his mother?"

Otash thought for a moment. "Labella...Labella Sounds familiar. He and his mother were raising Cain... yeah, I remember that little fairy. But ya seen one, ya seen 'em all. Know what I mean, Skip"?

I turned red and shouted, "Well, I'm that little fairy you tricked."

Talk about speechless, "Uh...well...that was my job. I took in d-d-dozens of queers every day, you have to understand-"

I'd heard enough. I lunged at Otash, ready to kick him off the set.

But you now what? We got to talking after the show and he eventually apologized. And the greatest
miracle of all – we actually became
good friends after that.

Imagine, the fairy and the
homophobic vice cop. A match
made only in Hollywood.

Radio was in its glory days. I
didn't do a lot, but the people I got
to work with were extraordinary.
And I loved working on a show
that glued the listener to the set to
play along with us, using his own
imagination.

Working with Lionel Barrymore
in The Mayor of the Town, I found
a kind man, who brought me Coca
Colas and sandwiches between

Sam Labella –MGM Studios

rehearsals. He taught me to enunciate and sat and helped me with my
lines. Al Jolson showed me acting and speech techniques, as did Agnes
Moorehead, a tough, tough lady, who was exceptionally kind and helpful
to children.

I also had the honor, after years of imitating him, to work with "da
shnoz," Jimmy Durante. He was a sweet and decent guy, as funny and
casual in person as he was when he was on the air. One day I asked him
who Mrs. Calabash was. He told me she was just some woman whose
name he'd heard walking down the street! That dear Mrs. Calabash,

whom Jimmy bid goodnight at every performance, meant absolutely nothing to him. But the expression caught on, so he kept it in his act.

Growing up in 1940s Hollywood was like a beautiful dream. Every stop along its Boulevard was special. Diving into my fabulous fudge sundaes, I was regaled by C.C. Brown's Ice Cream Parlor legend that Judy Garland and Mickey Rooney had met there for Judy's first date. And back then, when Mann's Chinese Theatre was still Sid Grauman's movie palace, I played hooky to see my favorite stars immortalize their foot and hand prints in its exotic forecourt.

Drugstores were a favorite hangout and – whether it was Schwabs, Thrifty or the Gower's – I loved sitting at the counter with my lemon Coke, gazing as the stars strolled in to buy their Max Factor makeup or pick up a trade paper.

And, best of all, after an exhausting day of work and school, I'd hop on the red streetcar. I can still see those ruby wonders as they clackety-clacked down the tracks, delivering me to my North Hollywood home, where we lived in a charming English-style cottage near Bob Hope's Toluca Lake Home.

But Mama was starting to feel guilty. Being separated from Father and her other children for so long, saddened her. And I couldn't remain a child actor all my life. I was approaching 16, and my baby face was melting.

So one day, Mother packed up all her things, bought two separate bus tickets, put me on a bus to Manhattan and took her own to Rockford.

I didn't understand at the time, but Mother sent me to my Aunt Sadie because Mama knew Daddy could never accept me and that I'd be in better hands with her lovable sister.

With a parting hug and her kiss on my forehead, I boarded the bus, as she called after me-

Sammy, get out there in the world and never be afraid. You've got talent, enough to build an empire. So, open those gates, and give 'em bloody hell, my darling! Give 'em bloody hell.

CHAPTER THREE

The Singing Newsboy

Like Moses, in the bulrushes, I plopped on Aunt Sadie's doorstep. She lived in a fourth floor walk-up, so between climbing the steps and running from her force-fed prune juice to the john, I stayed in marvelous shape.

Aunt Sadie's apartment was on the Lower East Side, a straw hat's throw from Sammy's Bowery Follies, where she knocked 'em unconscious every night with her deep-from-the- diaphragm vocals. Sadie loved me like my own mother, and when I was 16, she took me with her. I hopped up onstage, sang a few numbers and landed a gig. Sammy's was a famous vaudeville house right in the heart of New York's Bowery, a fun neighborhood back then, lived- in and worn, like a pair of old jeans.

Sammy Fuchs and his sweet Yiddish wife, Betsy, owned the Follies. Betsy took me under her wing. My warm, cuddly, hug-me-till-I-turn-purple mama. After the show, my second hefty- hugger, Sadie, would take me to her bountiful breast. So many loving, big-bosomed mamas... no wonder I was such a happy boy.

Billed as The Singing Newsboy, I'd shuffle onstage in patched knickers, dirty tennis shoes, a rumpled turtleneck, baseball cap tilted to one side and a grimy face. With a sack full of newspapers draped over my shoulder, I'd shout, "Extry! Extry! Read all about it!" Then I'd go into my song and dance routines. I'd developed a decent hoofing and crooning repertoire in Hollywood, so I was ripe for strutting my song and dance stuff at the Follies.

I was the baby of the Bowery, but that didn't stop me from giving those old vaudevillians a run for their money with great Gus Edwards tunes like "He's Me Pal," "How Ya Gonna Keep 'Em Down On The Farm," "School Days" and some George M. Cohan numbers like "Yankee Doodle Dandy."

Aunt Sadie took center stage with her rowdy hotter-than-hell tunes like "You Gotta Hot Mama," "Some Of These Days," "A Good Man Is Hard to Find," and all the naughty ballads that got the guys all worked up and put the women in a playful mood. The audiences loved Sadie's raucous style and industrial strength pipes that could sink a German U-boat clear across the continent.

People would throw us tips onstage, and we'd stash them in a big pot. At the end of the night, we'd split the till, usually taking in over a hundred dollars, leaving me with at least forty. When I bought my own sodas and candy bars, I felt like Daddy Warbucks buying up a fleet of yachts.

Aunt Sadie handled my tips. She was unofficially my manager. In fact, Aunt Sadie was everything to me – mother, father, manager, counselor. She was bursting with love for me, always making me feel so wanted. I was a skinny little bean pole, and nestling in her colossal arms, we made a striking pair – like Jumbo raising her tenderfoot, teaching him how to be the best performer in the circus.

Most of the performers were in their 80s. The person closest to my age was the 65-year- old blind piano player, Bernie. Born blind, completely untrained, he played by instinct, feeling your tempo and style. Nobody could tell stories about the early days like him. Society people would pat him on the back, open his pockets and stuff hundred dollar bills inside.

Everybody came to our shows, from the bums to the elite. Jane Powell stopped in with Roddy McDowell one night, but didn't recognize me. The ham in me wanted to put an arm around her and proclaim, "Janie, baby, welcome to my Bowery Follies," but all I could manage was a gulp.

When I got up on stage, it was fun pretending I was the star of the show, and Sammy's was my follies. Hey! Mama always told me to think big – not a bad idea when you're 5 feet 5 inches.

Every night we started work at eight o'clock, and didn't call it quits till three in the morning. Afterward, we'd go down to Rapoport's for some heart-jolting java and the squishiest, stickiest prune Danish around. Then home for my four hours' beauty sleep and off to Greenwich Village's Catholic school. Where else would a good Jewish-Italian boy go?

I walked all over Greenwich Village, where people felt free to be as flamboyant and bizarre as they pleased. Writers and poets sat around chatting, and I got an extraordinary education. Jack Kerouac, the beat generation's spokesman, was one of my teachers. I often asked him if the mind truly had anything to teach the soul. I couldn't figure out whether the human condition that he saw was real, or simply colored by the tattered gauze over his eyes. Whichever it was, the burden was too much for this dimming light, who liquored himself to death when he just 47 years old.

Aunt Sadie encouraged me to remember my Jewish roots and often took me to the Yiddish Theater on 2nd Avenue. Yiddish – derived from German, Hebrew and various Slavic tongues – is a lively, expressive language born in the shtetls of Eastern Europe. At every opportunity, Aunt Sadie took me to those emotional performances and though I barely understood the language, I was deeply moved.

My mad love affair with New York City started at Sammy's Bowery Follies. Manhattan was the town for me. I came alive in New York City, and I knew I was in my element there. Still, I needed to get away...establish some independence and take a break from the work-till-you-drop school of performing.

I was grateful to Aunt Sadie for her unselfish devotion but, after spending a good two years as The Singing Newsboy, I was ready to burst out on my own. I was fast approaching my eighteenth birthday, and anxious to experience life.

Once I left the nest and dared to fly solo, I wanted to look back, at least wave goodbye.

"Don't look back once you're airborne, Sammy," a wise voice whispered. "If you do, you just might crash into a tree."

CHAPTER FOUR

G-String Goddesses

I was well over 18 when I finally clipped the umbilicus that stretched from Rockford to Hollywood to Aunt Sadie in the Bowery. The road to independence led me to the strip joints of Chicago, Milwaukee and Kansas City. Having landed smack in the raunchy heart of the burlesque scene, I realized all my movie and vaudeville experience would be helpful, but without an act, I'd sink into the sewer.

I met Frankie Scott, the "Undernourished Comic." With a celery stalk figure, he'd come out and fire "thin" jokes at the crowd. I loved his act, borrowed some of the shtick, added to it, adulterated it, and voila – I had an act.

I heard there was work for emcees, and all I had to do was step into those shoes. Build the audience into a frenzy with risqué jokes and silly routines, prime them for the big event and, at the same time, relax them. Professional foreplay. I was a quick study. The girls loved me and envied my "Betty Grable legs."

Faced with a room full of excited guys drooling in anticipation of those broads, it was a tough act, but I pulled it off. A flamboyant dandy, I ran around the room singing "I'm Small," telling jokes, and hurling insults. I jumped up on chairs and hopped onto unsuspecting laps:

"Is that you wife, dear? Well, better luck next time."

"If you keep your filthy mouth open, Sir, I'll throw a toilet seat over it and use it."

I played myself for every laugh I could squeeze. Audiences loved it – it told them, "Gee, he's a regular schmuck just like me."

I loved competing for the attention of hot and bothered guys, aching with desire for a buxom babe splashing in a tub or twirling her tassels. I always managed to earn the laughs, applause and respect from those G-string strung-out guys.

Calumet City, just outside Chicago, was an important marker in my life. I was 18, and I'd yet to feel sexual pleasure. Something shut down in me when I was 9 and strangely, it wasn't a result of the terrible rape. Rather it was my father's not believing me, not standing up for me, his beating and belittling me. Since that time, I didn't believe anyone could love me. And I certainly didn't allow myself any sexual joy.

Tony, my manager at the Calumet City nightclub, was a powerful, good-looking guy – a beefy, rough Italian with greased back, black hair.

One night he called me over, "Sammy. Sammy, c'mon, get over here. Come into my office, I wanna talk to you."

"What is it, Tony?" I followed Tony into his office, thinking I was going to get canned. He locked the door, leaned back on his desk and opened his pants.

I knew what he wanted and I didn't want to lose my job. He pushed me down on my knees, grabbed my head and shoved it into his groin, forcing himself into my mouth, and pumped, over and over and over.

"C'mon Baby, you're good at it." The more he talked, the more excited I became. Night after night I came to do it again. That's when I realized I wanted to satisfy men – straight me, men who liked women. And macho bisexual men, who loved both.

51

I visited Tony every night after that. Every night in his office, for the next three months. We both wanted it. There was no conversation.

I was still a babe in the burlesque woods, but I knew the big mama of strip joints was Chicago's Silver Frolics. Every city had its strip clubs, but the Silver Frolics was where the best of them took it off.

There I was, a sweet teenager emceeing 20 luscious Lolitas, who teased me about my Betty Grable legs. In particular, I remember...

"The Saucy Sudser," soaking in a sea of bubbles, gliding a foamy sponge along her soft, white skin as every guy gazed, wide-eyed, wishing he were the sponge lapping up her body. Finally, the young lovely stood up and bounced into her dance, as all eyes strained to see what luscious body part a fallen bubble might reveal.

"The Naughty Nightie," peeling away her negligee as she slid into bed. As she cast her eyes at the panting herd, every male knew she was waiting just for him to lead her down the path to ecstasy.

"The Jungle Jezebel," with tiger skin draped around her, swaying slowly, suggestively, as a snake slithered down her body. Whip in hand, she'd tame a live tiger, while gyrating about the stage, till the guys growled and roared like the primitive beasts they were.

The striptease was choreographed like a Vegas routine, where the tease was more exciting than the strip. It wasn't what these gals took off but how they did it.

The mystique tantalized you as the ribbons and bows fell from the loosely wrapped goods. Sure, they'd bump and grind their pasties and G- strings, but the seduction kept you hanging on, aching with desire all the way to the climax.

After one tease finished strutting, I'd keep the guys revved up while the next beauty powdered her nose and other sundry parts for the dame- starved hounds.

Between shows the girls earned their best tips. Sometimes they'd play "sausage tag" under the table, giving the boys a thrill with a twist of the wrist in strategic areas. Or order b-drinks. The girl got a stick for each dummied coke, and later cashed it in at a quarter a stick. Customers would buy me a drink or two, and I'd make enough to cover cab fare home.

I did risqué double entendre, but never used "vulgar" language – I saved that for my private life. Lenny Bruce was just the opposite. Different styles. Ironically, when I met him later in life, he had me sub for him. But I did it my way. I loved the idea that, with squeaky clean language and classy acts, strip joints could still be the raunchiest places.

After the shows, we'd all go down to the Corner House where the old timers met for coffee and laughs. Those seasoned vets had so much life and energy, they inspired me. I knew, I'd be making waves and raising hell till my very last moment.

My headquarters in Chicago were the Devonshire and Berkshire theatrical hotels, where the strippers, belly dancers and emcees lived. My room was tiny, with just enough to space to lay my hat, coat and a few friends. There was a bathroom I shared with my neighbors who'd always forget to unlock my side when they were done! and a common kitchen in the hall.

The Mafia needed to launder money so they had sizable interests in many legitimate clubs, including the Silver Frolics.

My relationship with the strippers wasn't strictly business. I knew a few in the biblical sense, and I don't mean we twiddled our rosaries and read scripture together. Strippers have the muscle coordination of an Olympic athlete, so a half-hour session with a stripper was a great way to keep the body limber.

There was one stripper who loved gangsters, and often invited me to join her and the hot, young hoodlums. I loved watching my friend have her turf invaded by those thrill-happy thugs. And if she liked their warm-up, she'd get them to tie her up for a blockbuster finale.

There was a popular Italian restaurant inside the Berkshire, called Valentino's, where all the gangsters congregated. Not surprisingly, it was also the strippers' favorite hangout after a show. A compact little dive, there was plenty of room for late night tête-à-têtes.

The Mafiosi lusted after those blonde buxom darlings, and went there to satisfy their appetites. There were plenty of girls to go around, so every gangster laid claim to a few. A gorgeous young lovely was a status symbol...like the machine gun you had the pleasure of breaking in yourself.

One night I went into the bathroom, and realized I wasn't alone.

"Hey, Sammy, come over here!" One of the gangsters opened his stall, pulled me inside and shut the door.

"C'mon, Sammy, do it."

When I didn't move, he put his huge hands on my shoulders and pushed me down. Dizzy and confused, I was already dropping to my knees. By the time I was finished, I'd nearly swooned. But I did what I was told, and was amazed at how it turned me on.

Sal Lamadoro was another big-league thug, who showed up every night to case the strippers and pick up the hottest one. After I emceed a show, Sal would motion me to his table. His line was always the same, "Sammy, fix me up with one of the dolls, and I'll let you in on our private show." I never disappointed Sal and the action exercised my blood pressure.

Despite all these sexual adventures, I was sad. There was never anyone special waiting for me after the show. These crazy sexual capers were retreats, something to rescue me from my loneliness. Throughout my career, I was always meeting people, but when I got back to my hotel, a television set and a cold bed was all that waited for me.

That's the life of the single entertainer. You're everybody's darling as they shower you with their applause, smiles and laughter. But when the show's over, they go home to their loved ones, and you go back to your hotel room alone.

One night a gorgeous stripper casually reached into her hefty brassiere and pulled out a hand rolled cigarette. Somebody proclaimed, "Reefer, all right!"

I'd never taken any illegal drug, but this thing seemed harmless.

I held it between my fingers and took a deep drag. Seconds later, sick, woozy and lightheaded, my heart racing, I felt like all systems in my body's engine room shut off. Dizziness engulfed me, and I was the Titanic going down into the dreaded black hole.

I had trouble breathing. I couldn't remember my name.

I thought I was Sonja Henie and I was late for rehearsal on the Fox lot. Where were my skates? How could I practice with no ice?

Suddenly the floor rose up and smacked me in the face. And I blacked out.

I came to as a hypodermic sailed in my direction. The hospital doctor said I'd suffered an anxiety attack but assured me I could return home.

I hurried back to my room at the Devonshire and dove under the covers. After a couple hours' rest, I felt ready to take on the world. I sprang over to the window and lifted the blinds, but...as I looked out, I panicked. I had a vision of opening the window, crawling out and leaping off the ledge to the pavement, eight floors below.

I rushed back to the hospital and told the doctor about my morbid urge. I had the weirdest feeling I was still high marijuana toke I'd taken hours ago.

The doctor suggested I check into the Chicago State Hospital, a mental institution, and see a psychiatrist.

Was I losing my mind from smoking one joint?

I left everything in my hotel room and checked into...the Chicago State Mental Hospital. This was a whole different world. I was terrified of everything, and now with good reason. Like a scene out of The Snake Pit, these crazed souls would lunge out screaming, spitting and laughing hysterically. They'd vomit on each other or me, threatening to cut out hearts.

There was one man who walked in his sleep, trying to strangle anyone in his path.

One Eye Norman, who'd been in institutions all his life, grabbed a pencil and gouged out his left eye. Someone got to him before he could destroy the other eye, but I understood why he wanted to shut out what he saw in the asylum.

A World War II vet thought we were in a POW camp. "You lousy

Japs can try whatever torture you want, but I'll never tell you a god-damned thing!"

The hospital felt like a prison camp and I wasn't well, because I was relieved at having my freedom taken. I had loved calling my own shots, but now I was frightened of the world, a prisoner of my own mind.

I can still see and smell the place...the attendants, with their masking tape and restraints, strapping down yet another horrified victim for shock treatment – electricity pulsing through his body, a sausage sizzling on a skewer. Like a skid row alley on the hottest day of the year, the halls reeked of every bodily function.

My room was a gloomy cell I shared with dozens of deep end dwellers. I'd sit and stare at my ID bracelet, "Sammy Labella...Sammy Labella." I read the name over and over, not sure who Sammy was.

I couldn't think a clear thought, but what was I afraid of? My doctor asked me about inkblots, had me mold clay, draw pictures and scream. This went on for two months and then one day I was summoned before a panel whose Chief questioned me-

Mr. Labella, I've never met a show-biz type who didn't belong in a place like this. What makes you think you deserve to be let loose with all the other half-wit entertainers?

The truth was, I was adjusting to inkblots and screaming sessions. Deciding what color finger paints was all the decision making I was comfortable with.

"Sir, I'm not sure if I'm ready to leave-"

That was all they needed to hear. When you hate being in a place like that, it's for your own good. But when you accommodate, they want your ass out.

The board of doctors laughed at my arguments, "Congratulations,

Mr. Labella, you may leave at once."

I hadn't any idea what I'd do with myself. The thought of reentering the world felt like my first day of nursery school, "Mommy! Help me!"

Could I still make it as Sammy, or was I better off in the institution, with my tasteful white gown and matching ID bracelet?

When I first stepped out, I was blinded by the sunlight. And then, that hot fireball beating down felt so exhilarating, I didn't care if I melted. Once I stepped into the light, my apprehensions vanished. I could walk outdoors again...all by myself! I no longer needed a warden shadowing my every move.

Until my time at the Chicago State Hospital, I had no idea how fragile the mind is. That one toke triggered something, shook me up like a bottle of seltzer, and popped my lid in one swift burst. I don't know what made me snap, but I prayed I wouldn't slip off that brink again.

As soon as I got to the Berkshire, I got a call from the Silver Frolics offering me back my emcee job. I was so glad to be returning to the strippers and the whole gang. I was welcomed and felt needed – a feeling I hadn't experienced in a long, long time.

I swore off drugs forever after that. It was my own brain that cranked up the volume, but a one-puff overdose, "Forget about it," as my Mafia friends said.

I found a psychiatrist (one who didn't tell me that my inkblots were over-sized vaginas trying to smother me). Every day I didn't feel an urge to jump out the window or run naked through the Berkshire lobby, I knew I was rebuilding my confidence and sanity.

In spite of my stint at the institution, my strip joint days were some of my brightest. I was happy doing those shows even thought they didn't make me rich. Strip joints revolve around tips more that salaries, so emcees rarely get to see all the crispy green the strippers are exposed to.

Of course, there aren't many things that a stripper isn't exposed to.

When it came to finding happiness, I followed the strippers' lead. They work hard, and have decency and compassion for others. That's always been what's most important to me.

I've worked with so many strippers and found they're some of the nicest people in entertainment. There are people out there with noses forever up in the air, whining that strippers are sinners and lowlifes. Nonsense.

One of my dearest friends, Hope Diamond, always said, "With a little kindness, you can get along with just about everyone. You'll get anything you want in this life as long as you treat folds decently."

I live by those words.

Strippers were hardworking ladies. Many were single moms who'd work all night to support their children. Stripping was their nine-to-five; not that much different from any other job, except maybe the uniforms were less confining.

If there was a saucy stripper popping her pasties, or rocking her rump, chances are I emceed for her. I worked with Hope Diamond, Rose LaRose, Sally Rand, Irma the Body and Titian Doll, the Atomic Redhead.

Titian was the most buxom gal around – the mother of all milkmaids. Her home turf was the Miami Club, a hot Staten Island joint.

One night, Titian was giving me a lift to the ferry when suddenly her car sputtered and conked out. We'd just gotten paid, and I was looking forward to the weekend. We didn't know what to do when lo and behold, three saucy Italian boys stopped and offered us a lift.

As we rode along, I noticed we were going in the wrong direction.

I started to ask the boys if they'd realized we'd drifted off course, when the one behind me shoved a knife up under my throat!

Minutes later we'd driven up on a long dark stretch of beach. As they dragged Titian and me out of the car and into the darkness, I had a sickening feeling.

Finally, well away from the road, they threw us down and then slowly, grinning, circled around Titian. It was as though they were about to string up a helpless lamb, ripe for the slaughter...

And then, one by one by one, each of the three entered her...from in front, from behind, from on top.

Brutally, violently.

I didn't know what to do. I wanted to scream, I wanted to fight them off, I wanted to run for help, I wanted to stay with her. Just a skinny little guy who didn't know how to defend myself, I was terrified that anything I did would inflame them more. In the end, I stood there, helplessly, as one of the thugs bent me over and repeatedly thrust himself inside of me, slicing away at my insides.

Having resigned myself to being raped, I just tried to shut down. But finally, I couldn't take any more. Sammy, the little boy, escaped and shook me out of my numbness, crying and screaming.

But my attacker came down hard, "Shut up, you fucking faggot. This is my gift to all the fags."

The attack seemed relentless and unending. But finally it stopped. The three of them just walked away, cursing and laughing. Dazed, bleeding, we sat for a long time, not knowing what to do, where to turn.

And then we realized...our clothes were missing. There we were, on the beach, naked and bloody, with no clothes.

I looked at my hand. My ring was gone and so was Titian's. All our jewelry had been stripped from us. All at once we remembered the car and everything that we'd left inside. They were gone. We'd been raped and robbed of everything – Titian's car, her gorgeous gowns, my tuxedo, our money, jewelry, even my sheet music and arrangements.

Petrified, naked, we somehow made it to the house of one of Titian's friends. It was three in the morning. Her friend gave us clothing and called the police.

But when the cops came to file their report, they kept grinning at Titian's sizable breasts, as though her body alone were justification for what had happened.

We didn't dare tell them what had happened to me. I'd already heard "fag" enough for one day, and didn't feel like yet another bashing. After subjecting us to more grilling and humiliation, the police filed their report and drove us to the ferry.

Titian and I remained good friends long after that nightmare passed.

Besides emceeing for strippers, I worked with some wonderful belly dancers. The leader of the belly bunch was beautiful Nadula Ates from Turkey. She made a name for herself in the Broadway cast of Fanny. Years later she moved back to Istanbul, where she still dances. Pushing 70, she still has the tight torso of a 20-year-old.

Strippers, belly dancers, showgirls – whatever the title – are artists, pure and simple. I thank all those special ladies for the pleasure of working with them and being so entertained by them over the years...onstage and off.

Yes, I'm a gay comic, who's always surrounded himself with beautiful women, but I find nothing "queer" in that. I love and admire women. Their beauty and brains light up the world. They are God's perfect creations. Sure, I had moments with strippers and showgirls, but there was never enough sexual magic to lead me down the straight and narrow path...until I met Jean Wallace. What accounts for this unlikely transformation? Read on.

CHAPTER FIVE

Club Crazy

Nightclubs have been my playground ever since Aunt Sadie weaned me. Whether they were tiny, dark and intimate, or raucous, large and impersonal...whatever they were, they were my home. Whatever the location – hotels, strip joints, Moose Lodges, convention halls, cruise liners, or the front lines of Vietnam – clubs were the place to hang my hat and shtick.

When I was 20, I left the strip joint circuit, raring to stamp my name on larger marquees, where more people would see my act and bigger bucks might fall into my near-empty pockets. The strip scene was a great experience, but I didn't want to live my entire life in pastieland. Ironically, just as I was maturing as a performer and stretching my talents, destiny called me to the Palace Theater, back to a little stretch of hell called Rockford.

I was booked there with a brilliant young comic, my good friend Shecky Green.

In my act, I poked fun at my hometown. But in truth, Rockford was still a scary place for me. I wasn't sure I could handle returning to a place that had branded me a pervert less than a dozen years before. I could still see that nun lecturing me on sin and wishing me well on my "slow descent into Satan's pit."

Opening night the marquee bragged, "HOMETOWN KID RETURNS. ROCKFORD'S OWN – SAMMY LABELLA." That dreaded place I ran away from at nine was welcoming me back with open arms.

When I arrived at the old vaudeville house, I was scared to death. I stood backstage, listening to Shecky doing his comedy bits, waiting to perform my Singing Newsboy routines. My poor heart was fluttering around loose in my throat.

But the moment I heard, "Rockford's own – Sammy Labella!," I thawed. And before I knew it, the Singing Newsboy was out on stage in his knickers and knee socks. I sang and danced up a whirlwind, and they loved me! They absolutely adored me! As the applause grew louder and louder, the walls in my mind dissolved. And, looking out, there were Mommy and Daddy, sitting on the first row. Even Daddy seemed approving.

Suddenly I wasn't afraid of Rockford anymore. I felt for the first time. God! What a feeling! Several old schoolmates came up after the show to congratulate me. And I didn't remember them. Maybe I'd blocked out all memories of Rockford, even the good ones.

I knew I still had a painful journey to make before my three days' booking was up. I walked around all the old familiar streets of my childhood, and it felt so sad and strange being back.

When I reached the park, anxiety overwhelmed me. But I went in and forced myself to stand and breathe.

Finally I walked all over the park, when suddenly...I stopped. The tree I was slammed against by those four boys hovered over me. I could see its branches rising into the air and half expected hell to blast from its trunk.

But the tree stood there, in its stillness, being just what it was – an innocent tree, oblivious to everything but the evening's beauty.

Conventions were a rich source of work, and I emceed every imag-inable gathering in Chicago and New York. Policemen, doctors, lobot-omists, nudists...everyone loved a weekend out of town to get drunk, were nametags, and call it learning. One of my favorite times was the Policeman's Ball at Madison Square Garden, where I opened for the incomparable Johnny Ray and Patti Page.

All roads out of Illinois led to Kansas City, Missouri, where I worked on of the greatest Drag Clubs ever – the Jewel Box Revue. There were ten acts, and each did a female impersonation. I was the emcee, the only one not in drag. My clothes were tailored, but my material was high camp. The twisted straight man for all those "ladies." Miss Rude-Paul could take a trash lesson from the Jewel Box beauties.

Like strippers, female impersonators get a bum rap. They're a rare and talented breed. Female impersonators, more than make-up and fals-ies, is an art form not as easy as it appears. Highly polished, few imper-sonators are actually transsexuals. Drag shows attract a skeptical straight crowd. I've emceed for many over the years, and even I am constantly fooled.

One great tart was Butch Ellis. Old then, he'd come out, all made up and dressed to the hilt in skyscraper heels. Today, Butch is still a golden knockout, performing at the Queen Mary, a lively drag club in Sherman Oaks, California. The straight tourist crowd loves the place, where every-thing's camped up for laughs.

One of my good friends was Ray Bourbon. Back in the 1940s, when Hollywood was carving its way through the orange groves, Ray owned a drag club where the infamous Viper Room now sits. Eventually he packed it up and headed for the Jewel Box. Everyone loved Ray's wild washerwoman and mother-in-law bits. Way ahead of his time, Ray was branded the Lenny Bruce of drags.

Living in a trailer outside Kansas City, big hearted Ray could never turn away a stray. Even when the numbers neared sixty, Ray simply finished his show and used all his tips to bring home the kibble.

Ray loved his dogs, but kept them locked up in his trailer, too busy working for them to take proper care of them. We all felt sorry for the dogs, but didn't know what to do.

And then Ray got booked into England for a few shows. He wanted to go to make money for his brood, but had no idea what to do with them while he was gone. Till someone told him about a man in Texas...

Ray gathered up his dogs, drove them to the man's farm and paid the man a month's rent up front. But when Ray became a big hit in England, he stayed on for five months, and forgot to send more money.

When Ray came back, the man shrugged, "Ain't got no dogs!" Ray couldn't believe it. "I board dogs, Mister. I don't run no goddamn charity." Ray was livid, "I trusted you with my babies, where are they?" The man wiped his brow, "When you didn't send me money, I...I put them to sleep and...rendered them into lard..." Ray couldn't believe it. He stormed off and hired two punks to carry out a "hit." Eventually Ray confessed and was sentenced to the Texas State Penitentiary for life. One day while he was out in the field for recreation, he was knocked down by two thugs, shouting, "Here, drag fag. Try this on for size!" as they cracked his head open with a rock.

Ray's murder tore me apart. I still hadn't fully recovered from the Chicago State Hospital experience.

Running away seemed to be my fix of choice. So I said my tearful farewells t the Jewel Box lovelies and, as the mascara on their painted faces started to run, so did I – on the next train out of town.

I didn't have a clue where I was going when I grabbed the mid-nighter out of Kansas City, but I prayed to God the grim reaper didn't travel by rail. Rest in peace, Ray Bourbon. You were one of the best.

My getaway took me to Pittsburgh – a strictly first class town that attracted all the celebrities on their side trips from the Big Apple.

My elegantly cheap Edison hotel was just off East Liberty, overlooking the river.

East Liberty was hot club territory, and I made my mark on all the clubs there.

Down a dark flight of stairs was Lenny Litman's Copa dimly lit only by candles. There was a powerhouse blues singer named Dakota Staton and a talented exotic dancer, Rita Grable, who married singer Jerry Vale and lived the lush life in Beverly Hills.

At the Horizon, I worked with my old pal Johnny Ray and a new fresh face named Johnny Mathis, a hot stallion, who got his break because a lust-smitten kitten had the connections to get him hot-wired into the business.

At the Carousel I emceed for the great Connie Francis. Her first big hit was tearing up the charts, and the whole world had a crush on America's newest darling.

Connie loved to play cards, and we'd sit around in the dressing room before the show and deal a few hands with her father always a whisper away. He traveled everywhere with Connie, keeping the wolves away from his sweet teen dream.

Pittsburgh was a turning point. I was starting to feel comfortable in the night club scene, and my routines were a natural. Like kid gloves, the life of an entertainer was a perfect fit for me. That instant gratification from the audience as they hollered and applaud was a high I never wanted to come down from.

In my early twenties, I was having the time of my life. My job as emcee was to prep the crowd for the main event. And did I ever learn to get out there, night after night, and do some hard core peddling.

A thrilling first for me was the critter circuit...the Moose Clubs, the Eagles, the Elks, and all the other beasts of the wild. Chances are, if a creature runs free in the woods, it has a secret order and a fanatical following with initiation rites, silly hats and insignias. They're a jolly crowd, and many a Moose has come to an entertainer's rescue on a high- and-dry or lonely weekend.

With my confidence high, I was eager to climb entertainment's Mount Sinai – The Catskills. I heard Ray Evans was booking acts and thanks to him and the Shirnoffs, I worked with great performers on those Catskill stages including the Platters and Joni James. People may joke about the place, but the food's great and you couldn't ask for a better place to practice your skills.

The Wonder Bar's star emcee, BS (Bullshit) Pulley, had a mouth like a septic tank. A tall, mean-spirited tweedledee, he'd waddle over to a woman, straddling a cigar box between his massive thighs, rub up against her and purr, "Go ahead, Dear. Take a cigar. It's on me."

The unsuspecting lady would lift the lid, and find his own petite "cigar" peeking out from between his legs.

Though a singer and belly dancer were the featured performers, my favorite was a chunky old piano player named Belle Barth. Belle looked like a sweet grandmother, but her off-color songs and jokes could make a sailor blush. BS made you queasy, but busty Belle split your seams.

One insane day BS came over to me before the show and said,

"Sammy, let's be friends. Come in the kitchen with me for a cold one."

BS never invited me anywhere, and I suspected something devious, but I took my chances. We entered the kitchen and BS unlocked the huge walk-in freezer.

"Sammy, go in there and fetch us a couple chilled ones, will ya?"

The mouse trap was open, and the second I stepped inside, the freezer shut tight. I panicked when I heard the door slam, but the worst sound was the tumblers of the lock clicking into place. I screamed for my life, but nothing could penetrate that airtight ice-coffin.

As I grew more and more numb, I noticed a cow tongue hanging on a hook. I could just see the tongue flapping up and down, laughing at my stupidity.

I banged on the door, yelling, "Please, somebody. Help!"

Finally, a cook opened the door and I slid out, shaking like a junkie with a bad case of the joneses.

I ran to the stage and there was BS, bragging to the audience, "So I locked the little fegala in the freezer."

When he caught sight of me, he gasped, "Oh look, Ladies and Gentlesperms, it's the frozen fegala. The world's only walking, talking fegacide."

I hopped up on stage, kicked him in the shins and jumped up and down, trying to slam him. The audience couldn't stop howling.

But I was furious – "You crazy old warthog! What's wrong with you, trying to freeze me to death? You better pray I never get your blubbery butt in that freezer; there'd be enough schmaltz to get us through next winter."

Belle Barth took BS from behind, tackling his ugly ass down to the ground. "Is this what you were trying to do, Sammy?"

I was about to thank Belle for slaying Goliath, when the beast got his second wind, stood up and started chasing both Belle and me around the stage. The audience was howling over the little dwarf being defended by the 300 pound gutter-mouth grandma.

Just another crazy day at the Wonder Bar, complete with a Keystone Cops chase. Even on days when we weren't trying to be funny, we gave people their money's worth.

That's comedy for you – two parts talent, one part plain dumb luck.

CHAPTER SIX

The 1950s – Toe Sucking at The Park Savoy

Home again in Manhattan. Somewhere between the bobby soxers and the beatniks, I reentered the New York scene and found my wallet-friendly palace, The Park Savoy Hotel. It was everything I was looking for – cheap, comfortable, and roomy enough to stack a few friends end to end. And best of all, it was in the center of things – 58th and Broadway. The Park Savoy was my Manhattan castle.

Things were cozy. Each floor had its own bathroom, shower and kitchen. Bouncing off the patched-up walls was a stack of cooking odors from the kitchen on each floor – pork chops sizzling...on top of fried fish...crackling over garlic-drenched pastas...layered over toast...croutoned into beef stew.

Along with the food, the Park Savoy mingled the up and coming – artists, writers, poets and actors – with the down and all-the-way-out. The price was always right, so that even those who'd hit their ass on the pavement could find a welcome there.

Back in the early 1950s a blond angel, in the guise of an Indiana farm boy, showed up hoping for a place to lay his broken wings. One look at his delicate, unspoiled face, and I was hooked. The understated grace of James Byron Dean hooked everyone.

Born February 8th, 1931, in Marion Indiana, Jimmy got the middle name, Byron, from his mother who predicted her son's soul would be crippled like the poet. When she died in California at the age of 29, 9-year-old Jimmy had to accompany her body on a train back to Indiana for her burial. Her death wounded Jimmy deeply, affecting him for years to come.

As Jimmy got older, hot cars, fast bikes and Shakespeare helped assuage the pain. But after the role of Malcolm in UCLA's Macbeth brought only minimal success, he took off for the big Apple, showing up on our door-step on borrowed Norton bike.

Shy and awkward, Jimmy would stay alone in his room for hours on end, painting, writing poetry and staring out the window. But his moody, hypnotic gaze was nothing like the leather-clad, "fuck-`em" stare that covered his public vulnerability.

Jimmy loved reading new plays, and begged me to act out scenes with him and whomever else we could dredge up.

On snowy nights, he'd knock on my door and we'd meander over to 42nd Street and watch movies all night. Sitting in the balcony, stuffing ourselves with popcorn, we'd watch Montgomery Clift, Shelley Winters and all the great George Stevens' movies. Then we'd walk up and down 7th Avenue, drinking coffee and people-watching. Occasionally, we'd interrupt our strolls and wrestle in the snow like schoolboys.

During an innocent wrestling match at his place, Jimmy suddenly pushed me down on the bed. He could be very rough, especially when he rubbed his body up against mine. Again, like schoolboys, we compared our endowments, and Jimmy's was much bigger. After that, we mastur-bated each other. A few nights later, Jimmy dragged me outside to rough-house in the snow. When we were completely worn out, I said, "Jim, why don't you come back to my place and take a shower?"

Jim hesitated. "C'mon, we're fuck buddies, Jim! Don't be ashamed." He was shy, as usual, but I persisted. Jim smelled like the Indiana farm boy he was. I discovered that you can take the boy out of the country, but you can't take the smell of the country out of the boy. Jim's body odor consisted of urine and smegma, or "head cheese," and made me gag. What marketing genius came up with that name for a luncheon meat?

While we showered together, I rubbed his back then used a washcloth to wipe his genitals in a futile attempt to get rid of the eye-watering smell. Jim pushed me down on my knees, grabbed me by the neck with two hands and shoved his cock down my mouth.

All the time I kept saying, "No, no, no...yes, yes, yes..."

Another unlikely thought popped into my head about Molly Bloom's masturbatory soliloquy at the end of Ulysses. "...yes I said yes I will Yes."

Eventually I stopped struggling and gave myself up like a helpless kitten and did as I was told. After a while, my jaw loosened and I enjoyed the experience. Exhausted, we fell asleep on his less than ample bed.

Jimmy and I never had "fuck buddy" sex after that or discussed it. I adored Jimmy and we were very close the whole time we were together in New York. Jimmy loved men, women, the 42nd Street scene, the nightlife, the whores, the food, the movies. He loved that whole life.

Jimmy had a reputation as the consummate ladies man, but in a way few people knew, he was much more relaxed in the company of older women.

One glorious winter weekend my pal, Robert Ruth, invited us to his lovely old Connecticut farmhouse. Arriving first, we snooped around and discovered a frozen pond out back.

Delighted, Jimmy wanted to "ice skate." Sliding and slipping on his leather shoes, gliding and falling, Jimmy was suddenly gone. The ice had given way and he was under water.

A non-swimmer, I panicked and screamed for help, until I thought my vocal cords would rip.

Lucky for us, Robert was just driving up. He jumped out of his truck, dove into the pond and plucked the non-swimming soaking hunk out of the water.

It gave us a terrible fright, but at the end of the day, Jimmy just laughed. He expected death early, he said, though he had no idea how it would come.

Jimmy had and antique map of Paris hanging in his room. He'd fantasize walks down the boulevards where we'd introduce ourselves to café life, become society's darlings and be adopted by Picasso.

"Can you climb the Eiffel Tower and see all of Paris?" Jimmy would ask. "We must stop at the Café Lacopa and have dinner at the Ledoyon." His imagination and his love of food, guided us through a fantasy journey.

All day, every day, Jimmy drank his coffee and smoked his cigarettes to the nub. His fingers were always burnt. I loved to take him to the deli off 58th Street for cream cheese and bagel (and lox when I was flush). Jimmy would reciprocate with spaghetti and meatballs at Jerry's Deli, where the food was cheap and good.

Actors frequented Jerry's, figuring a good cheap meal was the best deal. One day we saw Marlon Brando, a man who was to become important to both of us. For me, the reasons came later. For Jimmy, they were immediate. Brando played a motorcycle gang leader in the 1954 movie, The Wild Ones. His line "Nobody tells me what to do," would forever define Jimmy's maverick spirit.

Life was so carefree back then. And the future, was just a dream.

One day I heard the buzz that Jimmy would be asked to Hollywood. He went, did a television piece and came back, unimpressed.

Shortly after that, Elia Kazan invited him to audition at Warners' New York office for East of Eden. Three weeks later, Jimmy packed his clothes in a paper bag and boarded the plane for California.

That was the last time I saw my friend.

Decades later I interviewed James Bacon, a great Hollywood columnist. He told me one night in 1955 he was sitting at the Villa Capri Restaurant in Hollywood when Jimmy sped recklessly on to the lot. As Jimmy got out of his silver Porsche, Bacon hollered, "Better be careful or you'll get yourself killed!"

Jimmy laughed, "Life's too short, James. You've gotta take it like it comes."

Three hours later, on Route 466 near Paso Robles, California, James Byron Dean lay dead, that beautiful body mangled in his beloved Porsche 550 Spyder after a head-on collision while driving only 10 miles over the speed limit.

❦

Actors weren't the only ones shacking up at the Park Savoy. A young man with magnificent, creamy white, shoulder-hugging locks took an apartment just off the main lobby, and henceforth Mozart's and Beethoven's sweet notes filled the lobby.

With Leonard Bernstein caressing his piano keys, our old Park Savoy was a grand movie with its own orchestral soundtrack. How I loved making my dramatic entrance into our great but shabby hotel. With concerts booming through the halls, I got a fabulous second-hand education. Imagine, free music lessons in a welfare hotel.

Leonard Bernstein maintained his apartment for many years, sharing great music with anyone who could plunk down a few pennies for a room.

On the other side of the lobby, a favorite of Leonard's, the Italian painter, Horace Costello, sold paintings from the gallery of his room. Walter Winchell was a big fan and wrote Horace up often, attracting the likes of Jessica Tandy and Nat King Cole to our humble home, as the aroma of wet oils added to the cacophony of smells floating through our cultured mist.

The Park Savoy was home to many of my favorites. Judy Holliday lived there for years before her dumb blonde comedy landed her more ample digs in Hollywood. Ralph Meeker escorted young showgirls to his room "to help with his lines." And there were times when a kindly drunk, Red Farrar, let Marlon Brando spend an occasional night on his floor.

Mrs. Rose, the hotel manager, was our official Jewish mama. Everybody knew she was there for us, and never held on to a dollar when she thought it might help someone else more. We called her "Ma," because she treated us like her kids, even giving us a good scolding when we needed it.

One day, when Marlon was appearing in A Streetcar Named Desire, he stuck his head into Ma's cubbyhole, asked how she was, and then shocked her by asking her if she could spare a few bucks till the end of the week.

As Ma reached into her tzedakah (charity) drawer to help out the biggest name in Hollywood, Marlon landed a big kiss on her cheek and laughed, "Keep it, Ma. You'll need it to get in to see my show."

David Hadley was a bright young thing from St. Louis, Missouri, with the hot blond looks of a California surfer. David loved the City and longed to act. But despite his passion, he simply had no talent. His notes didn't land in any particular key, and his acting barely landed him in the audience.

But bless his heart, David kept on plugging. Day after day, he went to bars and clubs, looking for singing gigs, but all he got was liver rot and a nasty hangover.

I'd have an occasional drink with David, but realized early on, I was out of my league. He lapped up enough vodka in a day to fuel the Russian army.

David's breath fermented the hallways. Working as the Park Savoy's switchboard operator, he exhaled a pungent odor that tackled you as you entered the lobby, leaving an alcoholic veil on your clothes.

David could barely walk without a swig from his "medicine." But drunk or sober, he was blessed with a Bette Davis/Clifton Webb wit. So despite his liquor lust, David could be a lot of fun and made friends easily.

One of David's closest friends was a Southern gent named Tom Williams. Actually, Tom signed all his plays Tennessee. Tom was from my home state, Mississippi, but "Mississippi" Williams sounded more like a blues singer than a playwright.

So Tennessee Williams it was.

Tennessee had a foot fetish, and got off on sucking David's toes in particular. Tennessee would come up to the Park Savoy and play tootsies with David. Their relationship never went any further than that.

Toe sucking – safe sex, as long as your feet are clean.

Tennessee Williams often invited me to go with him to the Lincoln

Center revivals of his shows. He loved Brando in Streetcar, and Shelley Winters in Night of the Iguana, as well as Ava Gardner in the film version.

He told me he loved Ava's "great soul," but never had the nerve to tell her so in person. Tennessee was just a bashful kid, with an innocent, little boy's shyness.

I learned so much from Tennessee about treating people fairly and with kindness. Besides being one of the fines playwrights of his generation, Tennessee Williams was an upstanding, considerate man, who showed respect to everyone.

A regular guy, he said he liked me because I was "an honest sort and when you're up front and honest with people, they'll automatically like you. Sammy, you must always remember to just be yourself."

Although Tennessee and I became good friends in New York, our paths didn't cross again until the late 1960s in the strangest place...

Whenever Tennessee showed up at our hotel, he'd say "Well, here I am, back at the YMCA." The narrow halls and miniature rooms had a musty, locker room feeling. Tennessee was smitten with David Hadley and wanted to help him, but David wouldn't take favors...

David was an opera fanatic and eventually found work at the Met as a chorus boy, where he'd sing and dance in the background, providing atmosphere like extras in a movie. The thrill of being near the great opera stars and magnificent sets every night was all David needed...along with a tubful or two of vodka...to make him happy.

One night while David was slurping his fermented poison, he got sick and blacked out. Just before losing consciousness, he told me he was certain he must be dying. When David came to in the Emergency Room, he was so thankful to still be alive, he swore off drinking and smoking for good. A taste of death was the best way to scare the life back into my friend.

Christmas time 1994, some 40 years later, I got an urgent call from David, "Skippy, you'll never guess what I found!"

"With you, there's no telling."

"Skippy...I found Marilyn's watch! She gave it to me when I was at the front desk, and I was so sauced I completely forgot about it. Skippy, I've got Marilyn Monroe's solid gold watch!"

I was absolutely floored.

In the 1950s, when Marilyn was studying at the nearby Actors Studio, she often stopped at the Park Savoy to see her friend, Nina Varela, the actress who'd costarred with Marlon Brando in Viva Zapata!

Apparently, one day when David was ringing Nina's room to announce Marilyn, he saw this fabulous gold watch draped casually over her lovely wrist. When he remarked on it, she handed it to him, "Here, honey, you take it. You'll enjoy it more than I do. Go ahead, I'd like you to have it."

But the biggest shock was yet to come. "Ho, Ho, Ho, Skippy! Merry Christmas! I'm sending Marilyn's watch to you. I want you to have it."

"David, you're crazy, dear. I don't need that watch."

As usual, David didn't listen, "Shut up, Skippy. Do whatever you want with it. It's yours."

It takes a lot to make me speechless, but that did it. When the watch arrived, I cried, not so much taken by its beauty, or that the one and only Marilyn had owned that precious legacy.

As the front desk person at the Park Savoy, David often had to enforce the rules. Droves of people would congregate in that cramped lobby, and he had the honor of tossing them out.

On several occasions silver screen golden boy Lawrence Tierney, looped as a roller coaster, staggered into the hotel with a gorgeous blonde thing. One night, as Tierney (who was famous for playing Dillinger on screen) screeched and ranted, David ordered him out.

Afterwards, David broke into a sweat, "Jeez, I thought he was gonna send the boys to rearrange my body parts."

David still lives at the Park Savoy, in the same furnished one-room apartment. Still a chorus boy at the Met, David couldn't be happier. He's in show business, surrounded by the richest operatic voices ever to thunder across the stage. And you can't get any closer to show business than being on stage, night after night, playing to a packed house of 5,500 fans.

David Hadley, unselfish as they come – I've seen him give his last dollar to the homeless – the Park Savoy's reigning good Samaritan.

The Park Savoy's the only New York place I've ever called home. Ironically it's surrounded by the classiest hotels. Occasionally a society lady would present herself inquiring if there were "any suites available."

When those uppa claaahss ladies were told there were only "rooms" available, and...gasp!...community kitchens and baths! They took their turned up noses and left.

Everything at the Park Savoy came cheap except the phone. Even in the 1950s, it cost $.50 to dial out from your room, probably to discourage ladies of the night from making their offices there.

Me? I'd grab my morning coffee, rush across to the Essex House, go in the back entrance and use the pay phone. That was my office. I'd sit there with my sacred book of phone numbers, my coffee and cigarettes, a couple of pencils and stacks of dimes, and call all the agents.

If I wasn't plopped down on my buttocks, I was out gallivanting the streets. New York's a walker's paradise, and my day was never complete without a brisk constitutional to New York's West side, East side, right side, and wrong side. I walked everywhere. My best pair of patent leathers was the only cab I needed.

And there were all the great nameless faces I'd pass along the street. Stone faces, never looking at you. Walking statues.

You could lose yourself in a New York street. I used to see Greta Garbo schlepping along, all bundled up, totally unnoticed, except by my star-crossed eyes.

On the East side, was the young, feisty Katherine Hepburn, on her bicycle en route from the bakery, a fresh loaf of bread bouncing up and down in the basket. Or Roddy McDowell stalking around with his camera, in pursuit of the perfect picture.

The Art Theater was a quaint little movie house on 58th Street across from the Plaza Hotel. I loved to walk there and lose myself in foreign cinema. Or catch Josephine Baker's stunning performance at the Capitol. Little did I realize that I'd one day work with the incomparable Ms. B.

The Palace Theater was a lovely old vaudeville house, in the middle of Times Square. For me, it will always be "Judy's Palace." I saw Judy Garland perform there over and over. Once, I jumped up after her performance, ran down the stairs and up the aisle, and presented her with a huge bouquet of ruby red roses. A devoted fan, I readily forgave her long ago snub in Hollywood.

In my fanciful New York days, you could pretty much roam wherever you pleased without worrying. Crime was something you read about in cheap novels. My late-night jaunts were the best. Two o'clock in the morning, three o'clock. I walked everywhere.

My favorite season for walking was winter.

Give me Manhattan on the rocks. Manhattan with ice and snow crunching under my boots, a chilling breeze settling on my face. I loved piling on the sweaters, vests, scarves and berets, the fur-lined jackets, the down packed coats, and underneath it all, warm thermal underwear.

A blustery gust of wind would grab hold and carry me down Broadway, past Second and Third, over to Carnegie Hall, and drop me off wherever I pleased.

Now that's what I call public transportation.

My favorite wintry walks took me down 57th Street toward the Plaza, up down and around 5th Avenue, Park Avenue, Madison Avenue and every other street that laid out the snowy white carpet for me.

I sang snappy show tunes to keep my engine revved. There was great musical theater in those days. Everything was new, new, new, and I loved it. When West Side Story was the big Broadway hit, I'd be walking around belting out "Ma-reee-aaah, I just me a girl named Ma-reeee-aaah." The scores of Gypsy, Sound of Music. All the singable, danceable show medleys of the day were the anti-freeze that kept my feet plowing through the white Manhattan way. I didn't give a damn who might be listening. People I passed would join right in. New York was truly my winter wonderland, offering one snow-scape after another.

Eventually, I was playing clubs all over the East Coast, then skipping back and forth to New York City.

One evening, listening to the Arthur Godfrey television talent show in my hotel room, I heard a satin-voiced singer, Richard Roman, singing "Love is a Many Splendored Thing."

Captivated by his voice, I shouted at the TV, "If there's a God, I'll meet that guy."

From that one appearance, Dick won a week's engagement at New York's Latin Quarter and through divine hocus pocus, my friends, Bobby Darin and Rona Barrett introduced us at Hanson's drugstore, where all the theater people hung out.

Bobby had just recorded "Splish Splash," and back then, Rona was in charge of his fan club!

When Dick introduced himself, I was taken with him, and an instant spiritual kismet took me over. Our friendship blossomed on a train ride to New York.

We were chatting about an engagement we'd just done together, when Dick asked me, "Sammy, we need to find you a name that fits you better."

That's a hell of a thing to tell somebody you've known just a short while, but I knew he was right. From the moment I first answered

Dick Roman gave Skip his name

roll call at school, I felt I wasn't Sammy. Sammy were heavyset guys with tough Brooklyn accents who pushed around hot dog carts or carried a submachine gun. Back in my Chicago strip joint days, a worthless gangster named Sam Latroco had grabbed me and spit, "A sissy like you with a name like Sammy? You gotta change it, ya hear? You're not man enough, boy."

So what could I call myself that would ease up on the ethnicity with just a hint of healthy WASP appeal?

I'd bought a pinkie ring when I was working strip joints. Gangsters wore monogrammed rings on their pinkies and despite its pansy-ass sound, the pinkie was their favorite ring finger. It had power in the underworld and I wanted to be hip, so I bought the ring and had my initials inscribed.

Noticing the initials on my pinkie ring, Dick pondered, "S.L. Let's see. Skip...Skip...Skip Lowe. Nah, something's missing. Skip E. Lowe. Yeah, that's it!"

Skip was a natural for me because of the way I frolicked around the room when I'd play a club. So, from that moment, Sammy Labella retired, and Skip E. Lowe was born.

Returning by train, I thought I could hear "Skip E.–Skip E.–Skip E. – Skip–Skip–Skip E.–Skip E.–Skip E.–Skip–EEE," emanating from the engine. And then the whistle would shout out loud for all the world to hear, "Looooowe! Looooowe!"

Skip E. Lowe. I loved my new name. I didn't care if it brought me fame or fortune, it had already blessed me with one of the best friends I'd ever have.

When I got in to Manhattan, I ran to the community bathroom at my trusty Park Savoy and went over to the mirror, "Hi Skip! Mr. Lowe, how are you? Skip E. Lowe. Skip E. Lowe. Skip E. Lowe."

I kept repeating the name out loud to get the feel of it. I locked the bathroom door and stayed in there for an hour christening the newborn Skip E. Lowe. People started banging on the door, but I kept right on with my mirror monologue.

When I'd first met him, Dick Roman was living in a comfortable apartment on 63rd Street and studying voice with Carlo Menotti, Frankie Avalon's vocal coach.

The Park Savoy was just around the corner from Carlo, so Dick and I would jaunt over to La Scala for an Italian feast, and afterwards, the theater, a movie or the opera. I loved our opera evenings – the showy theatrics, the dramatic scores, the lush style, and best of all, the breathtaking costumes. Not to be upstaged by the performers, I'd wear my long-flowing capes and scarves and with Dick, quite the flairmeister himself, we'd bask in the onlookers' attention.

Afterward, it was back over to Lindy's for cheesecake, a cup of java and a private scoop. Walter Winchell parked in front, late at night, conducting all his business on his car phone – a dial phenomenon in those days. When he'd see us pass by, we'd tip our hats and he'd throw a choice tidbit. Winch was truly decent to us, kind and generous. Though he had the scoop on everybody, he chose carefully what to publicize.

Dick Roman was one of my true friends from the early days, and wherever he played, I tried to be there. His career was going full guns when he got booked on the Ed Sullivan Show. My heart just couldn't stop pounding when I heard Ed announce, "Now, Ladeeeees and Gentlemen, for the first time right heeeere on our stage tonight, a very talented young man...Mr. Dick Roman."

That was a rrreeeally, rrreeeally big shew, with Dick managing to charm old granite-faced Ed.

Dick had a beautiful girlfriend at the time – a model and actress named Pamela Draper, the daughter of Paul Draper, the wonderful dance coach and entertainer. Pam was chic and sophisticated, with a lofty air about her, but I loved the way she carried herself.

Dick and Pamela were madly in love, and the three of us often did the town. Some of my most joyful evenings were our Wednesday night Christian Science Church meetings on Central Park West. I was content with the world after getting my dose of sin insurance, and I knew I needed to get my little hands on as much of that good stuff as I possibly could.

Dick always treated me with respect. My sexuality was unimportant to him – it simply had no bearing on our friendship. Our wonderful relationship was tested during a fierce snowstorm, when the two of us were stranded for three days inside Dick's beautiful apartment. As the snow piled up outside, it built an icy fortress all around, preventing either of us from stepping foot outside. After a while, we forgot we were stranded. We were simply two great friends enjoying each other's company. There was lots of time to read, play cards and work on new material for my act, and Dick came up with some inspired ideas that helped jazz up my stage routines.

There was never any tension, sexual or otherwise, between us. Dick and I more than survived the storm. We enjoyed it. There are so many wonderful memories attached to each snowflake that fell during those three magical days, and I'll never forget a single one of them.

Although those Manhattan winters were some of the happiest times of my life, I was missing something. I was a restless kid and the last thing I wanted to do was settle down.

As I sat in my room and glanced up at the map of Paris Jimmy Dean had given me, I could smell the fresh-baked croissants and taste the sweet, intoxicating French champagne. New York had a continental flair all its own, with its wonderful restaurants, museums and galleries, and it made me hunger for the European life.

It was 1951 and I was twenty, when I got a call from Burt Jonas. He was booking American acts into Europe. This was my dream! to work in countries I'd only seen in newsreels or fantasized about as I ran my fingers over Jimmy's great map.

My first plane trip, I was so exited! As soon as we lifted off, I was ready to take on the planet. When we touched down in Wiesbaden, Germany, I was raring to go – Europe, land of royalty!

But once I'd unpacked, my dreams of becoming an international sensation detoured. I arrived at the Wiesbaden Officer's Club, all set to jump into my routines and the shrapnel-filled hearts of those arrogant stiff- collars. But from the moment I set foot in the club, I sensed something was off. The place was empty, except for one long table of bulldog military brass, a cloud of cigar stink hovering over the belching lot of them.

I knew I'd have to prove myself on foreign soil, but I had no idea I'd be facing a firing squad.

"Skippy Lowe!" A voice bellowed out. "No, it's Skip E. Lowe." "Perform!" the voice barked back. "Geez!" I thought, "Is this some kind of military training maneuver?"

I knew the grunts had boot camp, but the entertainers too? As I hopped up on stage, I noticed each officer whipping out a notepad and scribbling something down. First, I let loose with some of my best ice breakers and those hard-asses didn't react. Hell, with that crowd I'd need a frigging blowtorch. So I ran off the stage, jumped onto the table, snapped up one of the pads and began to read their scratchings out loud:

"Joke #1, 5 points. Joke #2, 3 points. Joke # - say, what the hell is this anyway?"

It turned out that these base-side junior critics decided if you worked or not. I considered myself a seasoned performer by then, and the thought of traveling halfway around the world to be auctioned off like a laying hen at a county fair, was insulting.

Infuriated, I tap danced over to the first officer, scribbled on his pad –

Skip E. Lowe- learning how to work the crowd

AUCTION OVER! THIS HEIFER IS NOT FOR SALE! and broke his pencil in two.

Then I buzzed all their pencils faster than a beaver with his tail on fire. With the red-faced buzzards still gawking at the kooky comic, I sprung off the table, shouting, "The slave auction's over, Boys!"

Having blown my chances of getting work in Germany – hell, I was on the official military drek list for all of Europe.

I left Wiesbaden and went to Frankfurt, searching in vain for a club to work. After a couple of very sparse weeks, I was tempted to peddle my strudel, but something told me to hang tough. So, I lived on schnitzel scraps for a few days...until wundebar!

The stink I made had echoed clear across to America, where my old friend, Walter Winchell, glorified my international hissy-fit in his column. A short time later the entire audition process for professional entertainers overseas was eliminated. I'd declared war on the U.S. military and won!

Soon my phone was ringing off the hook. The Wiesbaden sergeants appreciated my stand and had decided I was the ideal performer.

I returned and, thanks to Geisler, Gunther and Feretti, I now had steady work for officers', NCO (non-commissioned officers) and EM (enlisted men) clubs. There weren't many female agents then. Gunther was a fair-minded and generous businesswoman. She expunged any notions I'd had about ruthless Germans by her honest, forthright manner.

I'd been watching too much Stalag 17 and all those American-made World War II newsreels that weren't exactly endorsed by Germany's Chamber of Commerce.

Wiesbaden gave me first class treatment, and I emceed for the likes of the Everly Brothers, Dick Haymes and Joni James. At $200 a night, and $500 per on weekends, I had a king's ransom in 1950's currency.

These American NCO clubs paid so well for one reason – slot machines. The soldiers fed them, and the officers managing the clubs gave a little back in terms of great entertainment, and pocketed the rest.

I stayed at the elegant Blum Hotel. Its lavish dining room served up richer-than-sin German breakfast goodies. Ooooh, that deep, dark German coffee, and those warm, buttery Danish. Who needed hot sex with these daily orgies? From the simplest breakfast to the most elegant five-course dinner, European food became my obsession.

Across the street from The Blum was the Spielbank – a gambling casino, where I'd spend countless hours flinging chips and strutting about like I owned the joint.

The Spielbank combined the elegance of Monte Carlo with the glitz of Las Vegas. I loved dressing up for that crowd. The casino doors would fly open and I'd make my entrance in a flowering banner of silk scarves, capes and tuxedo...a get-up that screamed, "Achtung! Ze crazy Amerikaner has arrived!"

Roulette was my game, and like Midas, my pittance was always spun into gold. I never found out what the secret was, a gift or luck? But I won at the tables. I'd sit there with a glass of wine, playing the wheel for hours on end, collecting my fortune and meeting scores of wonderful young American and English entertainers.

With all my winnings, I felt gloriously tall. I adored being the evening's entertainment, Wiesbaden's flamboyant attraction.

Wiesbaden was a city full of surprises. Under its rich soil bubbled natural hot springs that attracted bathers from all over the world. A few minutes in those earthy pools and you felt rejuvenated. Whether it was truly a sudden burst of health or merely a reaction to being boiled like cabbage, is something I never found out.

Touring the military bases in France and Germany I worked as the emcee-comic for the Everly Brothers, Don and Phil. The soldiers couldn't get enough of the "Wake Up Little Susie" guys. I loved standing in the wings, watching those slick-voiced Casanovas perform.

We rode along with the band on their bus, and I'd sit in the back with the window open, enjoying the cinematic landscape. Don and his girl-friend also sat in the back, tripping on their own scenery as they toked away on their joints. Brother Phil, on the other hand, sat in front, talking to the bus driver and strumming his guitar. A real "square" man, and that was fine by me.

Tragically, one day in Wiesbaden, while turning into an NCO club,

Skip E. Lowe, best friend Margee McGlory & Wolfgang Boulhold

our driver struck one of our soldiers, who was rushing to get a good seat for the show. It happened in a terrible flash. I only remember hearing a sickening thump. When we ran off the bus, we saw the boy had been knocked down, crushed under the wheels and killed instantly.

We were scheduled to entertain, but we couldn't leave the soldier. About an hour later, after we were able to pull things together as much as possible, we went out on stage and entertained. That senseless death still overwhelms me when I think of the Everly Brothers.

When I moved to Paris France, my neighborhood digs were the tough, largely Algerian Pigalle district, in the heart of downtown, where I roomed at the world famous Monte Jolie.

During World War II, that magnificent hotel housed French and German soldiers. Later it became a theatrical hotel. A stay at the Mont

Jolie was like living in a stately palace, with its gorgeous grand entrance, marble floors and intricate cage elevator with exquisite sparkling glass doors in the middle of the lobby. A prominent French family built the hotel at the turn of the century, and has owned and operated it ever since.

As I was coming down the elevator one day, a deep purr descended about me, "Well, look, Dahling, it's Skip E. Lowe."

I turned around, in love with the sound of Margee McGlory. This French/Irish enchantress in high heels, had a mane of red hair and a sprinkling of freckles over a face of creamy perfection.

With the energy of the Folies Bergère and the attitude of Tallulah, Bette and Marlene, this sultry beauty exuded soul and I could never get enough.

A stunning mixture of black and white, always decked out in gorgeous Chanel, Margee's singer/impressionist roots swelled up from a swath, deeper and more ancient than her New York City origins.

Having jumped from a Chicago theater group to Harlem's Apollo, she caught Billie Holiday's eye while doing an impression of the Lady Day herself. After that, Margee was scatting with Billie, Duke Ellington and other members of that royal jazz family.

When I beheld this gorgeous chanteuse, it was a meeting of the souls. Throughout our years of traveling, no matter what our plans, we'd come upon each other at the perfect moment as if drawn by some cosmic radar. We'd get together for a moment, share laughs and tears, then one of us would be off to other lands...until our next chance meeting.

Even today Margee hasn't lost that crazy knack of appearing just when my world needs saving. My third scrumptious suitcase, that's Margee, my perfect travel-mate and best friend.

Margee and I worked all the U.S. bases in France – Camp Deloche,

Fontainebleau, Evirue – thanks to Rube Blakey. An African American jazz musician, Rube decided to make color blind France his home. In between engagements at Paris' Blue Note and Soul Club, he'd book talent into the happening little clubs and eventually became one of Europe's finest agents.

During the 50s and 60s, France became an artist's haven, tempting many American actors, musicians and painters. The romantic allure of Paris was only amplified by the fact that its work visa had no time limit. Many Americans settled in Paris and even set up their own businesses.

Hot American imports like jazz clubs and soul food were among the most successful. An American known as Hayes, a World War II veteran, stayed on and set up Hayes Restaurant, a sizzling joint whose black-eyed peas, cornbread and ribs attracted such Hollywood luminaries as Elizabeth Taylor, Ava Gardner, Audrey Hepburn, Paul Newman and Joanne Woodward.

American actors were always in Paris, visiting, working or shopping for whatever. While touring the exquisite gallery in Versailles, I happened upon Edward G. Robinson, walking along, enraptured. We sparked a long conversation and he confided in me his overwhelming love of art.

Funny how this warm, sensitive guy became typecast as a ruthless gangster. But who'd have paid to see his Sharpei mug as a sensitive art collector?

With all the film stars in France, you never knew where a movie camera would pop up. I was fetching my mail from the American Express office one morning, when I stepped in a pile of dog shit! Cursing, I looked up and voilà, I was gazing into bright lights, an extra in the latest Audrey Hepburn movie.

If only I'd had my union card back then.

Josephine Baker –International Performer

From the moment I set foot in France, there was one magnificent star I dreamed of meeting – Miss Josephine Baker. Since the 1920s she was among the reigning royalty of French cafe society and I fantasized that here in France, her adopted country, I might actually meet her.

Late one afternoon, I got a frantic call from Jeff Patterson, an Australian agent, "Skip, can you help me out? I need an emcee in Frankfurt, tonight. I know it's sudden notice, but I'll drive you down. Oh, by the way, Josephine Baker's the headliner. She's probably a little before your time but-"

My jaw hung in mid-air.

I'm not sure what was more incredible – that Josephine Baker, chanteuse extraordinaire, was playing a tiny U.S. military club, or that I'd actually be on the same stage as her.

I asked Margee to join me and share the once-in-a-lifetime thrill.

Jeff's Citroen pulled up to the Mont Jolie and I looked inside where Le Josephine sat in the front seat, as beautiful and classy as ever. I was stunned. I thought surely the great Josephine would be flying to Frankfurt and we'd meet here there.

My tongue just rolled over and played dead, as I managed to stammer, "G-G-Good evening, Miss Baker, what a pleasure to m-meet you!"

She looked so vibrant and sexy, it was hard to believe the young plaything of the French elite was now approaching...gulp... middle age.

Margee and I sat in the back seat, petrified, as Jeff chewed up the autobahn, desperate to get us to Frankfurt on time.

Miss Baker tapped the frantic Australian on the shoulder, "Mr. Patterson, do you have any children?"

Our driver replied that he didn't.

"Well," she smiled calmly, "I have 12 beautiful adopted ones, and I'd like to see them again. So if you must break the sound barrier, could you do it with someone else in the car?"

The delightful Josephine Baker

Jeff realized we'd all be able to enjoy our paychecks more if we weren't on life support systems, so he slowed down to a reasonable 85 miles-an-hour and we arrived at the club on schedule and in one piece.

"Club" was an exaggeration for a spot, so cramped and overflowing with rowdy enlisted boys, who didn't even know who Josephine Baker was! These guys were out to drink, have a few laughs, and kill some time. To them, this classy former ingénue was just "that old broad with the hot body."

But Josephine didn't care. She toured everywhere to bring in cash.

Even selling her gorgeous gowns to make ends meet. Her concern was her 12 adopted children, each from a different nation. Josephine believed that the world could live in peace, and her rainbow of children reflected that philosophy.

Maybe the world could get along okay, but it was doubtful that roomful of raunchy fellows could go five minutes without a brawl.

Since this club had no dressing room, Miss Baker had to change in the beer room – then push her way through the dingy kitchen, onto the plank of wood that passed for a stage. My heart plummeted seeing the awful treatment she was getting. So I gave her the royal send-up, presenting her as though she were playing Buckingham Palace. Then out she walked in all her splendor, slinking around as svelte and magnificent as ever.

The shoddy club had one feeble light, flickering with all the intensity of a sick firefly. Her star may have been out of the limelight, but Josephine Baker still knew how to create a glow. Purring through a repertoire of sensual French songs, she played the room like a command performance for the Queen. That was the only time I saw Josephine Baker, but I'll always remember the night she turned a zookeeper's nightmare into a world-class affair.

All twelve of Josephine's children are doing well. One of them, Jean Claude, a good friend of mine, runs the exquisite New York nightclub – Chez Josephine – a classy tribute to his beautiful mother.

The American military in France was a presence left over from World War II. By the 1960s we were merely a symbol. An ugly symbol. Beer cans and cigarette butts were strewn about by our own soldiers. Stationed in Europe to guard it from enemies, we were doing our own job of destroying the place. France had survived centuries of wartime pillaging, and our boys were virtually laying waste to it in peacetime.

When DeGaulle rightly ordered us out and shut down our bases, the American military was outraged. With American/French relations under major strain, Margee and I had a hard time finding work. I was ashamed of what our guys had done, but the great shame for me was being exiled from France. If the French had hated Americans before, they now had a new reason to thumb their noses at us.

During this time, I traveled back and forth from Europe to America.

On one of my numerous return visits to New York, I starred in a charming musical, If The Shoe Fits at Greenwich Village's Bitter End – a quaint little club where Woody Allen cut his show-biz teeth.

The show, a spoof on the Cinderella story, has a guy being the target of his wicked stepsisters, and later the beau of the ball. Jerry Lewis followed it up with the screen version, "Cinderfella."

After my off-Broadway success, I emceed at the Village's Bon Soir for Barbra Streisand, who was appearing in her first Broadway show, I Can Get It For You Wholesale. The out-of-breath diva would rush over to the Village after her last performance and sing her heart out. She'd often run up to the stage, panting for air, still in costume from her show. The club manager would hand her a glass of water, which she gulped right down, and within seconds, she was composed. She'd sit on a plain wooden stool, glowing in the toast warmth of the spotlight, and enchant the crowd.

Barbra went on to Boston and worked the Frolics in Revere Beach. Once again, I emceed her show and, as always, she sent sparks flying through the audience. She hadn't become a Funny Girl yet, but Barbra Streisand was obviously and always a Great Lady.

After the Bon Soir, I worked my musical comedy revue up through

the Village – at the Blue Angel and the Julius Monk room – and into Manhattan, where I got steady bookings.

Around two o'clock one morning, I was walking down 57th toward 2nd Avenue, when I noticed the Montgomery Clift stumbling out of a gay bar blind drunk. Anybody could have murdered this man in his condition, I thought.

This was just after his near-fatal auto accident in Hollywood. I'd heard it had become a nightly ritual for him to get blasted and stagger around until dawn, his raincoat draped ever so cavalierly over one shoulder, as he groped in the dark trying to find his apartment.

I ran over and offered to help him get back home. He slurred a semiconscious "Whereyagoin?" Humoring him, I straddled his arm over my shoulder, dragged the legend ten blocks to his garden apartment on 67th, guided him down the stairs and into his bedroom, where he passed out.

As I was tucking him in, the actor awoke suddenly and without saying a word put his hand on the back of my head and shoved his cock into my mouth. Or tried to. Alcohol kept Monty from getting a full hard-on despite my enthusiastic efforts. Eventually, I gave up and left him unconscious but safe. I borrowed his expensive London Fog raincoat because a massive storm had started.

The next day I returned to Monty's apartment with the coat, but he wasn't home. I later found out that he had flown to California the morning after our get together. I didn't want to leave the raincoat outside his door. I wasn't afraid someone would steal it in that upscale neighborhood. I wanted to use the raincoat as an excuse to see him again when he returned to New York.

He never did. Years later, I found the memento of our encounter in the back of my closet and sold in on eBay for $700.

Although worn out myself, I was glad to have been Monty's designated walker that evening, among other things.

In showbiz, when your star fades, too often the booze becomes your closest friend. But it eventually turns on you, Montgomery Clift.

When that crazy, congested isle of Manhattan got to be too much, Fire Island offered the smoothest cruise on dry land.

David Hadley shanghaied me there one weekend and introduced me to the wooden section lovingly know as the Meat Rack, where everyone went hunting for prime rib in the bushes.

We met a beautiful young buck there who took us to a house at nearby Cherry Grove, where we joined 15 others who were shacking up for the weekend. Male models were everywhere, with a sprinkling of young female star hopefuls roaming among the boy-bods. Pumping through their young, hot veins were scandalous quantities of drugs, booze and an untamed sexual frenzy.

Everybody was doing somebody. And who should walk into this fuck- hungry crowd but Andy Warhol, Mr. Paleface himself. And of course, it was his pad, also known as The Factory.

Andy loved David's innocent good looks, so he invited us to stick around for the weekend. While we were there, he kept walking around with his camera, capturing it all for his experimental films. The perfect voyeur host.

The guy that David and I had met turned out to be one of Andy's models, and he posed and pranced and paraded his goods, making sure to be the first course on David's platter of "whore" d'oeuvres.

I'd been to orgies before, but this was still shocking to me. There were solo performances, twosomes, foursomes, sixsomes – you name it. Some of the action got so complicated, it was downright acrobatic.

Though freed up and outrageous on the stage and dance floor, I've always been sexually shy, so I kicked back and watched.

Ironically, that's the one thing Andy and I had in common – shyness.

Andy and I became casual friends, and he'd often invite me to his dinners. He'd take everyone out, sit there and never say a word.

This soup can guru was not Mr. Personality, but he attracted every-one – the beautiful boys and girls, and the ever-so-fashionable jet set. While everyone was busy engaging in all the talking and joking and end-less banter, Andy would smile and nod his head.

Andy, the ultimate conversation minimalist, rarely bother to say a word. Soft-spoken is an understatement, but Andy's unspoken gestures packed a wallop.

One day I dared him, "Andy, don't you ever speak up?!"

He pondered a moment, and responded, "Yes, Skippy, I speak up," with a glance that stated flatly, "But why should I bother?"

By never speaking, he let everyone else have the stage. That was Andy's gift. Everyone felt like a star in his presence. He never hogged the spotlight.

All the finely chiseled young beauties wanted to become his next "15-minute" star. He thrived on them and they yearned to be part of his

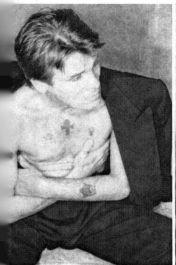

Chris Jones

fashionable underground.

Fire Island was Andy's talent pool. There was always a gorgeous young thing down at the Meat Rack choosing guys to be "discovered."

Andy wasn't famous when I met him. I never understood his magnetism, but I certainly admired him for climbing to the top without saying a word. And turning out all those avant-garde movies without doing the Hollywood scene.

If Andy had genius, it was his ability to draw people to him effortlessly. Andy had the toches everyone loved to kiss, and he never had to tell them to do it. Now that's talent.

I admit I didn't appreciate modern art trends in New York, but when it came to Manhattan's theater scene, I was a stage junkie.

Christopher Jones was a sexy, promising newcomer in the theater world when we met at the Park Savoy. Chris studied at the Actors' Studio, and throughout his long career he's proven himself to be noteworthy and accomplished. His first Broadway hit was Night of the Iguana, which he initially played one of Bette Davis's beach boys, along with another soon-to-be-famous heartthrob, James Farrentino.

After Bette left the show, Shelley Winters joined the cast. The audiences loved her...and so did Chris Jones. Besides her impressive acting talent, Shelley had a saucy pinup appeal. Chris was smitten with her, and they paired up offstage and on.

My friendship with Chris Jones extended far beyond the Park Savoy. When I moved back to Hollywood years later, we became roommates for a short while – talk about Odd Couples!

I still have his sexy brown leather trousers I wore all over Europe. Whenever anyone asked, "Where did you get those marvelous pants?" I'd tease, "Yanked 'em right off Christopher Jones."

I've never been a leather-hound, but that tight body-kissing fit was so comforting. And the fact that they'd been broken in by my stud-boy, made them a sexy endearment.

After all the great Broadway shows let out, everyone hit their favorite hot spots. My good buddy, Johnnie Ray, opened Johnnie Ray's Bowl-A-Bite and, in no time, it became the rave of the after-hours theater crowd. It was a popular place to go for a spicy little munch or two – and not all the munchables were on the menu.

Dorothy Kilgallen, the outspoken New York columnist, had a mad crush on Johnnie, and this otherwise lady-like gal did everything she could, short of spreading her legs in public, to snag the his attentions. She must have done quite a number on him, because it was common knowledge around town that when Johnnie got all hot and bothered over Dorothy, he was taking a breather from his usual gender preference.

One of the spiciest snacks at the Bowl-A-Bite was my belly dancer friend, Maritza, a raging bonfire of carnal delights, who lived at the Park Savoy. Exotic and sensuous in her bold, colorful turbans and luscious body, Maritza could draw men to her with her powerful stare. Never one to turn down an opportunity, I often asked if I could come along and join in the fun. Sometimes, I was let in on the action, and other times I played the voyeur, watching the two hungry savages feast.

Maritza's hot looks lured the most gorgeous men. Marlon Brando lusted for dark exotic ladies, and Maritza sizzled in any language.

Once, I banged on the walls, shouting, "Shut up! I'm trying to sleep! and if you won't, let me join in the fun."

Marlon cracked up and then Maritza chortled, "You'll have to take matters into your own hands, tonight! So, just get a good, firm grip on yourself, Skippy."

Marlon Brando, was no more than a casual acquaintance during his sexual serenades through the Park Savoy walls. Although I was always a big fan, Marlon was the last person I ever thought would come to play a role in my life. But in the mid-1980s, I found myself in the middle of a raging hostility that tore into the heart of the Brando clan.

But more of that later...

I first went to London in 1963 to study at the Royal Academy of Dramatic Arts.

Many of my memories of England are fogged over by the damp, gloomy London haze that always covered me like a trenchcoat. But there was nothing dreary about my cozy room at Olivelli's, the world-famous theatrical hotel on Storr Street. With its old world Italian flair, Olivelli's was a popular place for actors, and remains one of my favorite hotels.

There was a marvelous Italian restaurant inside where everyone got together at all hours for lively conversation, the smoothest wines and coffees, and sumptuous primo pasta dishes. The unlikely setting for this great restaurant was the hotel basement, which originally served as a WWI bomb shelter. During the World Wars, Olivell's was the place to go, because you never had to worry about getting blown up while having a night on the town.

After the wars, the restaurant remained just as popular – if you got bombed, it simply meant you'd downed too many, and your worst casualty was a killer hangover the next morning.

Many nights, I ran into Joan Littlewood, London's sought-after director/playwright/producer. Joan's room was down the hall from me, and we became fast friends. I often joined her at her corner table, wearing her trademark dark glasses and jotting down ideas. It was such a pleasure listening to this free-thinking woman whose play, What A Lovely War, was a smash in London's West End theater district, where the play helped shape the anti-war movement. Joan Littlewood's uncanny insights set her apart from the stuffy British literary community, where she was years ahead of her time.

In London's Mayfair area, I played the Blue Angel with Noel Harrison, the talented and handsome son of matinee heart-stopper, Rex Harrison. Margee worked her on-target impressions while I'd whip into my Carmen Miranda bandana and Anna Magnani shawl. Humor and camp, followed by "Danny Boy" and "Over the Rainbow" wrapped us up.

A little heartfelt pathos gets 'em every time.

My foolishness of running all over the room, jumping on tables and getting fresh with everyone, always caught the straitlaced Brits by surprise. They loved my Yankee zaniness.

But the Blue Angel audience was no ordinary crowd. I'd be skipping around like a crazy monkey with his tail caught in a light socket, and suddenly I'd be sitting in the lap of royalty.

Proper but funloving Princess Margaret and her royal entourage would often come by to see me carry on. Gayer-than-gay Lord Snowden was always with her.

She and the rest of British royalty seemed to prefer the dandy boys, especially in their servants. So many of the British help were gay. So much of the present tabloid tripe was started by the Royal Family's unloyal subjects shaking out the dirty royal linen.

When it comes to trashy tab rags, America has the Queen and her dishy little queens to thank.

There was a young mop-head who was just breaking into the music biz – a Liverpudlian named Paul McCartney. He and his girlfriend, Jane Asher, a lovely English actress, would often stroll in to watch me ham it up. I'd mimic Paul, exaggerate his walk and talk, and poke silly fun at him.

Noel Harrison was shocked, "Skippy, do you realize Paul's one of the Beatles?" Beatlemania hadn't erupted yet. Paul McCartney was just a terrific kid with hair.

"Well if the other three are half as nice as Paul, I bet they make a go of it."

Not long after that, I was in Paris' Olympic Theater with Margee and Nancy Holloway, catching the Beatles' bon voyage performance, just days before they took over America on the Ed Sullivan Show.

After the show, Margee and I strolled backstage to say hello to our lad with the scandalous hair. The minute he saw us, Paul started jumping up and down like a British kangaroo, shouting, "Skippy! Mr. Blue Angel! Over here, over here!"

With 50,000 teenage girls, he picked us out of all that pimply confection.

My friend, a regular, decent fellow, down-to-earth and genuine – if any Liverpool lad was going to become a bloody success, I was putting my money on Paul.

Blue Angel is the place of many memories. On the evening of November 22, 1963, I was on my way to the Blue Angel when I opened the door and Margee fell in – she'd just heart, President Kennedy'd been shot.

We felt as though we'd lost one of our own. News of the assassination had just broken over the BBC. The whole world would soon be in a state of shock.

The next day, London shut down to pay its respects to America's fallen leader. Margee and I walked to the American Embassy, and the sight that greeted us was overwhelming – a living tapestry – Americans, Londoners, people from all over the world, who were touched by the life and death of John Fitzgerald Kennedy.

When we returned to the Blue Angel that evening, Paul was there. He walked over and put his arms around me, "Everything's going to be okay, Skippy. I know it will."

A simple decent gesture from a decent loving man.

I felt so blessed to have seen President Kennedy in Wiesbaden in 1962 when he came to the base where I was working, to thank everyone for their hard and frequently unacknowledged work in behalf of our democracy.

I often wonder if the world ever fully recovered from its loss of this great man. Many try to trivialize his accomplishments, but that will never change my view of this true leader and patriot.

CHAPTER SEVEN

1960s – The Rich and The Horny

One of my grate traveling joys was meeting strangers, a pastime that often got me in trouble. Far too often, I took a vacation from common sense and ended up hoodwinked by a beautiful face. Basically, my brain was an excellent judge of character, but my brain cells dulled in the face of beauty.

My only hope is a high-tech blindfold that straps down over my eyeballs within a twenty-mile radius of a captivating face.

There were many stops along the Skip E. Lowe Ravaged, Robbed, and Beaten Tour, but my greatest sucker hit was It Happened in Tunisia!

I loved the adventure of charting my own course in a land where I had no friends or contacts. And so it was that I decided to board the boat to Tunisia.

I'd been warned about clean-cut college students waiting at the docks to rob Americans of their passports and money, but I knew it'd never happen to me.

When I got off the boat, a lovely young fellow offered to find me a hotel. He was so gracious and helpful, I took a chance. After all, he had an honest face.

We hopped in a cab, which he directed to an affordable little hotel, helped me haul my six heavy bags to my room, and then pointed out a restaurant next door, where I treated him to lunch. We had a pleasant chat over coffee, and I was so impressed with his fluent command of French, English and Spanish. The perfect companion and travel guide!

Phooey on all the warnings, I had found the most honest person in Tunisia and he had an absolute angel face.

As evening approached, I was dead on my feet, and went up to my room. My angel asked if he could come up and rest for a while, and I told him of course he was welcome, after all he'd done for me. I showed the virtuous young man to my room, then locked the door. After all, I didn't want any hoodlums to mess with me or my trustworthy friend.

My rest was cut short by the sound of fumbling in the room. A few hours too late suspicion kicked in.

"Excuse me, if you're going to rob me-"

My lovely friend swore he wasn't, offering the reassuring words, "I just wanna tie you up for a while."

Damnit!

So, my friendly stranger tied my hands to the top bedposts and my feet to the far ones...using my own neckties. Next he taped my mouth with a roll from his pants pocket.

I tried to scream, but my screams were sucked up by the tape. The jerk rummaged through my bags, tossing aside my money, jewelry and clothes.

Now, I was nervous. Other than my valuables and dashing good looks, what did I have?

My passport? Of course. The instant ticket to freedom for anyone desperate to avoid red tape. My guest drooled over my passport, but didn't take it. He just walked out, leaving me bound, gagged and utterly helpless.

I didn't know what the hell was going on. Was the kid leaving? Was he coming back? Death in Tunisia? That didn't even have a ring to it. Trust, it screwed me around once again.

I kept saying the words over and over...never again...never again...

Exhausted, I eventually fell asleep. When I woke up, it was seven in the morning. The door opened and my abductor entered bearing croissants and coffee. How lovely! A catered imprisonment.

After removing the tape and ties, and advising me not to yell, my thoughtful warden offered me the continental fare. I cried as I choked down my rations, and then begged the bastard to just take the passport and let me go.

I figured I could get a new one from the American Embassy once I told them what had happened.

I tried to assure him I wouldn't let on that it was stolen, but he didn't trust me.

After another full day of the rope and gag routine, the kid told me he needed a second passport. I explained I didn't have the connections to swing an extra one, but he'd have none of it.

"You're lying! You Americans can get anything you want. Don't you know that, you fuckin' retard?"

A banging interrupted our little party, as a hulking brute stomped his way over to me and spit in my face.

"Is this the American FUCK!?"

Reaching over, he grabbed my head and yanked my hair. "You filthy Americano shit! Where you from, little girl?"

I didn't say a word. "You fag, right? New York fuckin' American queer!" He yanked at the ties, making them burn through my raw skin. Then he slammed my head down on the bed, pulled a filthy kerchief from his pants and forced it deep into my mouth. Finally, he grabbed my passport from the table and stormed out.

As the kid was making his exit, he whispered, "Don't worry, Mister. They're looking for you. They'll find you. Please don't worry, Sir."

Two hours...four hours...eternities later, the door opened and two disgruntled police officers strolled in and removed the restraints.

I thought I'd been saved from the torture. Thank you God! I'd learned my lesson. I'll get a new passport, some sympathy and a little respect.

Wrong! The cops took me to the American Embassy for the ultimate degradation, assaulting me with every imaginable question and accusation.

"You sold your passport, didn't you Mr. Lowe? DIDN'T YOU MR. LOWE?! We weren't born yesterday. You tourists come overseas, sell your passports, and make five to ten-thousand dollars off the deal."

Shit, now they tell me. I could've put the thing on the open market and saved myself all that stupid aggravation.

Suffice it to say the charlatans at the American Embassy put me through more red tape humiliation in an hour's interrogation than the Tunisian student and his rabid wolfhound got away with in three long miserable days.

Other entertainers have reported the same unhelpful attitude from government servants, who have their jobs by virtue of our tax dollars. Often it was more effective to go to the English or Australian embassy, who were decent and helpful in crisis situations.

Ankara, Turkey was another stop on my hazard tour. Innocent and ignorant, I had no idea I was intruding on a revolution, where Americans were not popular.

With bombs laying waste to our Embassy, and American flags being burned, police urged us not to venture outside the bases.

But that didn't stop me. Since I was usually mistaken for English or French or German, I made sure to use that to my curiosity's advantage and continued to indulge my explorer's nature.

Nevertheless, the violent bomb-bursts and constant shelling finally convinced me that a inconvenient revolution was indeed taking place and that perhaps I'd not reached my destination. Yet.

Greece seemed the likely next step. But with all the fighting, transportation was shut down.

I ended up sneaking out on a freezing winter day with a bunch of peasant farmers on their primitive bus. Squeezed in with pigs and goats, Noah's nightmare beat walking, so I stayed aboard all the way to Greece.

My romantic vision of Athens made the cold, smelly journey bearable – and things began to heat up when I met a gorgeous young man on the back of the bus. Tall and blond, Tom Brown was the perfect specimen of youth.

The only Americans on the bus – and the only ones with no four-legged animals – we talked throughout the trip and ended up deciding to share a room and split the expenses. Tom was a writer from New York, traveling the world. Another wandering student of the universe. A mirror image of myself...except taller and better looking.

Tom and I had great fun in Athens, exploring the remarkable ruins and architecture. Tom was an impeccable roommate, kept our place spotless, and never hustled me for a thing, not even a cup of coffee. So while Tom was busy writing, I was out plotting where my next meal would come from and how I'd pay the rent while he waited for his check from home.

Once I learned the whereabouts of the American military bases,

I was off and working.

Then one night, several weeks into our stay, I came home to honest, thoughtful Tom and realized he'd cleaned up our place.

Thoroughly. He'd wiped me out.

Tom Brown, the professional thief meets Skip E. Lowe, the professional sucker. Another sour love connection. For the hundredth time, I swore, "Never again! The only people getting into my room will be room service...and then, only after I check their references."

Well sure, I'd had some bum luck on the road to Utopia, but I never let it sour me – good luck's always found me, even through the heaviest sludge.

I hit the jackpot when I took a boat to Tangiers, Morocco. I found a fabulous pensióne and across the street, Parade, a gay bar owned by Tallulah Bankhead's sister!

I'm no sooner inside the bar than I meet Will Rogers' daughter, Mary, drinking way too much, thought she already knew me – "Sippy! Get over here!"

Poor little filthy rich girl, that was Mary. We shared a lot of laughs and drinks that night. I had the most delightful time just hanging out with her. Mary was intent on financing everything. We were great friends, and I never took advantage of the situation.

I enjoyed my Moroccan holiday with Mary. We stayed in Tangiers for six months, and then she invited me to travel to Spain. First we took in Malaga, explored Seville, and finally on to Madrid.

It was great to have a traveling companion and live without a budget. I'm not the Ritz kind, but cruising in style is a lovely break.

During the afternoons, Mary indulged in a long siesta before her nightly round of dinner parties and society what-not. Her social circle was a pastiche that ranged from the sophisticated upper crusty to the rough and tumble bull fighters.

Mary tipped the bottle at every opportunity, though I tried to lessen her need for the stuff, by my ability to listen and amuse. I could sip the same glass of wine for hours where this sweet, beautiful darling needed her crutch constantly refilled.

Besides booze, Mary's other weakness was hot, young devil gods – Greeks, Italians...the sultrier, the better. She had steamy parties all night long. Actually, they started out as parties, and then the inhibitions and underwear began to fly.

One day Mary hauled us off to Greece, determined to leave no stud unturned. When she saw what an appreciative audience I was, she insisted I help her with her "carpentry." Share in the chores, I always say.

Papa Will made sure that working was not an option for Mary and she was intent on sharing the largesse. She gave me all sorts of things – including an exquisite pair of gold cufflinks with emeralds, that I treasure to this day.

We were both lonely, but we never spoke of the pain – just covered our need for intimacy by our perfect little club for two. But after months of tasting the fat extravagant life, I felt disconnected and empty. As though my ability to contribute had shriveled. Like Chaplin's Little Tramp, I was out of place and confused among the drifting privileged set.

It was time for this little tramp to move on.

Mary was a perfect companion, who would have provided for me indefinitely, but I had to say goodbye and pray she wouldn't run right back to her bottle.

Sadly, Mary Rogers drank herself into the grave. I'm sure the liquor

Barbara Hutton

store owners shed a tear when she left the scene, but I miss her the most. She was a great friend, and friends don't come easily.

Through Mary, I met America's "poor little rich girl," Woolworth heiress Barbara Hutton. "Rich" because when she turned 21, Barbara inherited almost $800,000 in today's money from her mother, Edna Woolworth Hutton, and her father, the co-founder of E.F. Hutton & Co., the investment and brokerage firm.

"Poor" because her mother committed suicide, and a five-year-old Barbara found the lifeless body. Several abusive spouses, among them European aristocrats of dubious lineage, reinforced her public image as a "poor girl." Instead of feeling sorry for Barbara, some reporters blamed the victim and mocked her propensity for marrying a series of Mr. Wrongs with faux titles.

I only found about the tragedy years after Mary Rogers introduced us around 1960. Barbara loved to surround herself with entertaining people who made her laugh and forget her troubled past and present.

As a professional if starving comic at the time, I formed part of Barbara's entourage, one of the court jesters who kept her relatively happy. She also got a lot of help, if that's the right word, from liquor and drugs.

Whenever I saw Barbara in public or in private, she was invariably enveloped in an alcoholic cloud and surrounded by handsome young men decades her junior. Her friend Josephine Baker adopted 12 orphans of various races she called her "rainbow tribe."

Barbara had a "rainbow harem" of Italian, Greek and American studs, black and white. Skin color meant nothing to her. She was an equally opportunity seducer. It didn't even matter what you looked liked like as long you were fun to be around and cheered her up.

The first time we met, she was at a Parisian jazz club, The Living Room, cuddling with a good-looking, tall, biracial Algerian in his early 30s. Barbara was 50something.

Generous to friends and strangers alike, Barbara paid the hotel bills and travel expenses of her entourage, which included me. I also stayed at her gated, walled palace in Tangiers along with the rest of the boys.

Barbara, Mary Rogers and I often went shopping for jewelry for the beautiful escorts. Back at her hotel or mansion, she'd distribute the costly baubles among the studs.

Besides dinner and travel, Barbara invited me to several orgies that Nero – or Hugh Hefner – might have envied. At one of these gatherings, I saw a beautiful biracial man with the largest cock of all time, 14 inches minimum. Arm-in arm, Barbara and her café au lait Adonis paraded among the other guests as she solicited compliments about his looks and endowment.

Barbara's trophy boy toy wasn't a male prostitute, just very friendly and open to anything. And I do mean anything. As I recall, all the men at these orgies, straight, bi or confused, participated in anal and oral sex with each other and female guests, including my best friend, Margee McGlory.

After that memorable night, I flew to the Far East to entertain our boys in uniform as a member of the U.S. Army's Special Services troupe. I never saw Barbara again.

When she died in 1979, I learned that her extravagant generosity had made her "poor" sobriquet literal. Depending on the kindness of a stranger turned friend, Hernando Courtright, Barbara spent her last years at his hotel, the Beverly Wilshire in Beverly Hills. Her room and food bills were paid by Courtright.

All that was left of her nearly billion-dollar fortune was a checking account containing less than $4,000.

With no particular place in mind except good food and wine, I headed off to Naples after I got off Barbara's dizzying merry-go-round of booze, drugs and orgies...

Napoli gave me steady work, and my search for the perfect casa Roma took me from the Via Veneto to the Piazza Del Popolo, where I stumbled upon the stately pension, Bella, right beside the Spanish Steps.

In the morning, I'd run to the American Express office for the mail, find an empty step, and sit with my coffee, reading The New York Times, making small talk with the tourists. In Europe, the American Express office was the perfect place for people-watching, making new friends, and the only mailing address, as far as I was concerned.

Rome is for roaming, and I loved exploring those ancient roads. It was a spiritual venture that put me in touch with my past. As though I'd actually stepped into some lost corner of a great civilization that had long since vanished.

I loved walking the Roman countryside, with its simple dirt roads, ancient barns, and acre upon acre of crackling-fresh barley. One look at the gorgeous landscape, while sitting under even the stormiest skies, and

On the Spanish Steps

I could see what inspired the masters to paint. A peasant's paradise – I could feel a hunger for that life.

But back in the city, the people and cafes called to me. The Cafe Rosati was one of my favorites. And it's where I discovered two of Rome's greatest treasures, the famed photographer of the stars, Sanford Roth and his beautiful wife, Beulah.

Both Sanford and Beulah had been high-profile Hollywood photographers for many years. Their phenomenal success took them all over the world, and they ultimately exchanged their rambling Hollywood mansion for a simple but charming Roman villa.

In the 1950s, Sanford had continued the tradition of the great glamour photographers of the '30s and '40s. A genius in black and white, he attracted all the royal subjects of the Hollywood glamour court – Rock Hudson, Charles Laughton, Anne Baxter, Noël Coward, Hedy Lamar, Anna Magnani, Ingrid Bergman, Louis Armstrong, Audrey Hepburn, Gina Lollobrigida and my all time favorite, the great French actor, Alain Delon.

The most gracious hosts, I spent so many memorable evenings with them. One night Sanford told me a great friend and one of their favorite subjects, was joining us for dinner. I didn't know Rock Hudson, only his image – the handsome, rugged, prince – so, I was surprised when this manly guy was fascinated by Beulah's knitting.

He watched mesmerized as she copied an expensive Italian design, which commanded an exorbitant price in the exclusive shops.

Rock loved the sweater, so Beulah told him to take it as a present. But that petite little patch of yarn could hardly fit his enormous frame. That night, Rock got Beulah to teach him to knit his own sweater. Rock, the he-man, knitting? I could hardly believe it!

It was fun to watch, big ol' Rock fumbling with a pair of knitting needles. But he got the hang of it, and left with a pair of needles, balls of yarn and written instructions. In later years he became quite skilled.

For many years, Rock kept his private life a secret. But as manly as he was, he liked his men even hunkier. He'd scout the gay rags for masseur and escort ads, and was always generous to his big, buffed guys.

Beulah was an incredible lady and made the most colorful clothes for us both. We'd have so much fun wearing those outfits. We'd take a plane to Madrid and go to the bullfights, so outrageously decked out, even the matadors paled in comparison.

When I met Anna Magnani in Rome, she told me she'd been attracted by my gorgeous jacket. It was, of course, a Beulah Roth original of embroidered red satin. Was this the story of my life? Rapturous over Anna Magnani, and she was crazy in love with my jacket?

Aside from Beulah's wild creations, Brooks Brothers was my favorite wardrobe – tweed jackets, grey trousers, penny loafers...and a long-flowing cape waving dramatically behind.

The Roths introduced me to their exclusive social circle and once again, the peasant American comic was given an insider's ticket to La Dolce Vita. What a splendid Roman holiday, being entertained every evening at the museums, galleries and the most spectacular parties.

When I first came to Rome, I heard tales of the lavish affairs given by Carlo Minali, the famed dress designer, at his magnificent palla. He was one of Rome's legendary hosts, and an invitation to a Minali affair was highly coveted. The Minali castle was the place to meet the nightly cavalcade of stars who paraded through his gold-trimmed halls.

Minali...Carlo Minali, there was something so familiar about that name. But I couldn't figure out why...until the first time the Roths invited me to join them at one of Carlo's soirees.

Not since the fabulous Berchtesgaden Castle in Frankfurt had I seen such an utterly breathtaking estate, and unlike the Berchtesgaden Castle, this historic knightly mansion was a full-time residence.

After we were introduced, Carlo stared at me, "Skip E. Lowe? You know you resemble someone I knew years ago...Sammy Labella."

Suddenly, I pictured this snot-nosed kid, who'd pushed me around in my old neighborhood of Rockford, Illinois. Not only were we childhood friends, we were born the same day and year – June 6, 1931.

Little Carlo Minali! I hadn't thought about that kid since we were both wearing knickers and scuffed-up sandals. Now here he was, a world- class dress designer.

Carlo and I kept in touch for many years, until I received the tragic news that he and his lover had died of AIDS.

Rome's cafes were the perfect employment agency. Networking, shmetworking. It's called opening your mouth, tooting your own trumpet and letting people know what you can do for them.

I heard through the cafe grapevine that the movie studios were look-ing for dubbers – people to voice-over the Italian movie dialogue into English. It's like doing radio, where you sit in a sound studio and read from a script. So, when Luigi confesses to Rosita that he's been getting his linguini sauced by Carlotta, it's liable to be my Yankee drawl looping the lurid news. I rarely refused a dubbing offer, because, good movie or bad, they paid the rent, handsomely.

The hot news in Rome was that Richard Burton and Elizabeth Taylor were shooting Cleopatra, the epic movie soon to become the epic flop. I was thrilled to be invited to the elaborate set and meet the Queen Vamp herself.

Eddie Fisher was sitting in her chair, reading his New York Times. I strolled over to him, introduced myself and exchanged some polite chatter. Liz walked over, during a break, looking dazzling as ever in one of those fabulous Egyptian gowns that only the Queen of the Hollywood Nile could carry off. Sweet and cordial and shy, she had a wonderful giggle.

Richard Burton stayed distant from the gorgeous star, but it was obvious from his longing looks, he was indeed Cleopatra's willing manservant.

Too bad they got married and spoiled everything. When I saw Who's Afraid of Virginia Wolf, I recognized this window into their life, proving the adage that marriage kills the best relationships.

Drifting along the breathtaking Venetian canals in a gondola was a great Italian treat...especially when the gondolier was equally breathtaking. I invited him up to my room for nightcaps and nookies, but I was determined not to be stupid. I had everything hidden away in the mattress, and gave him a sob sorry about an overdue money order on its way from America. Was I shocked when he not only didn't robe me, but gave me five American dollars to tide me over.

At last, a gallant gondolier.

Over the years, I've returned many times, full of visions of warm Venetian summers on balmy, sun-licked Mediterranean shores. The only problem was I always got my seasons confused and ended up going in the deep freeze of winter. Every time!

I still didn't care, even though frostbitten swim trunks messed with my social life. Give me those canals, those museums, those unmistakable specimens of Venetian beauty, and yes, even those sneaky gondoliers. I am a confessed Veno-phile, an eternal willing American slave.

Like most entertainers, there was one love-hate relationship in my life I could never resolve – me and my luggage. Whenever I traveled, my heap of bags went with me. I lugged those bags from one end of the globe to the other.

To show their appreciation for being escorted in style all over the world, those leather lead weights gave me a gift I'll remember forever. A hernia I carried for months, all the way to Frankfurt, Germany.

That thing was so painful, but I hated hospitals, and I was paranoid about Germany. Old World War II flicks were screening inside my brain, and I pictured a Peter Lorre SS officer, sharpening his scalpel as he prepared to experiment on me.

Eventually the pain was overwhelming and I reluctantly checked into the American hospital and told the doctors to get rid of the beast before it did me in.

After the operation, I desperately needed a recuperation period. Vonny and Harry Monroe, a dear couple who entertained at the bases (Vonny was a French singer and dancer with the grace of a young gazelle, and Harry was an American magician) let me stay at their apartment, while they nursed me and tended to my whims.

Every night, Vonny and her friends had a card game, and I enjoyed playing a few hands. But one night, while the poker hands were flying in the other room, I was lying in my bed, sick and exhausted, trying to sleep. The noise level reached such a crescendo, I marched my queasy self out there and barked, "Curfew! This casino is closed for the night, Goddammit!"

The gaming crowd took one look at my sour face and tore into laughter, screaming and carrying on even louder. Finally, they'd had their giggles at my expense and broke up the card party.

Victorious, I carried by bedraggled belly back into my room, and finally got to sleep. Two miraculous days later, I suddenly felt great. No more pain. What a relief!

At last, I was free of that dastardly pain-in-the-groin, and the ever-patient Monroes were free of their major pain-in-the-tush.

My darling Margee pitched in and got me an apartment in Frankfurt at her elegant building on 100 Odeweg Strasse. I had the most beautiful balcony that opened onto a breathtaking view of the city. I felt so peaceful and relaxed sitting there, enjoying it. It was a great time for reflection and meditations.

In Berchtesgaden, about a half-hour from Frankfurt, high atop a hill, sits another favorite of mine – an enchanting storybook castle right out of Sleeping Beauty. It was opened to the public after its owner, Adolph Hitler, left for his permanent underground address. When the monster hadn't been planning the destruction of humanity, he'd retreated to this sweet place of beauty. With all its intricate passages and ornate embellishments, the Berchtesgaden Castle is one of the more infamous and breathtaking man-made wonders.

So many American entertainers were staying in Frankfurt, doing shows for the military. Margee and I worked for the Special Service clubs on the American bases. Before calling it a night, I'd snag a ride to nearby Wiesbaden to see just how thoroughly I could bankrupt that Spielbank, the goose that laid my golden jackpots.

Train stations throughout Europe are works of art. Frankfurt's Bonhoff station was one of the more extraordinary. Every Saturday night hundreds of people cruised one another, walking for hours inside the massive building.

After checking out the Bonhoff, Margee and I would disco at The

Wolfgang Boulhold

Nunnery. It was owned by an order of Catholic sisters who lived upstairs. The hooded gals usually managed to stay out of sight, but early one morning, as I was stumbling out of their blessed bar, I spied two of them.

"G'mornin' sisters!" I called out.

They hurried upstairs, grabbing their rosaries, probably to erase my ungodly taint.

Frankfurt's Gurney Hotel had a wonderful bar where I often whiled away a few hours. During one of those times, I met my prince – Wolfgang Buhold. Nineteen years old, tall, blond, German and arrogant, Wolfgang kept tossing coins in the jukebox, selecting "Hey Jude" over and over. Finally I walked over to ask if he'd consider a little Edith Piaf.

When he finished laughing, he looked down at me, inquisitively. "You're awfully big for twelve!" I quipped. My joke made him roar, as I continued, "I was made in Japan." But when I tried to push my coins into the box, his large hands blocked the coin slot. As we bantered back and forth, I knew I wasn't angry, because the only tune I wanted to hear was his moaning on my pillow.

In short order, my German Adonis and I became an item. I never questioned how I'd found such a special person. I was just so glad he was

124

snuggled inside that lonely heart of mine.

Our relationship was every bit as fulfilling as my friendship with Dick roman, but this ventured further...into romantic love. We went everywhere together – the opera, the theater, fabulous dinners and all my shows on the military bases, often with Margee, making us a cozy threesome.

Although Wolfgang had a lot of attitude, he wore his arrogance with charm and taste. Eventually he moved in with me at 100 Odeweg.

One night, Wolfgang told me he wanted to travel to America with me.

"America?" I teased. "Oh Darling, there's nothing in America you don't have here."

I assured Wolfgang I'd love to show him the land of the fee and the home of the Whopper, but I wasn't ready to head back right then. I did promise him that I'd go to the American Embassy and do my best to finagle a visa for him.

Actually, I felt America might be a smart move for my darling. With his commanding German presence and cockiness, and those pin-up boy looks, he had the goods to make a mint in the States. I certainly wanted my fair prince to follow his dreams, but right now he'd have to go on without me, because I had other plans stirring.

It was 1966 and Margee and I were sick to death of the war raging in Vietnam, but we wanted to show our support for our boys. Surely there must be some way we could pay our guys back from throwing themselves into the fire while we were enjoying a carefree life thousands of miles away.

We knew friends were shipping out to Vietnam and entertaining the troops for the Special Services clubs in the foxhole circuit, smack in the middle of the action. And they were making decent money to boot.

Patriotism and capitalism, the perfect mix. Why not?

Above all, I felt a duty to my country. The least I could do was lift the spirits of our soldiers with some good old American nuttiness. This was something Margee and I had been mulling around for awhile. With Wolfgang getting antsy to leave, I was feeling my own urge to bail.

Margee and I decided to take the next available train to Marseilles, then set sail for the Far East.

Sure, we were acting on impulse. Plans? Who had time? With the destructive path the world was spinning in, there was no time to spare. We had to act now.

But suddenly I was faced with the fiercest challenge of all – how to let Wolfgang know I was leaving, without getting murdered by my he-man in the process. Wolf was so hell bent on shuffling off to America with me, I couldn't count on him to act rationally.

Before I even had a chance to break the news, he got wind of my plans, and charged into my room, "Skippy, you lied to me! You said you were taking me to New York. I can't even trust you to keep a promise!"

Startled out of my sleep, I stalled, "Yes, Wolfgang, I will. I will take you. Just calm down, Dear." I reached out my hand, but he clenched his fists.

"No you won't, you liar! I know you and Margee are planning to sneak away to Vietnam!"

The way Wolfgang carried on, you'd have thought we were running off on a madcap honeymoon.

I tried to set the record straight, "I've sort of been drafted, Wolfie dear. I volunteered myself for front-line duty in Vietnam so I could perform for the troops. It's hard to explain, but I have to go. I'll always hate myself if I don't. Please understand, Wolfgang. Please, Darling."

When I saw the veins swelling in his neck, I reassured him I'd earn enough money in Vietnam to send him to America and that I'd join him once my entertainment tour was over.

But there was just no reasoning with him. He grabbed me by the wrists, dragged me to the balcony, flung me over the railing and held me upside down by my ankles. Like a human pendulum, I swung from side to side, dangling above the traffic below. He threatened to loosen his grip and send me plummeting to a messy SPLAT if I didn't swear to take him to America right then and there.

By this time, all of the blood had rushed into my left eyeball, "Pl-pl- please, Wolfgang, pull me back up!"

My body was trembling so hard I was afraid I'd shake myself right to the ground and save Wolfgang the trouble of dropping me.

"Please dear, I'm not deserting you. I swear I'll get your ornery ass there as soon as I get the money. I won't leave you stranded. I love you too much to desert you, Wolfie."

Finally convinced, he pulled me back inside. I'm positive, however, it was sheer terror and nausea, not sincerity, that was doing all my talking at that moment.

Once Wolfgang had me back on solid ground, he grabbed me by the waist and hugged me with such intensity, I was faint. But this was my mighty prince showing affection. I knew his embrace could kill me, but right then it was the thought that counted. He finally let go of me and began to cry like an infant who'd had all his toys taken from him. I had hurt his feelings, and he felt rejected.

I felt guilty as hell, because Wolfgang meant so much to me, but I couldn't betray how I felt.

Since Wolfgang's tears were now at high tide, I knew it was time to send in the lifeboat. In all sincerity, I told him just how much I valued him and all our special times together, and that I'd bring him to America. We hugged for a long time, and fell asleep, each of us dreaming of his own foreign land – Wolfgang's America, and Skippy's Vietnam.

The next night, Margee and I packed our bags and armed ourselves with the performers' best ammo – killer shtick. We didn't even wait to be booked at the bases.

We just got some money together, moved out of our apartments, and made tracks to the nearest train station.

I was skipping off again, but for a noble cause. Auf Wiedersehen, my hot-tempered young Wolfgang.

CHAPTER EIGHT

Live From Vietnam!

Our great Asian adventure began on a train to Marseilles. Upon our arrival, Margee and I had to unexpectedly check into a hotel for the evening. Our boat to the Philippines, one of the gateways to Vietnam, was off-schedule and wouldn't be leaving until the next day, so we were forced to dig into our pockets for a room to hold us for the night. Already, the budget had been eaten away, but hopefully the Philippines would offer some club work to tide us over.

Our tiny room was a big enough excuse to stay out all night and soak up the local French color – blood red to be exact. A port town, Marseilles attracted more than its share of dirty little thugs who'd dock their ships filled with drugs, guns and other contraband at all hours. With all that shady intrigue, it's always been a dangerous place to hang out.

Margee and I didn't scare easily and we strolled those foreboding streets late into the morning, putting on our tightest face and walking fast so as not to get sliced into fish bait.

We located a superb French restaurant where some gracious natives treated us to wonderful food and casks of fine aged wine. The savagery right outside the door could have been a million miles away.

Early the next day, with a pleasant buzz still in our heads, we headed for the docks. We talked our way into student rates on an overcrowded boat. A boat? More like a cattle ship, where we were nothing more than sides of beef hauled across the Indian Ocean.

It was a grueling six-week sail that tossed us across the ruthless waters. Vicious typhoons trounced us at every turn. I can't recall a single meal I didn't wear on my sleeve, but as miserable as the journey was, I sweated it out, because this was the first leg of my passage to the unholy land of war.

Bombay was the first stop. A wretched land, the docks were paved end-to-end with the ravaged, barely-alive carcasses of men, women and children, sleeping in their feast of scraps we take for granted.

Many of those pitiful souls bound their children's arms, hands, feet, even poked out their eyes...whatever it took to give their clan an edge. The more pathetic they were, the more they brought home for their family.

I felt sorry for everyone in Bombay, and I was throwing change in every direction. They didn't speak English, but their eyes communicated perfectly – "Thank you! God bless!"

The saddest thing was knowing that no matter how many coins I gave, it would hardly prevent anyone from starving.

With death staring at them at every turn, it was easy to understand way they had cults that worshipped vultures.

I saw people dump their dead into huge crates, so their flesh would be quickly devoured by the birds. The families would then return, collect the bones and take them back to their homes as part of a sacred ritual.

After time in the ravaged, forsaken stretch of earth, my own worries – like paying the rent or making an appointment on time – seemed to take on less urgency.

Ceylon was another place wracked with starvation, and cursed with plague. I wondered why the gods were so angry at this part of the world.

Amazingly, in the bowels of this land of the damned and the dying, a spiritual Mecca was thriving. Hippies and other newfound fans of Easter religion, flocked to India and Ceylon. American's drug scene was afternoon tea compared to the far out Near East happening...and I didn't have a clue.

There I was at the "31 Flavors" of the narcotics world, and the only thing I ever scored was Pepto-Bismol, the only "bad trips" being to the toilet.

When Margee and I arrived in Manila, we had to negotiate through a huge parade in honor of Marcos, then newly elected President. The Philippines Hotel gave us fabulous accommodations, and in no time we were booked at Clark Air Base and the Subic Bay Naval Base.

Adding to my first night performance anxiety was the fact that when I asked who I'd be opening for, all I got was "three Negro girls."

When they came on, I indeed recognized the modest little trio...Diana Ross and the Supremes.

What an incredible first gig in Manila, emceeing for Lady Di and the girls for three nights in a row. Like all the acts on the bases, the Supremes had to furnish their own back-up band. It was a major undertaking to haul all the equipment around from gig to gig, but this was the no-frills reality of playing the bases. We were well compensated, but we had to take care of our own junk. I emceed for all the stars that performed. I'd do twenty minutes of shtick, then introduce the main attraction – Johnny Ray, Johnny Mathis, Peggy Lee, Patti Page, Joni James...

The favorite on Manila television was Polita Correles, and Margee and I guested on her show. I did my comedy shtick and Margee sang through her gallery of impressions – even today nobody can touch her cast of characters – Bette Davis, Pearl Bailey, Gloria Swanson, and even

Walter Brennan and Louis Armstrong.

One of my funnier club dates was at the elegant Club Niles. During this one show, I busted my nuts trying to get even one of those soldiers to smile, till I all but yanked down my drawers. After a long pause, one of the guys finally cracked his mouth wide enough for me to see – every guy in the audience had had their jaws wired shut because of a training accident. Now that's a tough audience.

Inching toward Vietnam, we were booked into Hong Kong. We stayed on the Kowloon peninsula, just across the water, at Chungking Mansions, a popular theatrical hotel. The rich favored Hong Kong, but Kowloon is charming and cheaper.

During the day, the ferries would negotiate the choppy water, but when we wanted a ride back after midnight, we had to take a walla-walla – a small boat with a canvas top. And when those choppy waters were in full form, it was a frightening food-spewing experience.

Whether it was high noon or three in the morning, the heat sent sweat rolling down my body so fast, I was tempted to shuck my threads and bare it all. Until I discovered...pajamas. People were up at all hours, walking the Hong Kong streets like it was one big slumber party.

My nightly engagement was the chic rooftop club in the fabulous Ambassador Hotel. Similar to the Blue Angel, it was filled with an English-speaking crowd as well as our Marines on sabbatical.

Meanwhile, bunny Margee was earning her carrots at the Playboy Club. When she got word she was booked in Vietnam, I was too choked up to speak. Like an inductee waiting for his orders from the front, I was nervous as hell. I decided not to think about it, otherwise I'd freak out and go AWOL. I hated the thought of being dishonorably discharged from the Special Services and have them strip me of my shtick.

After several prosperous Hong Kong weeks, I booked a freighter to Bangkok and emceed in exchange for passage. On this cozy twelve- passenger expedition, I entertained at the captain's dinner table, feeling more like a guest that the help. Between the many delicious courses, I served up my choicest bits and, before I knew it, had dined my way to Bangkok... tastefully of course.

It was an easygoing sail, but there was one particular guest who, to pass the time, moved around the ship, docking at every available male hitching post. With nothing better to do than look for a strapping officer to invade her landing zone, she got loaded one night and called out, "Hey! you some kind'a weird fairy fella? Wassa matter, you scared'a me?"

"Scared?" I asked. "Check yourself out in the mirror tonight and you tell me."

A few weeks later, I came across the lady at an officer's club where I was performing. Sitting right up front, all lovey-dovey with her husband, she realized who I was, and a look of terror flushed her face. She knew I could blow her cushy Mrs. Officer routine, publicly. I let Miss Popularity squirm in her nylons. Her secret was safe with me, but it was sweet to watch her suffer.

I was staying at the Miami Hotel...owned by an American, of course. No matter what the country, big or small, whatever the native tongue, you'll find a hotel with the name of an American city. It's a great way to get the Americans to check it out.

The Miami was first class all the way, and packed wall-to-wall with GIs on leave and entertainers of every sort. I knew I was getting my money's worth right off when I spotted a pool in the center. One big splashfest, with all those hot and bothered enlisted guys – my kind of place.

It didn't take me long to get work. Whenever I'd go to a new city, I'd walk in and say, "American comic here. American comic here." Boom, I was in. It's not so much about talent as having a big fat mouth...and using it at every opportunity.

Bangkok is a noisy town, the pollution is outrageous and the people rude and obnoxious. Still, it's a first class club town. A lot like New York – as crowded as a subway, but you'll never get bored for lack of nightlife.

Sometimes the wild club scene got too hot. I was playing a club downtown, and one night when I arrived there to work, I couldn't find the place. I kept walking the block trying to figure out where it had disappeared to. Suddenly, I noticed a charred up hole in the middle of the block.

Someone had declared war on the owner and set a fire at three in the morning. I'd gotten off at one, so I'd just missed becoming the hottest item in Bangkok by two short hours.

Not long after I got settled in Bangkok, Margee caught up with me at the Miami. She was grabbing some R&R after several long months in the jungle.

"Margee, what the hell are you doing here?"

Shaking her head in disbelief, "Skippy, just one day there is like a year on the outside."

As I swallowed hard, reconsidering, she added, "But it's all worth it! You'll see, Skippy. You'll see soon enough."

That was the moment I realized I wasn't going to play just another silly club circuit. When I got word I was booked, Margee was ready to return, so she joined me on my maiden trip to Saigon.

It was reassuring having a friend along on my first, and I prayed, last war. All at once, that faraway land of death and chaos I could barely watch on the black and white newscast, was about to become my living-color reality.

Hell's gates opened as we approached Saigon. Our arrival occurred only days after the April, 1968 Tet Offensive, the heaviest confrontation of the war.

We landed smack in the bull's-eye of the fighting and, to avoid being attacked, our pilot maneuvered crazily – soaring then plummeting and zooming right back up. I felt like my intestines were slung over the propeller, dangling me by a cord of oozing guts. The airport lights were dimmed, and it looked as though a web had been draped over Saigon. When we finally landed, I prayed for the first time in years.

With bombs blasting over the war-gutted city, Vietnamese were running and crawling in every direction, carrying what they could strap to their backs and balance on their heads.

As I stared at the never-ending procession of men, women, children and babies, my heart was torn apart. When war kicks you out of you homeland, where do you go?

As our taxi approached the Caravel Hotel, right next to the USO, I saw a filthy Vietnamese boy merrily chomping on a handful of big, round, brown nuggets. I brightened.

"Oh, Honey, I could go for some yummy chocolate right now."

The driver exploded with laughter, "Beetles, Man, beetles. It's a delicacy. Very healthy. Lots of protein."

Now I knew I was in hell.

Since this was Margee's return visit, she knew the turf, and that sexy singin' soldier made her rounds. Right away, I started working the Special Services' EM, NCO and Officers clubs, as part of their foxhole troupe – entertaining on the front lines.

One thing I looked forward to was witnessing the great Bob Hope in action. But what I found, was not what I'd expected. Sure his spectacular, patriotic USO extravaganzas were beamed across the world, and only a Communist wouldn't have loved watching Bob entertain the troops.

But while Bob's star-studded shows entertained thousands on the bases, he never went to the guys on the battlefield.

In the thick of the blood bath, between the land mines and trenches, our boys couldn't ask the Vietcong to hold their fire while they took in a show. So we came to them. Like doctors making a house call, we came on the scene to give them a quick shot of entertainment.

Everyone thinks Bob Hope sweat it out in the killing fields. Sadly, not true. Bob was concerned with one thing – giving NBC good footage so they'd buy up his shows. Once the cameras were off...so was Bob.

Spend a night in Saigon? Are you kidding? He was a show-boy soldier, though he let the world believe otherwise. He did his shows, then flew off to his deluxe hotel accommodations in Bangkok.

One night, it was pouring buckets in Danang. Tens of thousands of sopping wet soldiers waited in the downpour for Bob to make his appearance.

I happened to be backstage and overheard Bob, "We'll never get decent footage in all this rain. Put on some go-go girls so we can get outta here. They'd rather see the girls anyway."

Sure, the guys were crazy for the girls, but they came to see Bob Hope. Those guys didn't care about the rain. This was their once-in-a-lifetime chance to see their hero. Hell, most of them would be dead, they didn't get second chances.

Bob waited a few minutes, and when the rain didn't let up, "Let's pull out of here!"

So they put the go-go girls on, and that was that. The great Bob Hope no-show!

Those guys would have stood in the rain till they got pneumonia just for the chance to see him.

Thanks for the rainy-day memories, soldier Bob!

Surprisingly, when you play the war circuit, you not only learn more about pain and death than you ever wanted to, you get one hell of an education in entertainment.

There's no applause more satisfying than soldiers' hands thundering together; no laughter more gratifying than that of war-battered soldiers tickled into an uproar by a silly joke; no reaction more delightful than the yelping, whistling, screaming and crying of a collection of soldiers unselfishly pouring out their love.

We may have been there to boost their morale, but they were the experts at giving our spirits a lift, as we made do on our little makeshift stages, without the benefit of fancy props or costumes.

The marines were always ready in their choppers, to scoop us up from the field and lift us to our next "club" date in Danang, Latrang, and every other godforsaken scrap of land you could imagine.

It didn't matter how much encouragement I received from the ever-helpful marines, I never got used to the bobbing, diving, weaving and yo-yoing as their choppers played hard to get with the bombs. There wasn't enough Bromo-Seltzer to calm my tummy on those crazy airlifts. Once on land, I recovered quickly. One look at the beautiful faces of all those servicemen and women waiting patiently for their entertainment fix, and I was in tiptop shape.

Everywhere we played, we were so well received. Why should those soldiers, who were so fed up with looking death in the face, care how flamboyant or over-the-top I was? They were just tickled we were there to entertain them in those remote regions of enemy territory.

The greatest thrill for me is when I can snatch people away from their heartache and help them forget all the craziness going on in their lives. Whether I use a goofy joke or a sentimental song, it's all about reaching them when they need a friendly pick-me-up. Those soldiers happily gobbled up our entertainment buffet, savoring every morsel of punch line and sappy lyric.

A war zone is not the kind of place that makes the troops feel like laughing, so every chuckle was worth its weight in platinum. They just couldn't get enough. Our troupe included a belly dancer (you can't lose with a bare belly button and thousands of lusty soldiers), and an extra singer. When any of us needed a rousing big band in the background, we got it, compliments of my tinny tape player cranking out the hits. Margee joined us whenever she wasn't off performing at the bases.

Ours shows often became jungle-side pep rallies, leading off with "Yankee Doodle Dandy," a guaranteed rah-rah, flag waver that sent the crowds cheering. Since it was impossible to special deliver each guys' hometown to him, we did the next best thing. They'd holler out a town, and we brought it to life, with "Banks of the Wabash," "Give My Regards To Broadway," "Alabama Bound," "Back Home in Indiana," "California, Here I Come," "In New York," "Deep in the Heart of Texas," "Dixie," and everyone's hometown heart-tug, "America, the Beautiful."

I didn't just clown onstage. When I'd lassoed their funny bones and they were cracking up hard enough to put themselves in traction, I'd land them with a dose of "Danny Boy." In my best Irish brogue, I'd sing the poignant tale of the man who sits on his rocking chair, remembering his brave boy whom he lost in the war. That heart-yanker left the most macho dude teary. I felt like a shrink, giving them a chance to vent their emotions. Like a mass healing, it reassured them that their mission was not in vain, and that they'd never be forgotten by their loved ones.

Singing "Danny Boy" in Vietnam gave it new meaning for me. It wiped me out, and I'd have to take a few minutes to compose myself and get it together again.

Today, I can't listen to "Danny Boy" without thinking of those soldiers in Vietnam, soldiers who left their families with only cherished memories.

I found my niche entertaining the troops, but the Vietcong had a nasty was of booing you off the stage. No cane from stage right to gently nudge you away. I thought I was a pro at handling hecklers till I went one- on-one with grenades. Talk about tough rooms to play.

Once, when Margee was in the middle of a rousing number, and the shelling was getting closer and closer, ever the trouper, she kept right on singing even though we had strict orders to stop. We managed to drag her off the stage and, after the bombing let up, she ran right back on and picked up exactly where she'd left off. Ain't no war gonna stop Miss McGlory!

No matter how much fun we were having, it was hard to forget the bloodbath. One evening, I was on stage, singing and feeling great, when I looked up and saw choppers overhead, with body bags dangling from the side, stuffed to overflowing with dead GIs.

The relationship between the entertainers and the soldiers was astonishing. Those GIs were so protective of us, they treated us like family from the second we got inside their chopper. Though we were fired upon many times, somehow the deadly spray always missed. I don't know what I did to deserve it, but with my guardian angel Marines at my side, I could always count on the heavens beaming down on me to save the day.

Before coming to Vietnam, I certainly didn't have wholesome images of John Wayne movies in mind, but I could never have imagined the unspeakable carnage that I witnessed.

I admit it – Vietnam was the scariest joint I ever played. When I wasn't performing, I felt like crawling into a foxhole and hiding our forever. Nights in Saigon terrified me, with bombs exploding everywhere.

Many nights when I'd return to my hotel, the lights would have to be shut off, sometimes for hours at a time. Alone in my room, I'd sit there petrified, as the war roared overhead. Sometimes I'd scurry under the bed or into the closet and burrow in the dark. With violent noise all around, I'd lull myself to sleep by singing and rocking.

Having barely survived my Chicago Mental Hospital stay, I'd try to remember, war is just another insane asylum that never closes.

Margee wasn't afraid of anything. Compared to her fearless abandon, I was just plain wimpy. She went out with the white mice (the local code word for "police") nearly every night, shimmying and shaking it at all the clubs around town, just having a grand time.

Scared stiff or not, I joined Margee on a few occasions. In Saigon, discos were as plentiful as discarded shell casings, and we went out dancing and drinking at all hours. Sure, there was a curfew, and if you were inside a club or disco after midnight, you had to stay until four the next morning. Otherwise, the white mice would snag you. Where else but in a nutty war zone could you be forced to party all night?

Marijuana smoke clouded all of Vietnam. The weed was inescapable. The mellow high of a joint was like a coffee break for so many, a breather to help them escape the insanity. Vietnam was not a wholesome, Ronald Reagan GI training film.

At least once a week, I made my rounds at the hospitals where the shot-up and shattered American GIs were being treated, and it was gratifying to be able to relate one-on-one with these guys, at their bedside.

Whenever I visited the long-term bedridden patients, I had to remember to keep my smile in the "on" position, even though my heart ached, seeing what they were going through. As I was gabbing away, making small talk, I'd look straight in the eyes, careful not to stare at a gaping wound or other obvious deadly souvenir.

Too many times I had to catch myself from unaskable, "So, how you feelin' buddy?" But through all their agony and loss, these soldiers had the ability to laugh and show how pleased they were someone actually cared enough to pay them a visit.

The almost psychic connection between performer and soldier was never more dramatic than when I was sitting on the bed of a paralyzed, or full body-casted soldier. His body may not have been in working order, but when that kid smiled at me, or winked, or sent some beautiful unspoken gesture my way, it warmed my heart every bit as much as the loudest laughter or applause. It was like seeing the medicine work right before your eyes. That was one incredible feeling for this entertainer.

It was so easy to become attached to those kids. So many times, I'd have a great rapport with a soldier, and the next day I'd go into his room and see an empty bed.

"Oh, great!" I'd gasp, "He's been released!" Only to have the nurse bring me back to earth, "Yes, Mr. Lowe, he's gone. They took him away this morning."

Another statistic in the ever-rising body count. That's war. What has it ever solved?

Many GIs contracted a devastating disease that started with bruises all over the body. Back in the 1960s, little was known about the "Black Rose" other than that death followed months after this bruising appearance. Swept under the rug, this disease had no treatment and attracted no research. I think it was AIDS.

Those who knew they had the Black Rose were given a choice of which telegram would be sent their family – KIA or MIA. Many, who were listed as missing had in fact died long before, from the Black Rose or drug overdose or other hushed-up consequence of war.

There was a medical ship called the Good Hope where most of the boys who had the Black Rose were quarantined until they died. Anonymous soldiers buried unceremoniously at sea – still more "missing" casualties of the Vietnam tragedy.

When the American officers needed their R&R from the battlefield, they often stayed at the elegant Embassy Hotel in Saigon.

I'd rented a room there for a couple nights' relaxation, and asked Margee if she wanted to go for an early stroll. After ten o'clock every night the curfew was in force, so there was no way to venture outside.

We noticed a stairway, and decided to walk to the roof and check out the scenery below.

From the outside, the Embassy looked like any other posh hotel, but we quickly discovered that this one had a nifty little surprise inside. After wheezing our way up several flights of stairs, we arrived at the rooftop. This was a war zone, after all, so I wasn't expecting a particularly thrilling sight, but Margee stumbled upon quite a view. "Oh my God! Skip, check this out!"

Looking out over the balcony, we realized we were staring into a huge whorehouse below. There they were in all their bare-ass glory, the American military's top ranking officers, laughing and necking and grinding away with Saigon's finest ladies of desire. Row upon row of fancy cabañas provided little privacy for the big brass as they partied with Saigon's choicest whores.

Margee and I were a rapt audience, when two South Vietnamese soldiers charged us, fully armed and ready to fire.

I thought, "Jeez almighty, it's okay to kill people around here, but spying on them while they do the hump tango is a capital offense?"

The soldiers explained they saw us from their lookout at the U.S. Embassy, and anytime they spot walking targets on rooftops, they're ordered to shoot.

"You two better get down from this roof or you're going to find your asses in a muddy unmarked grave," they advised.

And what a target I must have been, standing on the roof in my blazing, glow-in-the-dark yellow shirt. So, we went back inside and stayed put for the night, and I thanked God for having sweet mercy on my wandering butt once again.

Across the street from our hotel was the swank Continental Hotel. In the thirties and forties, all the glamorous movie stars and writers stayed there, and it was now the premier hotel for military brass, journalists and TV reporters. I spent many afternoons at its restaurant, La Cava, lounging on the patio.

During a quiet lunch of people watching, I noticed a Vietnamese she-boy, frilled out in a satin shirt and pants, his face all made up, daintily sucking on his cigarette holder.

I was sitting there munching on my salad greens, when Madame Butterfly alighted at my table, his snow-powdered white face turning red. "Listen you, stay away from him! He's mine, do you understand me,

Yankee cocksucker?" I was completely dumfounded. "I beg your pardon?!!" "He's mine! You go out and find your own shit!" In seconds, the she-boy had opened a switchblade just under my chin.

Just what I needed, a Vietcongette, dicing and slicing me like moo shu pork.

Figuring I'd better humor him, I said, "Okay, Honey. He's all yours. Enjoy the ride and buck that bronco."

There had to be a lesson, but I didn't know what it was. I told Margee and, laughing, she shook her finger at me, "Skip – you cruise it in 'Nam, and you lose it in 'Nam."

Although Bob Hope wouldn't dream of doing Special Service shows, many of the performers on his USO shows got down and dirty with us. One of them was Martha Raye, the sweetest, funniest woman it has been my pleasure to know.

When we first met in the early 1950s, Martha owned The Five O'Clock Club in Miami, where she also performed. Ever since, we kept in touch and reconnected in Vietnam during the war. We appeared together in Special Services Shows in Da Nang and Saigon.

All the guys knew her lovingly as Colonel Maggie, and I was her longtime admirer. Not only did Martha do her part to entertain the troops with that powerful, sexy voice of hers and those great comic routines, she also sewed 'em up and bandaged them. Martha Raye was a registered nurse! I'd see her out on the field, patching the boys up as quickly as the choppers brought them in off the stretchers. She was great and they loved her.

Colonel Maggie was certainly no stranger to war zones. All the way back to World War II, my lovely friend Martha could be found belting out a fabulous tune as she poured on the iodine and wrapped the bandages. In Vietnam for seven years, Martha nursed and entertained, running

Dear friend, Martha Raye, joins skip for his birthday

back and forth between Danang, Latrang, Saigon and every other place that cried out.

Martha was a popular screen comedienne, sexy and beautiful with a yen for the limelight, but she was in her element caring for the troops.

She was always there with a generous helping of love and tenderness. Our soldiers loved her, men and women both.

But Maggie had another job besides entertaining her "boys" in uniform. She was also a registered nurse, and when she wasn't belting out a tune or delivering a punch line, you could find her running to meet a helicopter that had just landed with GIs who had been wounded on the battlefield.

There was Maggie, a real trouper, bandaging the injured and even sewing up their wounds, a singing, wise-cracking Florence Nightingale. I think it was the danger we were exposed to in Vietnam that turned our camaraderie into a friendship that endured for the rest of her life.

Years later, Maggie would gain new fame as the spokeswoman for Polident on TV commercials, where she introduced herself as "Martha Raye, entertainer, denture-wearer."

She was already wearing false teeth when were in Vietnam and decided to have some fun with them – or more accurately, without them. One night in Da Nang, she said, "I think I'll take my teeth out." We were at a club popular with young Marines who all loved Maggie because she was so much fun. They were about to learn just how much fund she could be.

Maggie took out more than her dentures that night. She called over a handsome Marine, unzipped his fly, pulled out the Marine's whopper and started gumming it. I was happy to watch all the fun until Maggie shouted, "Skip, let's have a contest to see who can get this young man off first." I accepted the invitation, which the Marines didn't object to.

Pretty soon other Marines crowded around, watching a "stage show" they had never seen on any stage. Laughing and shouting, the jarheads cheered Maggie on, saying, "Keep going! We love you!" The contest seemed to go on forever. She gummed those boys to death. Her mouth was like a pussy. Maggie won the contest, but only because she had the advantage of removable teeth.

Her stamina and endurance while entertaining the troops one by one seemed to prove her personal motto: "I didn't have to work till I was three. But after that, I never stopped."

Most of the Marines we did were very young, but I remember Maggie also gummed an older officer, a Marine captain. I guessed that between the two of us about 100 boys in uniform got off, giving new meaning to the term "Special Services" show. I think they gave us their dicks as a way of saying thank you for raising our morale...in more ways than one.

Maggie was such a kind and giving person, everybody loved her. I still tear up when I think about the sad end of a life that had been so full of joy and fun.

In 1991 while she was living in her ranch-style home in Bel Air, a stranger showed up at the door and said, "I'm Mark Harris, the hairdresser from Vegas." He then began to fix her hair and apply makeup, which Maggie loved. She was not quite herself because of all the medications she was taking following a series of strokes beginning in 1988 that had left her in a wheelchair.

Maggie was so out of it, the sudden appearance of a stranger on her doorstep didn't seem strange to her at all. At the time, Maggie was all alone in her home except for a maid. The woman saw how much Maggie enjoyed the attention Mark paid her so the maid offered to let him stay there...for the night.

I happened to drop by the next day with my friend and fellow Special Services entertainer, Margee McGlory, a biracial beauty. I thought Mark and Maggie were best friends the way they were talking. Mark claimed he had known Maggie for years even though he had just met her for the first time the day before.

In 1991, Mark married Maggie in Las Vegas only a few months after he showed up at her door. He was 42 and she was 75. "Mark schmoozed her like a pro," according to an on-line obituary. He ended up playing Svengali to Maggie's aging, ailing Trilby. Mark took control of Maggie's life and career. One of the first things he did was fire her long-time agent. Then he had her phone number of 30 years changed.

Noonie Fortin was one of Maggie's best friends. He also wrote an authorized biography, Memories of Maggie – Martha Raye: A Legend Spanning Three Wars. For all his meddling, it seems that Mark was a devoted husband although he refused to take a lie detector test on Howard Stern's radio show to determine if the marriage had been consummated. Mark told my friend and neighbor, writer Frank Sanello, "It happened" – "it" being sex.

"During their marriage," Noonie Fortin writes, "Mark, a licensed cosmetologist, would dress Martha up and wheel her around to parties and drag shows. Martha would often fall asleep in her wheelchair."

In 1993, the year before her death, Maggie lost her left leg below the knee due to circulatory problems. After years of drinking, her liver was shot, and her medical team predicted she'd be dead within three months due to years of alcohol abuse. As I recall, Maggie did like her grappa. Always the trouper, she proved the doctors wrong by surviving – barely – for another year.

But her remaining time on earth was not happy. Eventually she lost the right leg as well. Alzheimer's, cardiovascular disease, and cataracts also plagued her. But what troubled Maggie most, according to her friend Mike Pare, was the fear that friends would discover she was functionally illiterate. "She had terrible shame about that," Pare writes.

Near the end of her life, Maggie was in and out of hospitals, vomiting and suffering from diarrhea. On October 17, 1994, she was taken to Cedars Sinai Medical Center in Los Angeles and died two days later.

During her final hospital stay, Mark Harris refused to let her daughter, Melodye Raye Condos, visit. Mother and daughter had been estranged at the time. Sadly, Maggie died alone.

Mark was in New York appearing on radio talk shows, and Melodye wasn't allowed to enter the hospital room where her mother lay dying.

The coroner's report listed pneumonia as the cause of death, but what finally killed my dear friend was choking on her own vomit.

Maggie cut her daughter of her will and left her entire $3 million fortune to her husband.

The funeral was held at the Pierce Brothers Mortuary in Westwood, California, where Marilyn Monroe had been laid to rest. The casket was made of cheap pine. Although Maggie was Catholic, Mark insisted on a Jewish funeral. Melodye learned the time and location of the ceremony from a reporter – only three hours before it took place.

After the funeral, a memorial service was held at the Friars Club in Beverly Hills. During his speech there, Mark embarrassed everyone and revealed how little he knew his wife by referring to her as "Martha." Her friends had always called her Maggie.

Melodye later found out that her mother wasn't even in the casket at the mortuary. The body had already been shipped to its final resting place at Ft. Bragg, North Carolina, where she was deservedly buried with full military honors for entertaining her "boys" during three wars. There had been talk of burying her at Arlington National Cemetery where other war heroes, including President Kennedy, are interred.

But Maggie insisted on Ft. Bragg, maybe to spend eternity with some of the Marines she and I had "orally" entertained so many years before in Vietnam. The Marines had returned the favor by making Maggie an honorary colonel. The Army was also apparently grateful for her services because it named her an honorary lieutenant colonel.

In 1993, President Clinton gave her the prestigious Presidential Medal of Freedom award. I was delighted she invited me to the ceremony in her home, and I shared that precious day with many of her closest friends- Cesar Romero, Anne Jeffries, Rose Marie, and a host of grateful officers.

Posing with Signa Hasso and Mamie Van Doren

As I gazed over at Martha – wheelchair bound, paralyzed, with one leg amputated – I realized, Martha was still fighting with the same tenacity with which she'd cared for her wounded boys over the years.

Colonel Maggie kept up the good fight right till the end. God bless Colonel Maggie, a courageous soldier, in every sense of the word.

The military and the President of the United States weren't the only people to honor Maggie. In 1968 the Academy of Motion Picture Arts and Sciences gave her the Jean Hersholt Humanitarian Oscar. A year before her death, President Clinton gave Maggie the Presidential Medal of Freedom.

If you believe in karma or "what goes around, comes around," Mark Harris' sad life after Maggie's death seems to prove karma's existence. During his final appearance on Howard Stern in April 2008, he revealed that he had blown all but $100,000 of the $3 million Maggie had left him. At the time, he was living with his adult daughter after having suffered two heart attacks.

I prefer to remember Maggie from happier days. In her TV commercial for Polident in the mid-1980s, she introduced herself as "Martha Raye, comedienne, denture wearer..."

I would add to that "my beloved friend."

Mamie Van Doren, a leader among those sizzling sex-tigresses of the '50s and '60s, was another super trouper who toughed it out in the fields with us.

When Mamie slinked onto the stage, the curtain wasn't the only thing rising. She knew how to wake up your battle fatigues and have you saluting in no time. One long, hot gaze from Mamie, and a soldier got third-degree burns or heat stroke, if he was lucky.

But Mamie's one cleavage queen who's no dumb blonde. She's a solid performer and as compassionate as they come. The guys were mad for Mamie, and she stayed in Vietnam for a long time, shuttling back and forth along the various hell-zones.

That gal's every bit as delicious today, and we often go to social functions together. You should see the cameras magically appear from out of the floorboards as soon as Mamie's in sight. A wide angle lens is the only one that will do her big screen figure justice. When the paparazzi appears, Mamie always insists on squeezing me into the picture and, as I'm standing there gazing into her monumental shadow, it's like one gorgeous total eclipse of the sun. You just can't find a sexier humanitarian that Ms. Van D.

I stayed in Vietnam for six or seven months at a time, then took a couple weeks R&R in Bangkok. But in 1972, this trouper was starting to feel the strain. So, I hauled my war-weary bones to the chopper and braced myself for the exhilarating takeoff from Saigon. To my ears, the deafening crackle of the exploding sky sounded like one loud round of applause, cheering me on to my raucous Bangkok Shangri-La.

Ahhh, R&R – Rudeness & Raunch –Bangkok's specialty. Rest and relaxation? Even when I took my trench leave, I kept right on working. But it was relaxing playing the military clubs, knowing I wouldn't have to worry about bombs and grenades hogging the spotlight.

Late one night, all pooped out after a booking, I was burrowed like a little chipmunk, deep inside my warm, soft bed when, one nod short of Mr. Sandman, the phone starts jangling off the hook.

"Skippy, it's Tom...Tom Williams."

I was groggy and I hadn't heard from him in years, but I'd know that whiskied old Southern drawl anywhere.

"Tennessee! Where the hell are you, old boy?"

My old friend, Tennessee Williams was staying at the wonderful Oriental Hotel just down the street, so I pried open my weary eyes and shot on down there. Nearly 20 years had passed since our Park Savoy days, and there were volumes to catch up on. We spent a lot of time together, renewing our very special friendship.

Feeling especially adventurous one night, Tennessee talked me into checking out a male whorehouse, where very young Thai guys lined up for inspection. Five dollars for a night's entertainment. Such a bargain! Wholesale cuties! Those youthful Thai-gers bared their souls...and their britches.

They were truly a feast for the eyes, but my body wasn't in the mood for Thai cuisine, so I passed them up. Whorehouses were not my cup of sake, but it was an interesting...ah...cultural experience anyway.

Tennessee's tastes were more exotic than mine, and I'm quite sure one of those guys stole his heart (not to mention his five dollars...and then some). He definitely scored a big bang in Bangkok, and on many a night I'd find him Thai-ing one on in an exclusive house of pleasure.

Tennessee was a gourmet, and knew his way around all of Bangkok's finest restaurants. When you were with Tennessee, the food and company were always first rate.

There was nothing stuffy or pompous about him. As down-to-earth as anyone I've known, he got pleasure out of coming to the base shows where I was doing my silliness.

Sitting in the audience with the enlisted boys, he was just another fun loving guy out on the town. He was much too humble to be singled out, but I wanted him to know how much I appreciated our friendship, and I wanted our guys to know his interest in them.

One night, I turned the spotlight on him, "Okay guys, quit your bottleclankin' for a minute and let me introduce to you one of the living legends of American literature and theater, Mr. Tennessee Williams."

As Tennessee reluctantly stood up, an officer with an accent soaked in grits and gravy, shouted, "Tennessee? Boy, you from Tennessee? What you wrote? I heard a Tennessee Ernie Ford, but I never heard a you."

Tennessee smiled and said, "I'm a playwright, Sir." "Oh! Well, Ernie, you ever play the Grand Ole Opry?" Gentlemen Tom looked at the guy, "No sir, actually I've set my sights on the Metropolitan Opry," and sat down, unrecognized and happy. I am honored to have know Gentleman Tom – a true Southern gentleman with an uncanny sense of style, and an inspiration to all. His brilliant life came to such an undignified close in 1983, when he was found dead in his New York City apartment, a "child-proof" cap from a decongestant lodged in his windpipe. Death by medicine cap – one of those freak ironies Tennessee would have loved to use to kill off one of his own desperate characters.

Shortly after Tennessee left Bangkok, Margee returned from 'Nam for a breather and, just like me, worked right through her "time off." The President Hotel had the fabulous Cat Eye Room downstairs, where the American businessmen and GIs loved her act.

And across the street in the Aaron hotel, we both got singing gigs and had a ball throwing our hard-earned money right back into the place, treating all the GIs to one rowdy good time.

A couple months into my merry making I got the dreaded call, "Can you do a few short weeks in Saigon?"

I was bummed out at the thought of returning after four years of morning ash and napalm, but my conscience kept saying, "For the guys, Skippy. Come on. What's one more time for the guys?"

Margee was ready to return, so we went to the airport and boarded the plane. But just as it was taxiing, I had an awful thought.

I sprang out of my seat, shrieking, "Stop this plane! For God sakes... stop this plane, Goddammit! Somebody make that pilot stop this thing NOW, NOW, NOW!"

The passengers panicked, scurrying around in every direction, looking for the culprit. Even Margee looked at me as if to say, "Skippy, you've flipped. You've finally cashed in all your chips."

Suddenly, everyone was running from me and pointing at me, like I was the maniac who was going to blow the plane to bits.

A lady screamed, "Watch out! He's carrying a bomb. I saw it! I saw it!"

I didn't help my case with, "Oh sure, lady. Like I have a ton of TNT strapped to my little fanny!"

Yeah, I'd flipped out, and for good reason.

I had reached inside my pocket, felt my hotel key, and realized I'd left my jewelry stashed under my mattress back at the Miami Hotel.

I was determined to get right back to the airport. I didn't care whose flight plans I wrecked. There was no way in hell I was leaving Bangkok with all my valuables sitting there, just waiting for someone to find them.

The frenzied captain circled back to the airport to deplane "that raving nut." I barked and convulsed my way to the exit, ranting, "Out of my way, everybody! It's life or death!"

The airport police arrived on the scene and ordered everyone off the plane so they could check for explosives. Everyone was searched and their luggage ripped open. The police shook me down, tore through my bags and dragged me to the airport interrogation room.

Once they were convinced I was harmless, they released me. In all the commotion, I didn't have time to tell Margee what was going on. I shot out of that airport, ran into the street and hailed the first taxi I saw, "Miami Hotel, NOWWW!"

I rushed into my old room and realized I wasn't alone. But the naked couple on the bed were so busy pumping and pouncing, they took no notice of me. I actually sneaked around and waited for them to roll to the other side, reached under the mattress, and there it was – the ultimate security device.

The Sock.

A smelly old sock – the guardian of my dreams. I turned it upside down, gave it a shake, and all my shiny little friends came tumbling out – sparkling gems, including a diamond bracelet, gold jewelry, and all sorts of pieces I'd collected on my travels.

I was so relieved, so thankful, I kissed my nasty old sock before stuffing everything back inside. At last, I could breathe like a sane person again. The couple continued their passion party, unfazed by my little visit, and I was out in a flash.

Reunited with my stuff, I realized I was so exhausted, I needed a good night's sleep. So I re-registered, flung myself onto the bed, and a couple snores later that sun was rearing it's fiery little head.

"Well, just a couple days more..."

Weeks passed, and I couldn't bring myself to return to Saigon. Like a foolish kid, I kept hoping if I didn't show up, maybe they'd cancel the bloodbath for lack of interest.

Calling it the "theater of war," made it sound like a long Broadway engagement. Vietnam was one show that should've closed years before the curtain fell. With such terrible reviews, couldn't Uncle Sam take the hint? I'd have closed that production opening night.

Who the hell ever won a war anyway? If you're lucky, you have fewer soldiers to bury. Some victory. When they send out the invitations for the next great "battles to end all battles," DON'T RSVP. I know it's rude, but just be honest. Tell 'em you don't have a thing to wear.

When Margee returned weeks later she told me that all the passengers on my "hijacked" flight were talking about the crazy American comic. Just what they needed, some insane party pooper spoiling their lovely flight to the Vietcong cotillion.

But Margee was concerned, "Skippy, are you okay?"

I had to tell the truth, "No, Margee, I'm not. I'm totally exhausted. I feel terrible – I know I should be going back to the guys."

And then I started crying.

Margee had some good size pools herself when she echoed back, "Skip, I feel the same way. I'm sick to death of that dirty war."

"Dirty war? Honey, is there any other kind?" That settled it. As far as we were concerned, our tour was over. Vietnam is permanently branded into my soul. Like some never ending movie, it plays over and over in my mind. I can't erase the images of those youngsters who came from every state in the Union to die on some crazy mission that adults didn't understand. Drafted into service, their lives volunteered away by old medal-chested war hawks who ordered them to get out there and kill, kill, kill?

I can still see those beautiful, uncertain faces...every image, frame by frame, chiseled deep inside my memory.

Every time a soldier died in my arms, I realized that war is not a harmless game. It's about fighting and dying...mostly dying.

Margee took off for Hong Kong while I ran away to the great clubs of Japan, Okinawa, Malaysia, and Singapore. After the chaotic R&R in Bangkok, I deserved a little R&R from my R&R.

In Naha, deep inside Okinawa, I worked many of the Marine clubs. Some of the guys would recognize me from my shows in Nam. "Hi, Skippy. Remember us?"

No matter how many months had passed, emotion overwhelmed me, and made me realize just how deeply attached I was to them.

The first time it was like seeing a ghost – a friendly ghost. One familiar face took me right back there, and I could smell the blood and hate all over again; but all the joyous moments came back too. Here was one more soldier who'd been spared. Another kid made it home alive.

I just choked up when I saw them, "God bless you guys. Welcome back! Welcome back! Thank you, God, for saving one more!"

When I saw even one familiar soldier boy, it was as if the kid had come back from the dead, because once you leave Nam, your deepest fear is that every single kid you're leaving behind is going to lose his life. I wasn't particular. I accepted every life as a miracle.

I spent Fourth of July in Okinawa. Fireworks sparkled all over the island, and I got so homesick. It's amazing how those silly fireworks were such a big deal to me in a foreign country.

Being so far away from my sainted land of Spam, Joe DiMaggio, I Love Lucy and bacon double cheeseburgers, made my country grow even more beautiful. You tend to think the flag-waving bit is just cornball until you step out of your own backyard. It's like leaving a loved one. They may be number one in your heart, but time and miles makes you long for them.

Penang, Malaysia reminded me of miniature towns people set up alongside their model railroads. Tiny two-seater cars motored all over this little toy land. What a charmer! No noise, no pollution, no stress. I picked up some spare change at an Officer's club, where the Australian soldiers were such a fun audience and, because Australia wasn't all that far, I decided to take them up on their invite to join the kangaroos and koalas and skip around the bust for a bit.

But first, I wrapped up my Far East follies with a brief stay in Singapore, where I didn't know a soul. In no time, I was working a club in the St. Croix Hotel. This was one of those "Show me your scrapbook...I'll try you out" kind of deals. When I left a couple of months later, I was still packing 'em in, night after night.

When kids tell me they want to be performers, I tell them – Hit the pavement with your raw resources. Singapore was a prime example of that kind of chutzpa. Sure, you gotta have the talent, and connections can never hurt, but it's the steel ball bearings that gets your talent through the door.

I took my time looking around Singapore, and discovered luxurious

Rafal's, an aristocratic hotel where the English stayed. At first glance, it seemed snooty and high falutin', but the folks were friendly and hospitable, and they'd invite me to afternoon tea and extravagant dinners every night.

After such coddled treatment, I headed out for Australia and traveled all over the continent. But before I knew it I was broke. Never good at saving money, I checked into a small hotel in Perth, hoping I'd get some club action fast.

Poor and hungry, with no idea how I'd pay the bill, I dug my way out of my little gopher hole and stepped inside the hotel elevator. As the doors closed, I felt something shifting under my shoe.

"Shit! What have I stepped into now?"

Disgusted, I lifted my foot and couldn't believe what I'd stumbled upon. A fat, bulging wallet. And I, all alone with my new pigskin friend. It winked at me, teased me, begged me to pick it up and open it. How could I resist?

One tiny peek inside revealed thousands of dollars...

Without hesitation, this goodhearted sap went downstairs to the front desk where a wealthy looking fellow paced, in tears.

I waved that fat thing in his direction, and instantly revived this man from the dead. Just the sight of that wallet was like a whiff of smelling salts.

I handed it over, and he thanked me with a thousand dollar bill. Skip E. luck.

In Sydney, I stayed at the Darling, a delightful theatrical hotel. From the outset it was apparent that the Aussies and the English despised each other. The English can be so proper and stuffy, while the Aussies are like a bunch of uncouth Americans – informal, fun-loving and high-spirited.

An English girl told me to check out the RSL clubs. The Aussie version of our Moose Club, they do us one better. A regular Vegas a-la-bush, they have slot machines. I'm not sure exactly what R-S-L stands for, but for me, it meant J-O-B.

Australians are fond of American comics, but you've got to be funny – and they love gay humor. Why? Because it makes them feel like real men. I could be as outrageous and flamboyant as I pleased. Just make 'em laugh, and they'll let you get as crazy as you want.

Decent as they were, though, Australians had an evil twin, bitchy as a drag queen breaking in a new pair of pumps.

Once I was performing my little heart out, and the dozen followers in the audience wouldn't put down their newspapers. Flashing back to the officers in Germany, I hopped off the stage, snatched those newspapers from under their noses and demanded, "Listen, man, the show's going on."

One of them shot back, "What show?"

I jumped on the chairs, on the tables, in their laps. Anything to get in their face.

I pulled down my fly, recited the Gettysburg Address in Pig Latin and stood on my head. Aussies could be a tough bunch, but I got their attention. They loved the show. But what an effort!

Agents in Europe were calling me, anxious to get me back. It was tempting.

After DeGaulle's death in 1970, Americans had been taken off France's merde list and, like a yummy croissant-flavored magnet, Paris drew me right back in. I'd missed my wonderful, rough Pigalle and I couldn't wait to return to the Moulin Rouge, just down the street from the Mont Jolie.

In no time, I was back into my wonderful morning java and croissant routine, reading The New York Times and jaunting over to the American Express for mail call.

Two seconds inside the Mont Jolie and, can you believe it Margee, my wandering chanteuse, tapped me on the shoulder!

During one of our wee-hours club outings, Margee and I met the singer, Nancy Holloway, who'd just finished touring with Sammy Davis, Jr. Soon to be a big star in Europe, Nancy spent a lot of time with us, and our new friends, the marvelous Jean-Paul Belmondo, and a Russian gentleman named Alexis...

One night Nancy crooned, "Skippy darling, I want to ask you a small favor – do it with Jean Paul and Alexis. I want to watch."

"Oh, is that all?" I bitched.

I can't say there were any sexual sparks, but we "did it" to Nancy's appreciative audience. France was always a wild place.

The French perfected "kinky" centuries ago, and they've been getting it up long before America's limp little sexual revolution.

We spent many evenings at the Blues Bar, one of the hottest jazz clubs in Paris, where Margee performed with American jazz greats Chet Baker and Memphis Slim and Paula Watson, a big-bellied singer-pianist, who was funny as hell. Chet would sing and blast away on his trumpet.

Blasted on heroin, he'd often doze off right in the middle of a number. Chet Baker and I were friends from Pittsburgh, Pennsylvania, and we'd worked together at a club in there.

Chet didn't make much money then – just enough to buy his junk. People thought he was rude, but actually he was just shy and scared of crowds. James Dean was like that.

Booked- on the last voyage of the Queen Mary

Many entertainers like to be alone, but Chet's solitude was self-destructive. In between shows, he'd hide out and serenade himself as he pumped the lethal crap into his arms. There was never a more romantic singer, and yet Chet didn't have a single love in his life besides the dope.

Chet had been such a good-looking boy, a James Dean type, but even his love for singing and the trumpet couldn't save him from his deadly addiction. Wasted and broke, Chet ended up unable to pay off his drug debt. He owed money to everybody in Paris.

In the early 1980s, he "fell to his death" from his Amsterdam hotel room. I believe he was pushed by drug dealers as final payback for moneys owed.

My friend may be gone, but his luscious voice lives on in the recordings he made while half-asleep in the clubs and music halls of Paris.

I was a hopeless road addict, but after Paris I was ready to fly back to Yankee soil.

After being overseas for so many years, when I pictured home, it wasn't a hotel or room or house or apartment, or even a city...it was AMERICA. And that's where I belonged.

Home is the greatest place in the world, because you can run the hell away from it, but you always know it'll be there when you return.

I contacted the American President cruise lines, hoping they could use an entertainer in exchange for a free voyage to San Francisco. I thought it'd be fun to check out the fogged-in, hillside version of New York City.

A representative from the President lines came into one of the Aussie clubs and watched me shtick it to the crowd. He liked what he saw and booked me on the spot. They required only two shows from me. Such a deal! A free trip, incredible meals, and a hot engine room just waiting for me.

Landing the voyage was the easy part. Surviving the voyage was the challenge. When we approached the island of Samoa, disaster overwhelmed us in the form of a typhoon.

As the fierce winds bounced me across the deck like a tennis ball, visions of the sinking Titanic kept creeping into my mind. I knew firsthand how destructive those typhoons could be, and this one threatened to wipe us all out. Miraculously no one onboard was injured.

Natural disasters aside, the climate onboard wasn't much friendlier. Onstage, I was beloved. But once I stepped off, all I heard was, "That American is so funny, but have you noticed how...uh...peculiar he is?"

Peculiar...whatever could they mean?

Yeah, I was flamboyant when I performed. Why not? That's who I am. I camped everything to the hilt. Exaggeration, that's what comedy's about. It was so hurtful to be treated like a demented sideshow freak just because I didn't fit someone's narrow idea of "normal" behavior.

Gay entertainers think they have it rough today, but they don't know. Until New York's Stonewall riots began to open up the gay community, being gay wasn't hip. Still there were those of us who dared to let our uncensored, flamboyant, outrageous selves shine through those ultraconservative years.

When the snooty crowd on deck became unbearable, I'd keep to myself, rather than put out the effort to socialize. Sometimes, in the face of hurtful comments and stares, I'd disappear into the engine room and carry on with the sailors. I was such a little engine room tart, and the sailors had a fun time, too. I'd let them do what they do best – drop anchor on ole' Skippy. Yo-ho-ho, blow the man down.

When I returned on deck, sure enough, someone would corner me and ask where I'd disappear to. I'd play dumb, "Well, I just...I don't know...just tidying up around the ship."

Fortunately, there were none of the deadly plagues that exist today so it was easier to carry on and have a naughty old time.

There was one promising note on that stormy San Francisco voyage. I found that, while the adults were judgmental and fascist, the kids would tell me, "We did you Skippy. You're not like everybody else. Keep the faith, man!"

That felt so good. It was the kids that kept the nasty storms from completely overtaking that voyage. The 1970s were officially underway, and I got the feeling the young people of the world would make changes in people's thinking.

Thank God. Change was coming. Hallelujah!

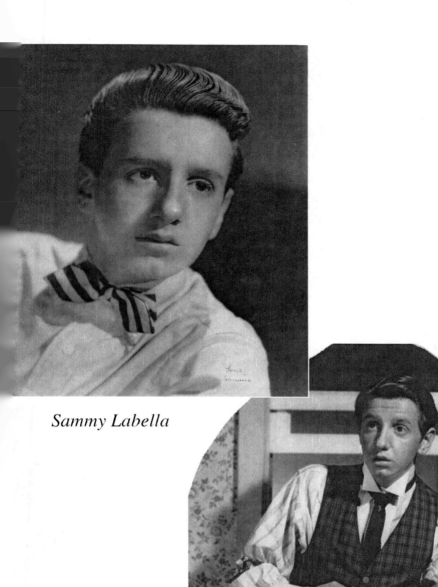

Sammy Labella

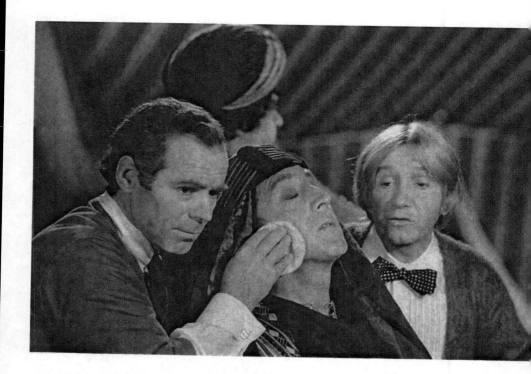

Performing with Gene Wilder in WORLD'S GREATEST LOVER

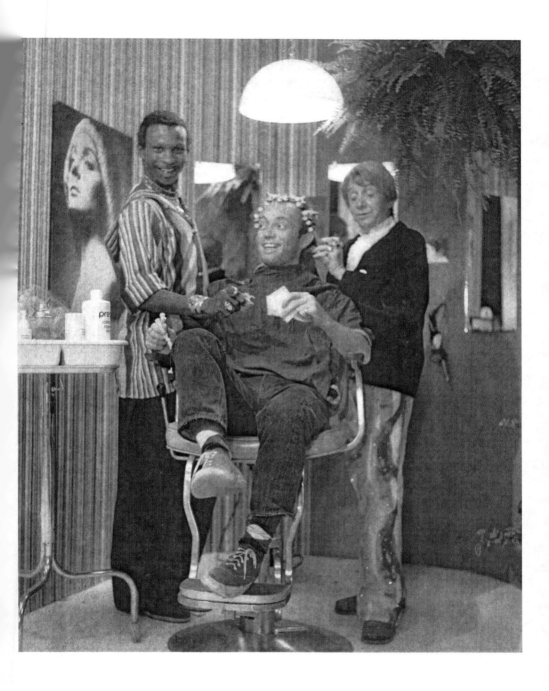

BLACK SHAMPOO starring John Daniels was a fun action comedy where I played "Artie" -an eccentric hair stylist.

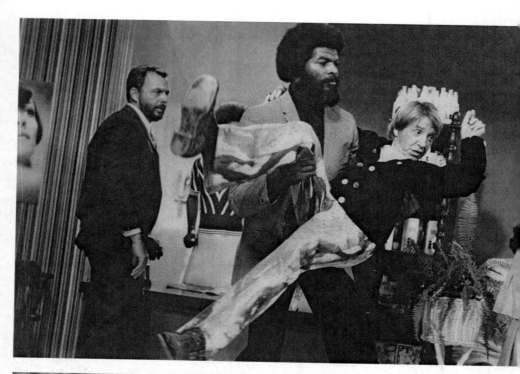

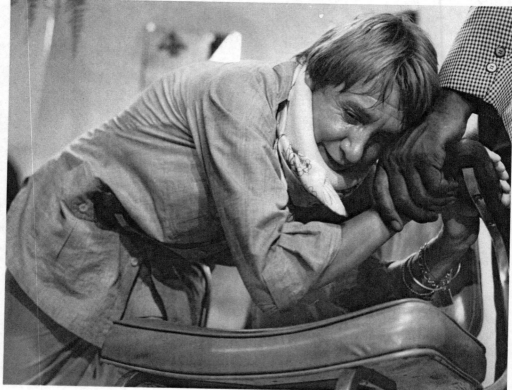

With Cesar Romero and Marie Windsor

Tempest Storm and Morey Amsterdam having fun

Skip with Edie Williams

Christina Crawford, Bill Cable, and Christian Brando

Christian Brando, Skip, & Bill Cable

Christian and Bill in the South Seas

Skip with Janet Leigh and director Curtis Harrington

Helping Joseph Cotton promote his book, with his wife Patricia Medina

Jim Bailey and Terry Moore

*Skip with Olivia Hussey and Leonard Whiting-
the stars of Zeffirelli's **ROMEO & JULIET***

Above: Skip and Aldo Rey at Skips' birthday party

Left: Skip with Rosemary Clooney and Mimi Hines

*With the elegant
George Blackwell*

*Lana Turner joins
Skip for his birthday*

*With Tommy Lee
and Pamela Anderson*

Skip with Helen Hayes

*At home with
Sylvester Stallone*

Cory Feldman, Skip, Madame, and Wayland Flowers

Skip and Marcelle Becker

Party goers: Billy Crystal, Milton Berle

Eartha Kitt, and Jacqueline Stallone

Right: visiting with Kirk Douglas

Below: Grace Robbins, Skip, Phyllis Diller, and Morey Amsterdam

Troy Donahue and Skip

Pauley Shore and Skip

*Skip and
Donald O'Connor*

*Visiting Tony
Curtis in his Studio*

With Cesar Romero and the beautiful Anne Jeffries

Jacqueline Stallone & Georgia Pelham (Cher's mother) celebrate my birthday

CHAPTER NINE

Skip Comes Marching Home!

When our ship pulled into San Francisco, I had to whip out my hand-kerchief. After watching the rape of Viet Nam's humanity, I'd developed such a longing for my country. Until I actually got sight of that harbor, I just couldn't be positive this great land was still safely glued to the map.

A tearing sentimental fool, I stepped onto the pier and kissed the ground, "Come to me, my lover!"

I looked back and waved farewell to the last of my working cruises. Performing on ocean liners month after month is a tedious way of life, but I loved the free passage around the world, sailing from port to port. Free trips on the world's most luxurious sea cruisers saved my life when I was too broke to afford even a dingy, much less the luxury of a liner.

As I walked down the pier, I noticed a crowd craning their heads at a belly dancer. There was only one person I knew who could draw crowds like that – Maritza, my hot Latin chum from New York. I pushed inside the crowd for a closer look, and Lord help me, it was Maritza, in the flesh...and not much more.

After being away for so long, it was wonderful seeing a familiar face the moment I hit American soil.

Just as shocked to see me, Maritza ran right over and hugged me, "This is my day job, Skippy. I get paid to dance while the ships come in."

She smiled at me, took my hand and offered, "Skip, why don't you board at my place for a while?"

Minutes on red, white and blue soil, and already I had a place to stay. Leave it to Maritza to dance me off that pier and right into her heart.

Seeing Maritza was my first jolt; adjusting to her lifestyle was the second. From the beads around her neck to the sandals on her feet, Maritza was a flower child. I couldn't believe it. Those kids in India were my first taste of the counter culture and at that time I didn't even know they were called hippies. America, my sacred land of the free, had become the land of free love.

So I crash-landed smack in the middle of Haight-Ashbury. Turn on... tune in...drop out! The lifestyle seemed bizarre, but I didn't mind the psychedelic music or the sweet smell of incense. After my toke on Satan's wee, I avoided the drug scene, but I'd kick back and check out the kids tripping, like a scientist observing Martians.

Too many of the kids searching of self discovery. There are many routes to getting there, and it's the most difficult journey we'll ever make. I'd have gotten there sooner myself if only it was as easy as finding the right travel agent to book the trip.

After my first few days in the city, I was finally getting adjusted to Maritza and the hippie revolution, when another shock wave zapped me.

While we were out taking a walk, a convertible pulled up on the sidewalk and screeched to a halt right next to me. That kind of curb service reminded me too much of the Chicago gangsters when they were about to do a hit, so I instinctively ran for cover.

Just then, a familiar German voice screamed, "Skippy! Skippy! I have found you!"

Before I had a chance to react, a hulking figure sprung out of the car, grabbed me from behind and locked me in a stranglehold.

"Wolfgang?!!" I gasped.

As ecstatic and overjoyed as I was to see him, I was frightened too. What if my hot-tempered German prince was so pissed at me for leaving him behind in Frankfurt, that he...gulp.

Nah, I didn't think so. After all, he was smiling. In fact, we were both thrilled to be reunited, and embraced, melting into one glorious hug. Two wayward souls, together at last.

Apparently, when he realized I wouldn't be able to take him to America right away, Wolfgang decided to take himself. With only a few German marks to his name, he managed to find a cheap flight to the States.

Once he arrived, his mission began – to find Skip E. Lowe. What an honor, to have someone so obsessed with finding me he'd actually set out on a nationwide search – friendly stalking, '70s style.

Even though I'd been in love with Wolfgang, I figured he'd thought of me as a fling. I had no idea he cared so deeply. I was very touched.

After giving me all the details of his journey, Wolfgang asked about Margee, the woman who, in his mind, I'd dumped him for and ran off with to Vietnam.

"Well, last time I saw her, she was in Hong Kong, doing fine. But that was several months ago."

Wolfgang just winked at me and teased, "Boy, Skip, you sure get around, don't you? You just dump them at every port, then move on to the next."

Oh yeah, just a little cad, that's me. Wolfgang took me to dinner that night, and I learned he was managing The Patio, a popular local restaurant owned by a prominent San Francisco dentist. As the friendly eatery

became successful, he turned it over to Wolfgang, and thanks to his hypnotic charms, that tasty little enterprise became an overwhelming success.

Everyone was hooked on Wolfgang's elegance and finesse. People were always telling him he had the ideal look and attitude for modeling or acting, but he wanted no part of the show biz glamour scene. Footlights and autographs weren't his style.

We hung out together, just two loving friends enjoying the miracle of reunion. But the winding hill ville by the bay could never be my town because, despite its European savoir-faire and Greenwich Village eccentricity, its constant London haze depressed me.

And somewhere, I had the oddest feeling that Mother was calling me. She'd moved back to Hollywood and I felt an urgency to see her.

I bid farewell to Maritza, hugging my lifesaver senseless. I then had to abandon my Prince Wolfie all over again. But this time around, he'd managed a comfortable life for himself and was far more mature and sophisticated than the nineteen year-old punk I'd left behind in Frankfurt. The reunion was my dream of a lifetime, and I knew that no matter where our separate wanderings might take us, my roving heart would always beat with his.

CHAPTER TEN

What the Hell Is a Showcase?

My first visit to the dream machine since puberty purged me of children's roles, shocked someone who thought he'd seen it all. One look at the hookers strutting their hand-me-downs on Sunset and the bum whizzing on Betty Grable's Hall of Fame star, and I'm thinking, "Toto, get me the hell back to Kansas!"

Where was the aristocratic glamour that had been so much fun back in the fantasy factory days of my youth. The Garbos, Gables and Barrymores had left to make room for the unwashed grunge and tattooed armpits of 1970s Hollywood, with its crime, dope and lung gasping pollution.

Hollywood had caught up to its dark ages, and as my mind wandered back to Rascotti's, the Brown Derby and Schwabs, I wondered, "Did little Sammy Labella live here once upon a time, or was that just a Technicolor dream?"

Still reeling, I got the sad news Mother was in a Long Beach nursing home. I couldn't imagine that unstoppable force who'd pushed me into the only career I've ever known, sitting idle.

I rushed over there, walked into her room, looked around and wondered, "Where is that pistol of a gal who herded me through the Hollywood cattle calls and prodded me into giving 100% all the time?"

All I saw was some frail old woman lying in quiet agony. I couldn't figure it out. But as I leaned into her careworn face, a shout came at me like a grenade, "Sammy! What's with you, boy? Never saw your Mama before?"

One brief glance and she'd brightened up like a Broadway marquee. "Mama? Mama?! Yes...yes it's Sammy!" Now I had to make way for the tidal wave of guilt that came crashing down on me. Had I abandoned my mother by traveling all over the world? But if I had to do it over again, I'm sure I would.

Sure, I resented Mother for shoving me into the limelight and dragging me all over the place to show 'em my stuff, even when I'd rather have been just a regular, normal, unemployed kid. But whoever said normal was fun? Much less valuable? Without her prodding and coaching, where the hell would I be today?

I couldn't desert that relentless force of nature in her final days. I thought to myself, "This lady doesn't have much time left. You can't leave her now."

After running amok, pursuing my cockeyed dreams, it was time to pamper Mama and stay put for a while...a long while, as it turned out.

I looked around for a decent place, but the beautiful, well-kept neighborhoods of my twenty-three year memory were nothing more than wasted, palm tree-lined drug cartels.

Finally, I found an affordable hotel along the demilitarized zone. It was far from a slum, but unlikely to make the Fodor travel guide. A pleasant little purgatory, sprinkled between the heroin needles and the boulevard rent-a-sluts.

A few months later, I actually located a charming apartment building with classic architecture reminiscent of New York City. Loaded with

Hollywood history, it'd been home to former and future friends like Shelley Winters and Susan Strasberg, and everyone's goddess, Marilyn Monroe.

I'd never owned any furniture, so picking out a sofa was serious business. Like springing for an engagement ring, scary stuff for this incurable wanderlust.

Okay, so I had a decent roof over my head, but how was I gonna pay the bills? What kind of work could I get in Hollywood? The movies had changed since the forties. No more singin' and dancin'. Now it was all screwin' and killin'.

I thought, what the hell, I was still an actor. I landed a bit here, a scrap there – Perry Mason, Gene Wilder's The World's Greatest Lover, Black Shampoo...

Eventually I took a shine to the new Hollywood's grit. I was making friends and networking all over town, but I needed a regular gig, not just scattered scraps.

One night a friend invited me to check out a show at the popular Ye Little Club in Beverly Hills. One of the best rooms in town, a chic little cabaret where scores of singers, comics and musicians had gotten their boost. The joint was known for packing in the celebrities and hot new talent.

After introducing myself to the owner, Marshall Edson, I got up on stage, did some comedy, a few songs, and had a blast...and realized how much I missed doing the live shows. Afterwards, I was delighted to meet Will Rogers, Jr. at the bar. We shared a few laughs, remembering my days in Tangiers with his dear saucy sister, Mary.

Still riding the high of a great show, I saw Marshall Edson motioning for me to join him. He told me how pleased he was with my onstage insanity and offered up an attractive salary to headline a twice-weekly showcase.

It sounded great but, "Showcase? Suitcases I know all about, but what the hell is a showcase, Marshall?"

"You know, Skip, the kind of deal where you bring on the singers and the comedians. An emcee."

Emcee, my middle name! It fit me like well-worn wingtips. I was sold, and "Skip E. Lowe's Showcase" was hatched. The show became popular and proved fertile ground for many talented newcomers. Joan Rivers had the successful Friday/Saturday night comedy show, and my talent fests on Sunday and Monday wrapped up the package. We enjoyed a long, successful run, till Marshall became ill and had to shut down.

I wasn't sure what to do, but heading down Sunset in a cab one night past the Hyatt Hotel, I had an inspiration – "I'm portable!"

I yelled out, "Stop! Turn this cab around."

The same madman that had commandeered the Bangkok flight took over the cab. I'd had a good vibe and the forgiving cabby reversed into a backward landing.

Instinctively, I set my sights on the food and beverage manager. "Go for the stomach first – all good things will follow."

I promised him I'd pack the room. Who knows if he believed me, but he said he'd try me for two weeks.

My Hyatt showcases became one of the hottest events on the strip. One of the acts starting on my show at the Hyatt was Billy Ray Cyrus. Four years later, we were still the place to strut you talent. Two Smirnoffs – Yankov and Bruce (no relation), Roseanne Barr and Tom Arnold launched their careers there.

But when new management took over, Skip E. Lowe was out and

jazz was in. I packed up my medicine show and went to the next tent.

At the Cinegrill Lounge in the Hollywood Roosevelt Hotel, I enjoyed a solid three-year engagement. But when they closed for renovations, I was winding down, feeling a peripatetic urge. The media interviewed me as the reigning king of Hollywood talent showcases, and I have to admit, the pleasure and satisfaction of that acknowledgment meant a great deal.

I discontinued weekly showcases after that, and put them on when the talent moved me.

Besides the wonderful new faces showcases sent my way, they also brought be together with dear old friends when I least expected it.

Hosting a series at Beverly Hill's Ramada Inn called "Skip E. Lowe's Celebrity Night," I held weekly auditions for singers, comics and musicians.

One day I walked in, summoned my piano player and started calling everyone to order. My back was to the talent, when someone touched me on the shoulder.

I turned around and could hardly get the words out of my mouth, "Margee...McGlory?!"

Margee was also in a state of disbelief. "Skippy? Is this soldier Skippy?"

We hadn't seen each other since our final parting in Bangkok, years before. After tears and hugs, I managed, "Margee, don't you dare audition for this thing. Listen, girl, you come down tonight and perform."

She did just that, and I introduced here as our featured guest star. I wasn't surprised when I found out she lived a few blocks away. I counted on that fiery feline being close as a heart beat...and she never let me down. What luck! Dare I think I'd never see her again.

If I've contributed to the Hollywood community, I'd say it was through our showcases. I'm proud of the hard work we put into each of them, but some of the brightest talents who started at the showcases, never acknowledged the help. I wonder about the amnesia stars develop about their humble beginnings. To hear them all tell it, they were born in a manger. All those virgin-star births.

And then I got the dreaded call – Mother had died. I owed her so much more than the too few visits I'd paid her in her final years. I knew I could have done more, and the guilt bore into me like acid, frazzling every nerve.

It was Mother's wish to be cremated, so I had her ashes placed in an urn which I kept for many years. Sadly, I spent more time confiding in her ashes, than I confided in her while she was alive. Maybe it was easier to empty my heart out to an uncoaching, uncritical silence.

Sometimes, when I felt like crying, I'd serenade her with my old Singing Newsboy song, "He's Me Pal," changing the words to, "She's the best that there was, and I love her because, she's me pal, she's me pal!"

Goodbye, Mother. My protector. My miracle worker. My lifesaver.

Mother's death sent me into a deep depression and, at first, I just kept to myself, holed up, crying. Mother had left me a handsome inheritance, and instead of investing it, I fed all those fresh, crisp bills to the new love of my life, Santa Anita, Our Lady of the Thoroughbreds.

Those horses grazed on every last dollar that I had and, in the long run, I didn't win, didn't place, and had absolutely nothing left to show.

The hundred thousand dollar cushion, I used to line their stalls. When you're a hopeless gambler, those four-legged animals are nothing more than slot machines with hooves that never pay off. When running down to the track got to be a hassle, I discovered the wonders of the bookie. I'd get up early in the morning, study the odds and jump on the phone to place my bets.

I was as desperate as any junkie needing that next fix. There was such emptiness in my life, and I filled it by making the bookies and the jockeys rich. It took a few years, but I managed to mow down all the green Mother had left me, right down to the last clinking penny.

I hadn't recovered from Mama's loss, when I got word that Dick Roman, my angel-voiced soul mate had suffered a fatal heart attack.

Living in Las Vegas, he'd recently separated from his wife, Honey Merrill, formerly one of Jackie Gleason's mistresses. Nobody knew where Dick was for two days, until Jerry Vale stopped by, pounded the window open and discovered Dick slumped over in a chair, the television on and the remote still in his hand.

That remarkable singing phenomenon died so unceremoniously, without ever having achieved the success he deserved. I'd never forget the man who breathed life into Sammy Labella, rechristening him Skip E. Lowe.

Dick's death struck me hard. Although I hadn't seen him in several years, I just took him for granted, comforted in the belief that my dearest friend would always be around.

Once again, guilt nagged me, asking me why I hardly ever bothered to get in touch with my best friend. For weeks, I'd wake up crying and just stay in bed all day, dogging around in those tear-drenched sheets. In time, the tears dried up, but the sense of loss never left. He was me Pal.

And then, a short time later, I got more devastating news. My dear Prince Wolfgang was driving an employee home. He swerved off the road and tumbled down an embankment. His companion was killed instantly, and Wolfgang was in a coma.

For two agonizing weeks, Wolfgang lay comatose. It was the worst two weeks of my life – a nightmarish period of not being able to do a thing to bring him back to the walking world. I couldn't sleep or eat and, on top of everything, I had showcases to put together, so I couldn't get away to see him.

I called San Francisco hourly for an update. One of the great loves of my life was drifting away, and I couldn't visit him.

And then I got the news that he'd died. My loved ones were vanishing – Mother, Dick, and now Wolfgang. The last slice of my heart had been scooped out.

Desperate, I cried out, "Damn you, Wolfgang! You were my immortal angel. You weren't supposed to die. I love you! Come back to me! Come back!"

Though I never realized it when they were alive, Wolfgang and Dick Roman were enmeshed in my soul. I couldn't imagine going on without them. I treasured their pictures and kept them constantly close, desperate for direction.

One night, a strange thing happened as I held these two pictures. Light radiated from the photos and a clear voice let me know, "Skippy, we're here. With you. Keep going, keep fighting – because you love a good fight! Be yourself, buddy. You're unique, and glorious and have so much to give. You're never alone."

In that moment, something shifted inside of me, and as it did, peace replaced the ache in my soul. I lay back in that magnificent feeling and felt a sense of connection I cannot explain.

Blanketed by loving gratitude, I continued to feel them with me, and to this day, at the oddest moments, I feel their presence nudging me, prodding me, reminding me to never let up, until God socks that last breath out of my feisty little carcass.

CHAPTER ELEVEN

Strange Interlude – I Fall in Love With a Woman

By the mid-1970s, I'd carved my name into enough Hollywood marquees to give me a healthy share of local celebrity. From Beverly Hills to Hollywood, news hounds were interviewing me, and new talent knew they'd be seen if they did one of "Skippy's shows."

But I was ripe for new excitement. During one of my shows, I noticed a guy at the bar. I'd seen him night after night, checking me out, and I figured he was either a talent scout or a demented stalker with a severe emcee fetish.

Finally, he approached me and introduced himself as an executive with the local cable station – "Skippy, why not do a public access show where you interview celebrities? It'd be a natural for you to sit and talk about Hollywood with the up-and-comers as well as the legends."

The idea sounded tempting. I certainly loved those glorious stars from Hollywood's glamour days, and Lord knows I love to dish. Public access was the cocky new kid on the TV cable block, and I decided to jump on it.

And with that...Skip E. Lowe Looks at Hollywood was born.

My first guest was Aldo Ray. Aldo rose to fame in the 1940s, and when I met him decades later, he was still a hot-blooded heartbreaker. This blond Italian hunk from San Francisco scorched a hole into hearts

with his hoarse sexy voice, massive neck and shoulders and magnificent chest in Miss Sadie Thompson, with Rita Hayworth, The Marrying Kind with Judy Holliday and Leon Uris' Battle Cry.

When he consented to do my talk show, Aldo gave me the secret to a great interview, "Look into my eyes – they'll tip you off how I feel and what I'm about to say. When I'm finished, they'll clue you in again."

I followed that advice, and it's served me well ever since. Aldo and I became close friends, but booze was corroding his livelihood, and he was having a tough time. I was more that glad to help him out, and let him stay at my apartment while he tried to sober up.

After our brief introduction in San Francisco in 1972 when I returned from entertaining the troops in Vietnam, I didn't see the hunky ex-Marine until six years later. Or more accurately, I heard him while I was hosting talent nights on Sundays and Mondays at Ye Little Club on Camden Drive in Beverly Hills, where Joan Rivers used to try out new material before taking her show to Vegas and other large venues.

All the stars showed up on the nights I hosted at the tiny, hole-in-the-wall cabaret.

Someone in the audience I didn't recognize was visibly drunk and disrupting the performers with his gravelly voice. His beautiful date looked embarrassed and seemed to want to be anywhere but here with this loud-mouth who was getting nasty stares from the other club goers.

I left the stage and went over to the muscular, middle-aged blond who was a boisterous but never a mean drunk. "Please, there's a show going on. I'd love you to be quite..." The stranger's froggy voice prompted me to ask if he had a cold."

In a good-natured way, the man slurred, "OK, sorry. That's the way I always speak, kid." The beautiful woman sitting next to him whispered to me, "He's that old-time movie star, Aldo Ray." I immediately remembered the name and finally recognized the face of the stranger whose films I loved.

When the show ended and the place was closing, I looked over at Aldo's table. His lovely lady friend had deserted him – and for good reason. By now, Aldo had passed out with his head resting on a table. I felt sorry at the site of this once great hunk of a movie star. I shook him awake and said, "Mr. Ray, you have to wake up now. The show's over. We're going to close up now."

I realized Aldo was in no condition to find his way home, so I ordered him a cab, which I had to pour him into.

Later that year we met again at Continental Hyatt Hotel on Sunset Strip where I was hosting a singer's showcase in the hotel's bar/lounge. Aldo was at the bar every night, drunk as always. Sometimes he was accompanied by the veteran Western actor, John Carradine, (Stage Coach, The Man Who Shot Liberty Valance), as drunk as his friend and with a voice just as deep and gravelly.

I thought to myself, "Oh, my! This is 'Frog Night'!"

To break the ice, I asked the two men whose voice was deeper. Without hesitating, Carradine graciously conceded that Aldo's voice was deeper and called "basso profondo," the deepest type of male voice. To my ear, it sounded like a draw between Aldo and Carradine as to who possessed the thicker vocal chords.

Carradine asked me if I knew that Aldo had been a major movie star in the 1940s, costarring with Rita Hayworth, among others. Aldo was too drunk to hear what Carradine also said about his drinking companion.

"These days, poor Aldo isn't making many movies. He has almost no money. He's so broke he's slept on my couch or on the floor at other friend's homes," Carradine tried to whisper but found it hard to because of his signature basso.

On another night at the Hyatt showcase, Aldo sat alone at the bar, buying drinks for beautiful women. By the end of the evening, he was in no condition to leave. It turned out that his friend, Carradine, had been right about Aldo's precarious financial situation and intermittent homelessness.

Aldo looked up from the bar where he was resting his head and said, "Hey, kid! Mind if I sleep on your coach."

I agreed and took him back to my cramped, one-bedroom apartment in West Hollywood below the Sunset Strip.

As soon as he entered my apartment, he went straight toward my tiny couch, and passed out. I took off his shoes, covered him with a blanket, then went to bed.

I was awakened later that evening/early morning when I found Aldo, stark naked, crawling toward my bed. Then, he climbed in and was all over me.

Sporting a prodigious erection, Aldo said, "Take care of papa. You know you want it."

I hesitated until he added, C'mon, baby. Touch it!" He didn't wait for me to accept or decline his offer. Instead, he violently shoved my head up and down on his thick, nine-inch cock. Somehow, I managed to take it all the way.

I was surprised that he was able to have an orgasm after consuming so much alcohol, but he did and, unlike President Clinton, I swallowed.

Aldo passed out again immediately after he ejaculated and spent the rest of the night in my crowded bed. When I woke up later that morning, Aldo was still asleep or passed out.

I went into my microscopic kitchen and fixed breakfast for both of us. When I finally managed to rouse him, he leapt out of bed and said he had to call his agent, Johanna Ray, who also happened to be his wife. He called from my apartment and heard good news. Johanna had just landed him a film role.

Then he drank black coffee while I ate breakfast. Neither of us mentioned what had happened the night before in my bedroom. He acted as though nothing had occurred. And nothing ever did again. That may have been a blessing in disguise because Aldo was very rough in bed... or at least in my bed.

Massage is one way of connecting with people and I often soothed him through the rough times. I had feelings for him and he knew it, but I never let my emotions stray. Aldo was grateful for my hospitality, and introduced me to a lot of Hollywood's influential people. I feel a debt to that wonderful man who gave public access its first taste of class

We became good friends and confidants after so many nights he spent sobering up on my couch. Although the subject of men and sex never came up again either, we did discuss women. A confirmed misogynist from personal experience, Aldo once told me bitterly, "Women are big disappointers. You can't live with 'em, and you can't live without 'em."

Maybe it was during the periods when Aldo "couldn't live with 'em" that he experimented with men. Are we all bisexual, as Freud claimed?

Like Aldo, straight guys are all pretenders. They don't discuss having sex with other men because it makes them feel guilty, especially if they like to suck cock.

I've had so many similar experiences with Marines. They would get drunk, have sex with me, then the next morning say, "I was so drunk last night I don't remember a thing!"

All the clichés about Marines are true in my experience. I never met one I couldn't seduce or who tried to seduce me. Most of them wanted to play the "male role" and fuck me or demand a blow-job. Sometimes, they begged me to fuck them, which I never do. I get fucked but I don't fuck because I consider myself a lady, not a man.

Aldo, although I don't blame him for pretending, was just like all the other "straight" men I've had sex with. Although he hadn't served in the Marines, Aldo had fought during World War II in the Navy. Sailors, away at sea for months at a time, are even more open, if that's the right word, to having sex with men because in those pre-feminist days, women didn't serve aboard military vessels.

Aldo had agreed to be the first guest on my cable access show because he figured exposure, even on cable TV, might find him work. It did, but not the kind likely to resurrect his non-existent acting career.

Desperate for money, about a year after he crashed on my couch, Aldo appeared in a porn film, Sweet Savage. Although only in his early 50s at the time, his body had deteriorated to the point where he was cast in a non-sexual role in the film.

When I asked him why he had decided to do porn, he only said, "A blow job's a blow job..."

Jean & Cornell Wallace's wedding photo; Jean and I on our way to get married.

Another reason for this exotic turn in his declining career was that Aldo was broke when he appeared in the porn film. After being diagnosed with throat cancer in the 1980s, the Screen Actors Guild's health insurance covered his catastrophic medical bills. Financial difficulties forced Aldo to work in non-union productions, which led to his expulsion from the actor's union and the loss of his insurance.

It was in some ways a blessing when my friend's troubled life ended on March 27, 1991.

He was buried in his hometown of Crockett, a suburb of San Francisco, where he had served as constable (police officer) before World War II. The entire town turned out for his funeral.

After years of neglect by his Hollywood "friends" and colleagues, the belated honor reminded me of Malcolm's verdict on Macbeth. "Nothing in his life became him like the leaving it."

Besides the occasional pleasure of his company, Aldo gave me something much more important. He introduced me to the love of my life, Jean Wallace.

In 1974 I met Jean's estranged husband – and my personal hero, Cornel Wilde. Nobody ever carved up the screen with Cornel's flair. Errol Flynn's sword went limp every time Cornel entered the scene. When I asked Cornel if I could interview him on my cable show, he accepted and I was thrilled! A generous man, he shared all his exploits and hot romances.

His favorite movie, surprisingly, was not one of his swashbuckling feats, but the beautiful Chopin bio, A Song To Remember with Merle Oberon.

The interview marked the beginning of a wonderful but unfortunately brief friendship.

Cornel was separated from Jean Wallace at the time. Discovered in the 1950s by Howard Hughes, Jean was a gorgeous, blonde California number – tall, slim but voluptuous like Veronica Lake and Lauren Bacall.

Jean chalked up quite a few husbands and wild affairs in her day. Hughes was just one of her many torrid liaisons.

Legend has it that when Franchot Tone first saw the star of The Big Combo and Louisiana Purchase at the Cocoanut Grove, he asked her over to his table, proposed to her, and tied the knot two days later. One of the shortest courtships in history. It sounds implausible, but Jean could bring out that kind of mating urge in most any man.

Jean, unfortunately, started drinking, and having produced two lovely sons with Franchot Tone, they divorced. She then married Cornel Wilde and they traveled the world.

Jean was a tortured soul who carried herself well and drank privately. But eventually the sickness spilled out. Cornel saw how infatuated Jean was with Jack Daniels and his 100-proof charms. She just couldn't keep her hands off him, and when she drank, Jean could be a monster.

Cornel tolerated Jean's crazy behavior for years. But when he couldn't get her to stop, he left her to save his own sanity.

Shortly after I became friends with Cornel, my good friend, the Baron von Susten, took me for a drive, which ended up at Jean's house in the Trousdale Estates, just north of Sunset Boulevard.

The Baron was halfway through his introduction, when Jean completed it – "Lowe. Skip E. Lowe. Yes, of course! I watch your show. You're the man with the tight close-ups! How wonderful to meet you!"

Ten seconds with Jean, and I felt like we were hatched from the same egg. It was a Crazy Glue instant bonding. She'd enjoyed my interview with Cornel and wanted to know how he was doing. I could see this was a tortured woman, still very much in love with her ex.

Jean Wallace's sex appeal awakened the lady-killer in me. All these years and she was still a knockout – a she-devil with skin as chaste as virgin snow. That face and that body with its sumptuous curves, conspired to me think hard (very hard) about my sexuality.

I couldn't believe how affected I was by Jean. I had such wild, intimate feelings that no woman had ever brought out in me. What was happening?

Yet on top of all this, I felt a terrible sympathy for her. A beautiful woman, isolated in this big house, with no friends, no interests and no passion. True, her son slept in one of the bedrooms, her home was more of a way station for him. Two strangers who greeted each other in polite, cold passing.

Jean and I talked well into the night. And the next day, I walked from my apartment all the way to her house, bringing croissants and scones. We laughed and chatted, sharing intimacies. I marveled that this woman affected me so.

I loved Jean Wallace, regardless of her drinking. Though I was not in love with Jean, I loved her deeply. She was my friend and lover, and her sensuality was something I'd never experienced. Jean was a full flesh and blood woman and, as I nestled against her, I felt the sweetest rose petals surrendering unto me. every time she touched my flesh, I was renewed.

I told Cornel I was seeing Jean. He never asked for details, and was simply delighted she cared about someone. And someone he felt was worthy.

For my part, I was incredulous that I was actually head-over-heels over a woman! Much less the ex-wife of one of my dearest friends.

Jean would take me to the celebrity affairs. It was so much fun being the escort of a classy movie star. We'd go to clubs and, while Jean drained the bars, I'd sip to be sociable.

Like many stars, Jean loved the sleazy little back-alley Hollywood dives. Thankfully, I was a light drinker. Maneuvering your swaggering sweetie out to the car is easier when you're not pickled yourself. Unfortunately, I don't drive, so I was always at the mercy of Jean's patented method of auto suicide. Miraculously, we never had a smashup.

Jean may have been an alcoholic, but she treated people with kindness and respect. She never held grudges or knowingly hurt anyone and somehow, the universe responded. She was never robbed or taken advantage of, even though her addiction made her easy prey.

One night Jean dragged me to a dingy dive and found a stray, "Come on Skippy, have a heart. Let's take him home and clean him up."

So, we brought the man home, tossed him a six pack of Ivory and ordered him to indulge in some steamy suds. While he was scrupulously scrubbing, I noticed Jean pacing back and forth.

"Jean, if you're so nervous about this guy, why did you invite him here in the first place?"

She ignored me, "Skippy, he's taking too long in the there. What's he up to?"

I pushed the bathroom door wide open and there was our boy, standing naked in front of the mirror, brushing his teeth.

Waving in our direction, he smiled, "I've got a dilly of a headache. Got any aspirin?"

As I pointed to the medicine cabinet, Jean nearly dissolved into an ashen heap. As the guy opened the cabinet, found some aspirin, the closed the cabinet door, Jean calmly rejoined the living.

Later, confiding in me, she reached into a hole behind her bathroom mirror, and pulled out a sock...filled with her valuables.

We're talking millions of dollars' worth of priceless diamonds, rubies, sapphires and emeralds, set in platinum and 18 carat gold. I'd never seen such treasures in one place outside the glass cases of Cartier and Harry Winston. All shoved into that hole behind her Anacin, No-Doz and Band-Aids.

Funny thing is, nobody ever discovered that toilet-side vault. Cornel Jr. and I were the only ones she ever told about her crazy hiding place.

Every time I was with Jean, our lovemaking grew steamier. What was happening to this effeminate little pixie-boy? Could Masters, Johnson and Dr. Ruth sort this out?

I did the only clinically reasonable thing, and booked an appointment with my good friend and astrologer, Jacqueline Stallone.

Jacqueline listened, read my chart, then Jean's, and her prognosis overwhelmed me – "Marry her, Skippy. The planets approve and it'd be good for both of you."

Marry her? Skip E. Lowe married?...Wolfie would turn over in his grave. To a woman?!! What a concept!

Jacqueline not only gave us her blessing, she offered to perform the ceremony in Vegas.

During one of our all night passion fests, I popped the question to Jean. At first she couldn't believe it. Then she thought for a few seconds, and gave me an enthusiastic, "Yes! Yes, Skippy, how sweet! Yes of course! Let's do it. I love the idea!"

She loved the idea, but she never said she loved me.

Nevertheless, that "Yes!" set the matrimony wheels in motion. Jacqueline was the most excited of all. She couldn't wait to pronounce us man and wife. Wedding in Vegas! Everything was set. Small ceremony or not, getting married still felt like a very big deal.

Jean and I were in the limo with Jacqueline and her pal, Jack Rapaport en route to catch a plane to Sin City, when reality hit me, "I'm getting married to one of the most beautiful, desirable women on the planet!"

As I gazed into Jean's eyes, I saw the only true love of her life reflected deep inside those spectacular green pools, the only man who lived in her heart – and it wasn't me.

Yes, we'd had great sex and great times, and I loved being with her. But we weren't in love.

We were great friends, who flew in the face of society's skepticism.

Great friends, who cared deeply about each other, and had sympathy for the other's denial and pain.

I, for the beautiful woman, who existed all alone, with no laughter, purpose or connection in her life. And she, for the little man who made the world his family, his love, because this life never offered him the love he yearned for, or the family he so desired.

Each of us wanted to give the other what we didn't have. She offered me her connections in and loving security. I offered up my laughing heart.

It could never be. Frightened at the thought of it all, I looked over at Jacqueline, lamenting, "Please. We can't do this."

At first, everyone in the limo thought – "Silly Skippy, he's pulling another gag."

But I was never more serious. We turned around and celebrated our marriage-that-never-was at Nicky Blair's. The wedding was off. No hard feelings. I knew that if marriage hadn't worked for Cornel and Jean, she and I had no chance.

At first Jean seemed disappointed, as if I'd rejected her or found her undesirable. But soon she could joke, "You're jilting me, Skippy? What nerve!" I suggested we could still have our hot honeymoon night – for "Skip E. Lowe – always the bridesmaid, never the bride!"

Besides our lovemaking and foolish antics, Jean and I had wonderful, quiet evenings together. Although we dined out often, we also made dinner at home. Jean was a marvelous cook and sang divinely. Nights in the kitchen together, cooking up pasta from scratch, or glazing crème brûlées are some of my warmest memories.

The tabloids portrayed me as a gold digging talk show homo, leeching off a drunken has-been. Had we not been so involved in our happiness, it might have hurt us. We brought all we had to our relationship, sharing our hearts and laughter.

If I'd met Jean earlier in my life, would I have taken a more traditional path? Mr. and Mrs. Skip E. Lowe...married with children? I can't imagine it, but there's a part of me that aches, wondering what could have been.

Not long after our cancelled nuptials, Jean expanded her cocktail hours and it was more than I could deal with. Just like Cornel, I desperately tried to get Jean to quit, but it had too strong a hold on her.

One Valentine's Day, months after Jean and I had ended our raunchy romance, Baron Von Susten and I were at dinner when I suggested we go by her place. I knew how torturous Valentine's Day can be when you're alone, so we agreed to go on a mission of love.

I knocked at the front door, but there was no answer. I went around the back and peered through the glass doors. There she was, unconscious on the floor, lying in a pool of blood.

I hollered for the Baron, and we crashed through the doors, fearful she might be dead. Blood was pouring from her head. I squeezed her lovely hands, but they felt icy cold.

"Jean, Jean! Don't leave me! Please!"

I grabbed her around the waist and pulled her to me. As I held her close, I felt her heart beating. Oh God, I was relieved.

I found a blanket, wrapped it around her, and we carried her to the car. The Baron took every short cut and back street, hell bent on getting to the emergency room before time ran out.

We rushed a still bleeding Jean into Cedars Sinai. They took excellent care of her, keeping her for three weeks until she improved. All Jean remembered was drinking a bit too much, and the floor rising up to meet her.

That horrible blow should have knocked some sense into her, but it didn't after her head healed, she was transferred into an alcohol treatment ward, but the day she left the hospital, she went right back to lapping up rotgut.

The doctor warned her and I pleaded, but Jean just shrugged, "Skippy my darling, when it's time to go, none of us has any say in the matter."

I was angry and tarted back, "You don't have to do such a good job helping the fates, do you?"

Jean just laughed, "In case you don't know, Skippy, I love booze. It's my one lasting love affair, and nobody's gonna make me break it off!"

It was hopeless.

Shortly after Jean was released from Cedars, Cornel was admitted... with leukemia. His doctors tried every new procedure, but Cornel was on a steady downhill slide.

Cornel's son and daughter were at his side at all times, along with Cornel's girlfriend, Colleen Conte, the former wife of actor Richard Conte.

Jean desperately wanted to visit Cornel, but it was her very desperation that he couldn't bear. If in life, he couldn't care for her, how could he be asked, in his dying, to care for the frightened hysterics of a woman whose main concern was with her own pain. Jean never meant anyone harm, but in this time of great loss, her emotions would have drained him, and us, when our focus had to be on Cornel.

Jean was heartbroken, and blamed Colleen for not being allowed to visit Cornel. But in truth Colleen liked Jean and sympathized with her. She simply had no say in the matter.

I pleaded with Cornel to let Jean visit just once, but even on his deathbed, he stood his wise ground.

It had been a long time since Jean had given selflessly to others. And now, in Cornel's final days, he couldn't trust her to be there for him.

Cornel celebrated his last birthday at Cedars. We brought a cake and had a little party for him. As we sang Happy Birthday, we were painfully aware that this was our friend's farewell.

A week later, Cornel could no longer eat solid food. Sweating, shaking, veering in and out of consciousness, he held on as long as God would allow.

I knew Jean was waiting by the phone, so I called her to let her know Cornel was barely holding on. She sobbed into the receiver, "Skippy, will you give Cornel a kiss for me? And let him know it's from Jean, damnit! After all, you don't want him to think you're coming on to him."

That was Jean! She could make me cry and laugh at the same time. But I could feel the incredible pain she was going through at that moment, and I hated for her to be so far away from Cornel as he lay dying in his room.

When I returned to Cornel, he was gasping convulsively, trying to hang on. I sat by him and stroked his head when suddenly the breath just left his body.

It was unbearably sad and so hard to believe. This amazing human being was gone forever.

It was Christmas.

Cornel was cremated and his ashes placed in an urn that Cornel, Jr. gave to Jean.

How sad not to have been able to visit Cornel while he was still alive. Now, Cornel's ashes were Jean's only consolation. I visited her often during that holiday season, and she loved to bring "Cornel" out to share in the festivities.

Sometimes she'd break out singing to him, or she'd have a lengthy conversation, filling him in on the latest dirt.

It all seemed morbid at the time, but that urn was Jean's only connection to Cornel in his passing, and she kept it until she died...just six months later.

Cornel, Jr. came home around midnight and, to his horror, found Jean dead on the bedroom floor. He called me and broke the news.

"Oh, Jean, no!" Poor Jean kept playing alcohol roulette until that barrel finally lined up in her direction. She died broken-hearted, but at last, she'd be reunited with her one true amour.

When I got home from her funeral service, I toasted her one last time – "Bottoms up, Jean. Now you can be with your Cornel forever. I know you're twirling around on some heavenly barstool. Save a seat for me, Honey. If they let me in, I'll join you, Cornel, Wolfie, Dick and Ma, and we'll sit around and share some laughs. You were always loving and kind. Thank you."

So why didn't I marry Jean, the only woman I ever loved emotionally and sexually? It wasn't a lack of physical attraction, although she was the only woman I ever made love to. Her skin was the color of pearls. When I touched her still voluptuous breasts, it felt like heaven to me, a "touch of Venus," literally. Jean made me feel like a real man, whatever that is.

To be honest, she was also a loud, boisterous drunk. Not mean or abusive, just very noisy and gesticulative while under the influence. Even when she wasn't drinking, she had a mouth like a truck driver. We used to go a buffet restaurant on the Sunset Strip in West Hollywood called The Cock 'n Bull for lunch. Everybody in Hollywood showed up to sample the restaurant's lavish all-you-can-eat meals. That may explain why

The Cock 'n Bull was a favorite watering (and eating) hole of the insatiable Orson Welles. Jean would sit at the bar as though she owned the place and make loud comments about all the celebrities there, not caring if they heard or not.

Jean was a nice lady, very sweet, when sober, which was roughly about 40 percent of the time. I loved her sober or drunk, but marriage to such a volatile personality would have been a poisonous nightmare I'd never be able to wake up from. As much as it pains me to admit it, I'm actually relieved we never tied the knot because I would have been miserable living with a drunk. And Jean probably would have been miserable living with anyone but her ex, Cornel Wilde, whom she never stopped loving.

I just don't like drunks in general, even beautiful, charming ones like Jean. During my career hosting talent shows all over the world, I traveled with a lot women who love the platonic company of gay men. They are unkindly known as "fag hags," and Jean was a huge fag hag.

She loved to hang out at sleazy hustler bars on Santa Monica Boulevard in Hollywood, although I guess "sleazy" and "hustler bar" are redundant. After buying drinks for all the boys peddling their flesh to men, Jean would pick up one of them and take him home, where they continued their private drinking party. They would spend the rest of the evening and early morning until they passed out. She never had sex with any of these gentlemen of the evening. I think she just liked to hang out with fellow drinkers who wouldn't judge her or give her a lecture about alcoholism.

The hustlers were all a bit star-struck by Jean, whom they recognized from her heyday in the 1940s as Hollywood star. She was in her 60s by then, but these supposedly straight hustlers who only had sex with men for money still considered her glamorous and gorgeous. And so did I.

I warned Jean about picking up what in the gay community is known as "rough trade," but she said, "Don't worry, Skippy. You'll protect me!" Hah! Fortunately, Jean was able to protect herself without my help, and despite her dangerous house "guests," she was never harmed or robbed by any of the male prostitutes she took home.

Typically, after a hustler left her home in Trousdale Estates, a posh neighborhood on the northern tip of Beverly Hills, just outside Bel Air, she'd give him cab fare home. Once, after waking up at her mansion, a hustler went to the medicine cabinet in the bathroom for an aspirin to offset the headache and other effects of the hangover from drinking the previous evening.

Jean always hid her jewelry in the back of the medicine chest. Thank god, the hustler only found the aspirin and never the thousands of dollars worth of precious gems she hid behind the medicine bottles.

Pills made her alcoholism worse. One time, under the influence of God knows what combination of alcohol and drugs, she allegedly over-dosed. On another occasion, she "accidentally" impaled herself on a kitchen knife.

It was the combination of drugs and booze that led Cornel to leave her. As much as we loved each other, Jean still considered Cornel the love of her life and they both made several attempts to get back together, if only for the sake of their children.

When Cornel was dying of leukemia in 1989 at Cedars-Sinai Medical Center in Los Angeles, Jean kept a lonely vigil outside his room in the ICU. She was drunk, as usual, and demanded to see her dying ex-husband.

Cornel Jr., his daughter, and I were at Cornel's bedside when he heard Jean screaming to be admitted. Cornel Sr. said to me, "Skip, don't let that drunken bitch in!"

So I found myself in the excruciating position of refereeing between the two until Cornel Jr., a high-schooler, volunteered to help. He left his father's room and said to Jean outside, "Go, home, Mama. I'll tell you everything when I get home."

Cornel died five minutes later after that, three days after his 77th birthday.

Cornel was cremated, and for some reason, Jean got custody of her ex-husband's ashes, which she kept in an urn on the mantle over the fireplace. At Christmas-time, she phoned and invited me over for a drink. When I got there, she said, "Let's sprinkle a 'little of Cornel' on the coffee table," which she proceeded to do. Then she laughed as she blew the ashes away and said, "That's the best blowjob you'll ever get from me!"

In 1990, at the age of 67, Jean suddenly died of an intestinal hemorrhage. I attended the wake and her burial at the Hollywood Forever Cemetery, at the time known as the Hollywood Memorial Park Cemetery on Santa Monica Boulevard in Hollywood.

Her resting place is only a few blocks from the hustler bar she loved to hang out at.

CHAPTER TWELVE

The Ghost of Molesters Past

In May 1989, Mamie Van Doren and I went to a charity benefit dinner at the Hilton Hotel. Seated at our table was a Canadian couple and two boys, four sense people we presumed to be a family. The father appeared to be the puppet master, with a firm grip on the strings of his clan. After introducing himself as Josè Menendez, he presented his lost-in- space wife, Kitty, and his two tormented sons, Lyle and Eric.

Menendez ignored me, but was determined to get to know Mamie, intimately. Arrogant and rude, this twisted Casanova actually removed his shoes and rubbed his feet against Mamie's legs, working his grubby toes up to her gorgeous thighs.

Here we were at a black-tie dinner, and barefoot Joe's playing footsies with an uncomfortable Mamie, while ogling her conspicuous breasts, and making suggestive remarks. He was treating her like his toy, all in full view of his stone-faced wife and sons!

Mamie signaled her discomfort to me, and set his feet and his eyeballs straight. Eric, the younger of the brothers, attempted, "You're very beautiful, Miss Van Doren." Mamie was flattered and thanked Eric, while she still had her hands full with Josè.

But Josè was furious. He yanked Eric's arm and barked at his son,

"Shut up, Dummy. You see I'm talking to the lady. Just shut your mouth and behave."

Eric, a frightened reprimanded puppy, turned bright red. Big brother Lyle reached over and patted Eric's arm, trying to lessen the impact of their father's shattering blow. "Just forget about it," Lyle reassured.

When Kitty left for the ladies' room, Josè whipped out his business card and forcefully placed it in Mamie's ample cleavage.

"Give me a call anytime." Then he winked and patted Mamie's breasts.

Mamie turned to me and, with nerves fluttering in her voice, whispered, "Skippy, I don't know what he's liable to pull and I don't want to find out. Let's leave."

The whole thing had me feeling uneasy and I was more than ready to call it an evening. So Mamie and I got up, said our good-byes and left.

That glimpse into the lives of the Menendez family left me disturbed. Lots of assholes behave badly in front of their wives, but what bothered me most was that this one shot his son down just for speaking. He didn't just scold him, he manhandled him in front of everyone.

Months later I saw an excerpt of a murder trial on the nightly news. A tennis player was on the stand, talking about Lyle and Eric Menendez, who'd been charged in the murders of their parents, Josè and Kitty.

I thought to myself, "Menendez...Menendez..." and suddenly, I flashed on that bizarre night at the Hilton earlier in the year. "Menendez. Of course, that's the strange family we sat with at the banquet."

Mamie Van Doren called shortly after that, and we talked about that bizarre evening, and debated whether it could have any bearing on the trial.

Not long thereafter, when the news broadcast Eric's breaking down over his father's sexual abuse of him throughout childhood, the events of that night haunted me.

Enraged, I decided to testify on behalf of the two brothers. If I could help the defense back up their claim of the father's abuse and the mother's apathy, I would.

The trial was conducted with alternating juries – one for Lyle and one for Eric. That way, only one trial was required instead of two taxpayer-money-sucking-ordeals.

I took the stand and talked about how Josè had such ruthless control over his family; and how the mother appeared to be taxiing over planet Earth, but didn't know where to land.

During Pamela Bozanich's cross exam, the pit bull pounced on my motives. I didn't know how to explain myself, but I was driven to speak in behalf of those boys. Though I may have appeared composed, racing around inside me was an out-of-control Indy car, crashing through every organ.

The intensity of emotions in a murder trial is so volatile and the stakes so high, it's like ten opening nights crammed into one performance. Added to this was an unknown compulsion, driving me into their vortex. All I cared about was the boys and the death sentence dangling over them.

With Bozanich's inquisition out of the way, I went home and followed the defense on TV as it presented experts on child abuse and its terrible effects on the entire family.

I was sitting at my desk one day, casually monitoring the trial, when I heard the screams of a little boy. Startled, I looked up...looked outside.

Nothing. Checked the hallway. Nothing. I couldn't be imagining things, but when I closed my eyes, I had a horrible vision of a fist swinging wildly at a little boy, who looked a lot like me.

It was me! I tried to get a closer look at the attacker. I could see him spitting, hear him yelling, "Sammy, you bad, bad sissy boy."

For the rest of that day I was distraught and frightened, wondering what I'd unearthed. That night, I kicked the sheets around for hours, wondering when the huge man with the angry fists would return.

Several days went by. I was watching the trial and doing some routine mail sorting, when I opened a package containing an old 78 record. A label with the penciled notation "Sam Labella – Hollywood, California" appeared on both sides of a well-worn disk, and an enclosed note indicated a fan had found the record in his attic.

After tracking down a dinosaur record player, I nervously placed the record on the turntable, eager to hear what lay beyond the "Cchtzkrriccch... Cchtzkrriccch" of the needle as it circled its way through the scratchy grooves.

Pushing through the crackling static was the most adorable soprano voice, proclaiming, "He's the best that there was, and I love him because, he's me pal, he's me pal!"

If I'd forgotten that Sammy Labella was once a little boy, that worn old platter brought it home to me. I was flabbergasted. Traveling through a time tunnel, the rickety trolley car in my mind chugged back half a century. I was no more than 11 years old.

Making a dub from that scratchy relic, I was singing along to my stirring Irish refrains, when suddenly the hateful vision of the pounding fist and little Sammy returned. I could see myself crying as the man began to hit me, screaming, "Sissy Sammy. Bad, bad, sissy Sammy!"

I struggled to get a look at the blurry face. Suddenly I heard a voice warning me, "You better straighten out your life, right now! You're a young man and you better start acting like one. If you want to be treated like a little sissy girl, then go somewhere else, because I won't have any son of mine making other boys do those queer things to him. Shape up or we'll ship your fairy ass out of here. Understood?"

Weak, shaking, I had to sit down. That was my father speaking. Saying those cruel things and whipping me like a useless mule. Father never did such things!...did he?

Then the awful revelation. Yes, my dad beat me. And abused me. Not sexually, but verbally and physically. Yes, now I remembered.

No wonder I was driven to testify in the boys' behalf. No wonder Menendez's humiliation of his sons infuriated me beyond reason, beyond anything else. No wonder, despite all my love of and compassion for people, the slightest look askance could drive me into a rage. Not only did my father beat me verbally and physically for "seducing those boys," he didn't believe me! He didn't believe they had raped me!

He didn't believe me, he didn't stand up for me. And he didn't defend me.

CHAPTER THIRTEEN

S & L Doughboy Takes a Powder

After my brief appearance at the Menendez media circus, many people, including some of my dearest friends, were angry I'd testified.

"Skippy, you're losing it. How could you!"

In the long run perhaps my testimony didn't do much for the boys, but I made no apologies. I knew why I had testified. My own agony over being abused and my father not only believing me, not standing for me, but beating and berating me for my being raped, created a fire within me that would not be quelled.

All my life I'd reacted to perceived slights with anger and haughtiness. Now I understood.

My protective stand for these boys may have seemed outrageous to some, but to my heart, it was right action. If I made a fool of myself before millions, so be it. I could live with that.

One reason I caught so much grief for testifying at the Menendez trial was that it wasn't the first time I'd ruffled the court.

When something bugs me, I go a little mad. My sense of self righteous anger kicks and fusses till I find a way to bring my opinions public.

Two of my more outrageous commotions come to mind...

Charles Keating made me mad. Everyone who invested in his S&L lost money. Many tossed their life savings. I lost several thousand, myself.

I felt bad for all us Unity Savings losers, but my heart went out to the senior citizens and those on limited incomes who'd invested every last cent of their savings in Cheating's S&L (Stealing & Lying) scheme. When you're well off, you can afford to diversify – put some cash here, some there, even toss some into a bonfire. But when you're not rich, you don't have a lot of choices, and no padding to fall back on.

That cynical, deceptive, germ of a human being loved flaunting his arrogance, and showed no remorse for screwing so many out of millions. As I watched him sneer at the cameras, I thought, "Skippy, it's time to give that Cheating hound something to bark about. I'm gonna give that scalawag some Skippy justice."

Step one of my plan took me to the house of that outrageous, confetti-cutup, Rip Taylor. Rip's a super guy and a great friend, but I didn't come to visit. It was one of his trollop wigs I was after. I pilfered it – stuffing it tastefully under my shirt – took it home and powdered it down with enough powder to cover the Aspen slopes for a holiday weekend.

Next, I called Margee – who'd also gotten swindled in the Unity disaster – and asked her to drive me to the Los Angeles Superior Court to see that S.O.B get fried. She told me nothing would give her more pleasure. Margee must've figured I was up to something lowdown, but she didn't ask, and I didn't offer.

Margee and I had just grabbed a seat outside the hearing room when the stench of greed and evil descended into the air. Mr. Living Dead whisked by me, accompanied by his attorney. Briefcase in hand, he escorted Cheating into the bathroom, no doubt trying to wash some shit off his reputation.

Perfect! The dominoes of revenge were stacking up in my favor.

Skippy-justice was about to begin its reign of terror.

I checked the overnight bag I'd brought. The weapon was loaded and I was all set, "Say your prayers, maggot meal, vengeance is mine."

The restroom door opened, and Cheating goose-stepped toward the courtroom: my curtain call.

Just as Cheating's shadow dimmed my face, I reached for my weapon and BAM! SMACK! POW! I slapped Cheating in the face, over and over, covering him and his precious Brooks Brothers suit in mounds of sticky lily-white powder.

Stunned, like a boar bagged with a tranquilizer gun, he tried to brush the powder away, but it stuck to him, like mud on a squealing sow

Hyperventilating, he lurched into the courtroom, smelling like a baby's butt.

Then everything happened in a blur. I heard shouting and screaming, and felt massive hands grabbing be and nightsticks jabbing me, as cops corralled me into a room, where they held me for questioning.

Once inside the room, I broke into tears. When one of the cops sternly demanded, "Why did you do this, Sir?" I tried to compose myself and answer.

But it was all blank. Had I just murdered Charles Keating? The police wanted answers.

"Well I-I got so angry watching that smug...embezzler...seeing he was gonna get away scot-free...I had to do something. For the seniors. For everyone he victimized!"

I rambled on, spilling my guts, and those tin badges actually seemed touched. I don't know if they cheered me on, or just felt sorry for the insane old comic.

"All right, Sir. You can go. But you are positively forbidden from setting foot in this courtroom while the Keating trial is underway. Is that clear?"

"Oh, yes. Yes Sir!"

The police politely instructed me to leave through the back doors, because a mob of reporters was waiting out front.

I followed police orders, but one foot out the door and I was swept into a tornado of media mayhem. A Current Affair, Hard Copy, CBS, CNN, NBC, ABC...the reporters knew the back door was the place to swarm.

I gave a few quick words, then sneaked into a cab and hightailed it back to my apartment. But suddenly, I remembered Margee, who I'd left in the lurch just outside the courtroom.

Having traveled all over the world with me, that girl knew what a nut I was, and got as big a kick out of seeing Charlie get pummeled as I did pulling it off.

When I arrived home, the phone was ringing like a fire alarm, blaring out every two seconds. The tape on my answering machine was gagging. All of a sudden, I was a media freak of the day. Everyone was asking me to the prom and I could have cared less.

The real treasure was hidden inside my TV. I aimed the remote and sat back as the Skippy blitz invaded the airwaves. How perfect! There was the filmed coverage as I dumped all over Charlie Cheating. TV is so convenient. The perpetrator can sit back with a cold drink and pretzels and relive his crime...over and over and over.

I flicked through the channels, catching each and every electronic headline as it scorched into the screen – "Crazed Comic Attacks Kingpin"... "Senior Zaps Keating"... "Skip E. Strikes Lowe Blow"... "Talk Show Host Slaps Screwball."

One five-second video made me the sideshow of the moment.

For once, I got to sock it to the bad guy. Thanks to that anonymous cameraman, wherever you are, for helping me battle Goliath. If I didn't slay him, at least I messed with his wardrobe.

After my Keating foolishness, wherever I went, people applauded me and cheered. At Matteo's and Hamburger Hamlet, everyone in the place gave me standing ovations. I'd walk up Hollywood's Crescent Heights and people would shout "Skippy, we love you! Thanks for socking it to Keating!" Or they'd sneak up next to me in the their cars and blurt out, "Keating! It's the Keating guy!" and scare me half to death.

Rip Taylor lit into me for ripping off his best wig. (Wouldn't you know it, he needed the platinum carpet that night for a show and couldn't imagine where it had gotten to.)

Still he admitted he loved what I did to the S&L Bozo and once the powder wore off and the wig no longer smelled like Baby Hooey's tushy, he forgave me. And, as the fumes disintegrated, so did my fleeting fame as the Keating powder-fairy.

In 1989, when Zsa Zsa Gabor's cop-slapping trial was hogging the headlines, I got another visit from the loony bird that flits around my head. I was so tired of hearing about this poor, traumatized movie star, who'd slapped a rude cop. It pissed me off that my taxes were helping to finance this idiotic trial.

The Soviet Union split up, the Berlin Wall toppled, and neither got half the coverage that that Ga-boring trial did.

Enough. I'd had enough. I decided to get a T-shirt that would bitch and kvetch for me. Unfortunately the Middle Eastern printer I went to didn't understand English. The shirt, which was supposed to read, "Hang it up, Zsa Zsa," ended up saying "Hang Zsa Zsa."

Not exactly what I had in mind, but it would do the trick.

Bright and early the next day, this court jester slipped into his sassy Zsa Zsa shirt, went to the courthouse and found a good seat in a spectator box. When the cameras caught it, it was an instant hit.

Zsa Zsa stewed for a long time over my vicious T, but eventually forgave me. Actually, not only are she and her Count husband good friends, but so is her sweet, unspoiled, daughter, Francesca Hilton.

Amazingly, through all that rice throwing and trips on the hubby express, Zsa Zsa raised a sane and down to earth daughter whose deep, honest friendship I cherish as I do her mother's.

CHAPTER FOURTEEN

The Lowe-Down on Hollywood

By this time my cable show was off and running, with a strong following both locally and nationwide. I favored close-ups, that created vulnerability and intimacy. Save the phony soft focus for Liz Taylor perfume ads, my audience wanted stark honesty. They wanted to be right there under the make-up and the facade.

Of course that's scary, but the payoffs is an honest, uncompromising interview. With the Norma Desmond treatment, I found some were "ready for their close-ups, Mr. DeMille" and some weren't. Often a star would confide they'd do my show if it weren't for the close-ups.

Esther Williams is a good friend, whom I've asked many times, pleading, "Esther, you're beautiful, Dear. they'll look into your eyes, those gorgeous eyes, and your beautiful face will tell your fans so much about you. Forget the lines, they're not important, not at all."

No sale!

Shelley Winters performing at Skip's showcase

Lana Turner, Jane Russell, and so many other close friends shied away because of the "wart shots," and it's a shame. Those great faces tell so much, and the fans love to see the whole gorgeous picture.

Shelley Winters is an exception, I admit. She comes into the studio and takes charge. She knows what kind of lighting is kindest to her and exactly where the cameras should be placed. Shelley's so tuned in to the camera's presence, she can instinctively feel it's cold beaming stare.

As a compromise to my great bold friend, Shelley gets medium close- ups, and we can both live with that. Pros like Shelley learn all they can about every aspect of the show – behind and in front of the cameras. And, out of respect to their diligence and uncompromising craft, I share the reins.

Shelley's one of my favorite interviewees because she lets me probe her heart. She digs right in and lets the caring, decent Jewish mother out, leaving the wild, outrageous eccentric for the other talk shows.

I met Shelley at our favorite local coffee shop, The Silver Spoon, when she came in with her then boy-fling, Richard Tate, a close friend of mine. Over a breakfast of bacon and hotcakes, she and I became fast friends, and have carried on our madness ever since.

Sometimes people get the impression that Shelley's rude or over-bearing. This couldn't be further from the truth. She's bold, courageous, strong and determined; never shy about her options; and compelled by her compassion for the world at large. A Democrat in the proud tradition of her role model, Eleanor Roosevelt, Shelley scrupulously reminds me, "Skippy, you don't own anyone, so cut the dictator crap."

Unpretentious and generous, she's never refused my spontaneous request for a Western tune or parody lyric flavored with her unexpected comedy flair.

Forever active, Shelley's priority is helping young people build their confidence. For years, she's balanced acting with teaching at the Actor's Studio and conducting workshops at shelters for teenage runaways.

Full of vitality, Shelley gets everyone involved. When she puts out the call for clothes for her "kids," all her friends empty their closets. When Ms. Winters calls, you know she's representing a worthy effort.

The lady doesn't deal in bullshit. If it ain't real, Shelley will have no part of it. She breaks the rules for all the right reasons and doesn't hesitate to stand in dangerous territory for her heart's truth.

In the late 1970s, I heard talk about my old Park Savoy pal, Christopher Jones. John Barrymore, Jr. had kicked Chris out of John's sprawling Sunset Boulevard estate, and Chris was without a home.

After Chris had left New York in the early 1960s, he did the Jesse

James TV show for a year, then married Susan Strasberg.

Drugged out and fighting through most of the sixties, they eventually dried out and ended their relationship. But unfortunately, not before Christopher beat Susan badly while she was pregnant. Susan kicked Christopher out, but the damage had been done to her unborn child. Susan spent the rest of her life committed to healing Jennifer and rectifying the mistake of staying with an abusive man.

Christopher, for his part, roamed about till John Barrymore Jr. took mercy on him and took him in. But once again this Wildman wore out his welcome. Chris was starting to feel like the homeless mutt that nobody wanted. Never being one to turn away a stray, I took in the shaggy dog.

Chris was a bright guy with a likable daytime persona. But at night the vampire in him came out, tormenting us both with gruesome stories of torture and dismemberment. His sick imagination never quit and I was about to kick him out when he broke down and told me the source of his ghoulish insomnia.

Not only had he hurt his beloved Susan and their wondrous daughter, Jennifer, but he went from that shameful devastation to a horrible good fortune...

When the beautiful actress, Sharon Tate, was butchered by the Manson family in 1969, she was survived by a lover who'd inadvertently escaped the mayhem.

Christopher Jones was living with Sharon while her fiancé, Roman Polanski was off in Europe making a film. Struck by a sudden nicotine urge, Christopher jumped on his motorcycle and headed for Turner's Drug Store down the hill. After that, he drove up to the Pool Pocket to strike up a friendly game. And was still there, hours later, when horrifying bits of conversation filtered through the cigarette haze – MURDERED! ... NO SURVIVORS! ... BUTCHERED LIKE CATTLE! ... UNBORN BABY! ... HOUSE UP THE STREET!

Christopher was devastated as one of his friends broke down with the news – Everyone at the Polanski house, including Sharon and her unborn child, had been slaughtered.

Christopher wept and screamed and, in the end, bottled up his insanity. But the guilt and anger inside him would forever deprive him of a peaceful night's sleep. For at the oddest times, he swore he heard Sharon's tortured shrieks as the life was being carved right out of her.

What could I say, but do my best to let him know I'd be there when he needed to talk things out. Knowing the constant pain that haunted Chris made it easier to overlook his annoying habits – like that he never worked!

I managed to ignore his lack of interest in such mundane matters and he stayed with me on and off. We remained good friends long after he moved out and had settled into a new life with his beautiful wife, Paula, and their four adorable kids.

When I interviewed Susan Strasberg, she confided that, though she loved Christopher Jones, the true love of her life was Richard Burton. She pined for Liz's lush lover, but alas, it was unrequited.

Marilyn Monroe studied with Susan's father, drama coach Lee Strasberg, and she was often a guest at the Strasberg home. Susan and Marilyn often shared their secrets and one night Marilyn confessed, "Oh, Susan, I wish I could just be like you."

Astounded, Susan couldn't imagine what the desirable Marilyn could possibly envy.

Monroe cried, "Susan, people respect you. What I wouldn't give for a little respect, ya know what I mean?"

Susan was floored when she realized how hollow this goddess' life was. Marilyn never felt she was respected, and she was right. Marketed as every man's plaything, she wanted sex and respect all in the same package? Certainly not in the 1950s. Perhaps it existed for Mamie and other stars, but these women owned their souls, respected themselves and didn't give a bloody damn how the rest of the world perceived them.

෪

On another show, I asked my friend Butch, Cesar Romero, how he got his nickname and if there was any truth to the rumors about him and Tyrone being more than just friends.

Butch smiled and hedged like a gentleman, "I loved this man. Were we more than just friends? Sometimes we don't know what we are."

The blunt truth was too dangerous for Butch, but I admired my then-84-year-old friend for not hiding his love for Tyrone.

In the early 1980s, I became acquainted with Butch at a gala fundraiser for Thalians, the psychiatric ward at Cedars-Sinai Medical Center in Los Angeles. Our wonderful relationship evolved from there.

Sybil Brand was his escort for the fundraiser. Cesar was what unattached female socialites call "walkers," platonic friends or men paid to escort rich ladies to fancy public appearances. The socialites are ancient and asexual, and Sybil's walker is what is known as a "beard,"" a woman who appears in public with closeted gay men.

Eva and Merv, Calvin and Kelly, Barry and Diane. (My vetting attorney made me redact the last names. Dead men don't wear plaid and they don't sue. Live men and women can and do.)

Writer-director Rod Lurie, at the time the local Los Angeles ABC station's Oscar commentator, once spotted an unshaven superstar and his wife on the red carpet and said live on the air, "Here's Tom Cruise with a beard and his beard, Nicole Kidman." The notoriously litigious Cruise and his pit bull attorney, Bert Fields, didn't sue Lurie.

In an interview with the Los Angeles Times in 1986, Cesar described his frequent and obsessed date:

"She just doesn't turn anything down. [Sybil is] a generous, big-hearted woman. I keep telling her she doesn't have to go to everything, that she can say no once in a while. She can't say no; that's her makeup."

Cesar had me over to Sybil's place many times or asked me to tag along when they went out to restaurants.

I used to joke that Sybil's wallpaper consisted of original Renoirs and Chagalls, plus some kitschy clown oil paintings by her friend Red Skelton.

I didn't have a car so Cesar would pick me up and take me back home whenever I joined him and Sybil for an evening out.

One night, instead of taking me home, he stopped at his home in Pacific Palisades where he lived with his mother until her death. We bypassed the main house and went to a cute little cottage in the back. I think he used the retreat for sexual rendezvous.

"My shoulder hurts," Cesar said once we got inside. "You probably need a good rub down. Why don't you take off your shirt, Butch?" "That sounds great, Skip!" Cesar was in his late 70s by then, I think, and I was shocked when he removed his shirt.

His physique was incredible! "OMIGOD, he's beautiful!" I thought but didn't say. After a few minutes of massage I suggested he remove his pants. which he did immediately. His huge cock was fully erect and wagging up and down like a dog's tail. "I bet you love this. Ever do that with another guy, Butch?" "My friend Ty [Tyrone Power] once, and, yes, he loved it!" Encouraged, I began massaging his cock and he asked politely, "French kiss it?" He didn't have to say anything more. End of conversation. I just worked and worked it then gave him a blowjob and he came in my mouth.

Afterwards, Butch said, "Don't tell anybody. Promise me, Skip. It's nobody's business but ours."

Cesar cleaned himself up, then he told about his affair with Tyrone Power when they were both under contract at MGM. According to Cesar, Ty, as he called the actor, really loved him and was "the greatest in bed." This was back in the 1940s.

Neither men ever discussed sex, they just did it. Butch was more upfront with me and said about his relationship with Tyrone, "Both of us knew we were gay but the subject never came up."

I asked Cesar why everybody in Hollywood was so paranoid about being gay. "It's career death, Skip. You do it then drop it."

A few years before her death in 2011, I bumped into Tyrone's ex-wife, Linda Christian, the mother of their four children.

"Ty was so beautiful," I said to Linda. "I think every guy in Hollywood was in love with him. Was he gay?"

"Of course he was gay, honey!"

After our sexual encounter, I asked Cesar the same thing about Robert Taylor, another Hollywood wet dream of mine.

"I don't know. I never sucked his cock," Cesar said, laughing – and stealing the line from Tallulah Bankhead when the actress was asked about Cary Grant's sexual orientation.

My 80-year-old neighbor, Anna Popper, told me an unlikely story about Cesar and Ronald Reagan.

Anna was a wealthy Holocaust survivor whose apartment had a magnificent Chagall screen which her Christian servants in France hid along with her other art treasures during World War II. She had donated her museum-quality art collection to the Padro in Madrid, I think. I'm 83. Gimme a break. She held on two T'ang Dynasty lions, one of which the maid broke in her apartment when we knew each other around 1990.

Anna was sharp and her mind undiminished by age. I used to see her power-walking up and down a very steep section of La Cienega Boulevard below the Sunset Strip.

She told me she, her husband, Cesar and Reagan during his Hollywood years often played bridge together. Originally from Vienna, Anna winked at me and said in her lilting Lili Palmer accent, "There vas somet'ing definitely going on between Cesar und Ronnie."

A real lady, Anna refused to tell me more.

On another show I asked Butch his secret for long life, and he told me he never eats meat. Another guest, the French actress, Corinne Calvet, piped up, "I don't eat meat either...unless it moves." In typical Cesar Romero fashion, Butch blushed like a little kid. Even at his age, anything risqué embarrassed him. I miss you, Butch.

ℭ𝔖

Lynn Redgrave offered a glimpse into her theatrical family, led by the aloof Sir Michael Redgrave.

Lynn never felt she knew her father at all. Sir Michael was private and proper and found it impossible to show his love toward his children.

Lynn cried as she revealed that she knew her father only as an actor. That he had a difficult time getting close to people in general, but that it was especially difficult for him to relate to his family.

And that finally, on his deathbed, he told Lynn how he wished he'd gotten to know her more intimately, sat her on his knee as a child, been a father to her. It was then that Lynn finally broke down and cried in her daddy's arms, at last feeling like his little girl.

As she wondered, "Why? Why did he wait till too late to tell us he loved us? she translated her pain into the one-woman show, Shakespeare For My Father.

☙

The Crosby Clan was another family with major papa problems. Bing and brother Bob may have packed the Cocoanut Grove, night after night, but inside their homes, they were box office poison.

Bob's son, Chris, told me what a tough time the Crosby brood had in Hollywood. Their drinking, womanizing dads raised an unhappy bunch, who hated their fathers and weren't so crazy about each other.

I also interviewed several of Bing's sons and got the scoop on the rude, crude crooner. Having seen him on the set at Paramount many times while I was a child, I can vouch that Bing was not a nice man. His smiles and good humor soured as soon as the cameras were off. He declared himself a man of great Catholic piety, but Bing knew his way around women, and had more than his share.

There's nothing I despise more than a holy hypocrite, and that was Bing.

Ↄ

John Agar clued me in on the life he shared with America's darling. Shirley Temple. John, a young, good-looking guy from Chicago, had served his time in the army before making tracks to Hollywood. He met some well-connected people, got into the movies and caught the eye of the young teen angel, Shirley Temple. In no time, they were married.

But John became an alcoholic, staying out all night, boozing with his co-star, John Wayne. When Agar didn't even come to the hospital for his daughter's birth, Shirley divorced him and vowed never to let him see his child.

At this writing, John's grownup daughter has never seen her father. I felt sorry for this fractured family and tried to ease a reconciliation. Alas, there was nothing I could do.

Ↄ

For every sour marriage in Hollywood, you'd be surprised just how many solid, happy love pairings there are. Craig Stevens, once TV's biggest gun slinging hunk Peter Gunn, had adored his wife, Alexis Smith, the enchanting Warner Brothers star and Broadway headliner. They were inseparable, and were blessed with a long-lasting, joyous marriage. When Alexis died, Craig was heartbroken. Her death nearly killed him. It took many years for Craig to finally move on, though it's clear Alexis will always anchor his heart.

૭ঙ

Joseph Cotton and Patricia Medina were another classy Hollywood couple. Joseph talked about his wonderful friend Orson Welles, and how Welles maintained close contact with him, Agnes Moorehead and the rest of the Mercury Theater Ensemble. Cotton loved working with Marilyn Monroe in Niagara, and she later told him it was her favorite movie – her dramatic breakthrough. Joseph adored Patricia, as she did him. When Joseph Cotton died, so did one of Hollywood's classiest, most enduring marriages.

Later, Patricia wrote her own book, Laid Back in Hollywood, about her life and marriage to Joseph Cotton. Touching and beautiful, it included many of his poetic love letters to her.

૭ঙ

Ageless diva, Eartha Kitt, shared that from her earliest days, she picked cotton in North Carolina, and she's proud of her roots planted in that rich Southern soil. Eartha's momma named her for that precious earth from which we all come, and Eartha loves that quality in people.

Nevertheless, cotton picking was backbreaking work for such a young girl. Toiling in the ground, her hands and feet were forever blistered and callused. Exhausted every night, Eartha dreamed of being a princess and leaving that hard life behind.

After years of crying herself to sleep, Eartha's mama shipped her child off to New York's Harlem to live with relatives, but the child's abusive aunt beat her and made her wish she'd never left the sweet Southern soil. Eartha took to riding the subway just to get away from her hateful guardian. Save underground, drifting from one station to another, she ran loose all over the city to escape the madness.

Despite her humble, abusive beginnings, this trouble uneducated child, developed into an extraordinary and knowledgeable performer. Having endured, Eartha transformed her own anguish and suffering into a profound understanding of pain and life's possibility.

Although hurt by racial inequality and our government's treatment of her when she spoke out against the Vietnam war years before it was fashionable, today Eartha is as in-demand as ever. When she's not busy recording or performing on stage and television, she is living the simple life in Connecticut with her loving husband.

❧

Robert Morse, came into my life in the late '80s when I met him at a Hildegarde concert. Bobby was staying at the Yamashiro Hotel, once an exquisite Japanese styled estate, an atmosphere where we were able to develop a terrific friendship. He was kicking alcohol, and asked me to go with him to AA.

It's weird how the same cocktails that introduced these people to one another in the first place were now bringing them together for the cure. I saw more "A-list" stars at the AA meetings than Spago's and movie premieres combined.

Hearing all those people letting their fears spill out, inspired me. Bobby would often bare his soul to his fellow recovering alcoholics. He even met his wife at AA, in every way the perfect training ground for a solid marriage. I've seen more honest communicating there than most couples experience in all their years of marriage.

One day Bobby dropped by my place with a manuscript tucked under one arm, "Skippy, I've been asked to play Truman Capote in a show called Tru!"

He tossed the script at me for my opinion, since Truman and I had been friends...

I was performing in DC with Don Rickles. One evening after the show, Truman and I were reading our respective papers in the hotel coffee shop.

Just a couple of effeminate Southern boys in awe of the world, we struck up a conversation, and talked our way into the night. We had a lot of mannerisms in common...our flamboyant attitude, style of clothes and uncut umbilicus – the telephone – reaching out to connect and catch up on the latest dirt.

After that we saw each other at social functions, and also one fabulous party Tru held at the United Nations apartment building. A great writer, but a sad man, my friend ended up drinking himself to death.

After glancing through the script, I realized Bobby was a natural.

This was a great comeback opportunity for my friend, whose big success had been the Broadway and movie versions of How To Succeed In Business Without Trying. Watching a tape of Truman, I looked at Bobby's reflection in the TV screen, and realized, "You were meant for this role."

Bobby accepted the part, and was brilliant. Our friendship gave Bobby an almost firsthand feel for Tru's mannerisms, but Bobby wasn't imitating anybody, he was true-blue Tru.

A new career blossomed for the rediscovered stage marvel. He deserved that success, and all the triumphs that followed.

ॐ

Jacqueline Stallone called me one evening after seeing my show, and said she just had to meet me. Her gutsy, straightforward attitude captured my heart, and I was equally anxious to meet her. The Polo Lounge at the Beverly Hills Hotel was still the favorite "Let's lunch, let's dish, let's deal" spot, so that's where we met.

She brought along her good friend, Jack Rapoport. I had a strange feeling, the name was so familiar – Rapoport... Rapoport... Rapoport's Restaurant on Second Avenue!...

"There was a fantastic restaurant in New York City called Rapoport's, are you familiar with it?" I asked.

"Are you joking? My father owned it."

Nearly falling out of my cushy leather chair, I proceeded to tell Jack and Jacqueline all about my days at Sammy's Bowery Follies and our early morning breakfasts at Rapoport's. Just thinking about that special eatery gave me a warm, comforting feeling that Aunt Sadie was with us at the table, smacking her lips over a scrumptious prune Danish.

Jack was as kind and hospitable as his father, and we became wonderful friends. Once again, my small world shrunk even smaller.

Jacqueline Stallone is an impressive, strong-willed lady, who speaks her mind. Once the conversation was in her court, she was in her element. A master communicator, never lacking for something important to say, she'd seen my show many times and thought it'd be fun to host one of her own.

I was astounded that this dynamic personality had never been interviewed, so I jumped at the opportunity, and told her the first step to becoming an interviewer was to be an interviewee.

From the moment we started taping, Jacqueline's charisma, charm and unbridled energy burst through. It was obvious this elegant powerhouse was a natural. There's nothing timid about Jacqueline, and her ballsy candor made for a fat-moving, highly spirited interview.

She's opinionated, and hates phonies. Her favorite beef is young lovelies who sleep their way up the career ladder and then brag to the whole world about every buckaroo who ever straddled their saddle. Or bed-kittens, who act so demure, innocent and hard working, without mentioning the men who got them where they are today.

Hollywood stars aren't the only heavenly bodies that fascinate Jacqueline. Her knowledge of astrology often guided me through difficult times.

Jacqueline had worked and lived in Las Vegas most of her life before moving to Hollywood, where she was still virtually unknown...until she did my modest little cable show. After that, one of Hollywood's best-kept secrets was suddenly in demand for talk show after talk show. Everybody fell in love with this feisty new star, and she was perfectly suited for life in the limelight.

She called me all the time, inviting me to parties and connecting me to entertainment people, announcing, "This is the man who changed my life and launched my career."

I'd have to chuckle, "Jacqueline, I can't take credit for that. You're a natural."

She'd laugh, but it was the truth. In fact, it was my life that changed through meeting Jacqueline Stallone. Besides gaining a wonderful new friend, I went from existing on the fringe of Hollywood to being part of it. Jacqueline and I spent many fun evenings at Nicky Blair's. What a paparazzi magnet! Every time I went out with her, I prepared myself for the unending burst of flashbulbs. The photographers swarmed around her, but the bursting bulbs never bothered Jacqueline, whose smiling sparks and sizzle blinded those guys right back.

CƁ

Jackie Mason chatted with me just before knocking the Broadway critics on their tchotkes with his brilliant one-mensch show and, contrary to his show-no-mercy image, was also a delightful, charming interviewee.

Shelley Berman, the wonderful actor-comedian, was another surprise. I understand he can be quite difficult, but I found him to be approachable and easygoing.

Yes, I'm happy to report that there are comics out there who actually do have a great sense of humor. Milton Berle was another cutup friend.

Until our interview, I had no idea that he was once a child actor and vaudevillian, sporting the first Buster Brown hairdo when he posed for their shoe ads with Nipper the dog. Traveling the Vaudeville circuit with his mom, young Miltie had a hard time because he was under age. But once he found the ham in himself, he never gave up.

Madcap Miltie loves to camp it up with me, but I tell him, "You're a bigger drag queen than I'll ever be." His drag act goes back to Vaudeville's cross-dressing shtick. He and Jack Benny got such a kick out of doing drag.

Milton, honey, nobody fills out their bloomers like you, dear. You're a natural woman, and you wear it well.

The late Morey Amsterdam was a great comic. A sweetheart of a guy and healthy well into his eighties, he was like a kid. When I asked for his secret to health, he'd always say, "You gotta laugh every day. You gotta laugh at yourself and at the world."

ↃↃ

On the darker side of the comic spotlight was Paul Lynde, now deceased. I met him at a Hollywood bar, where he'd go every night to get smashed. Wayland Flowers would drop in with his loudmouthed puppet, Madame, whom he'd perch at the bar in her god-awful getups and have her camp it up with the customers.

Paul Lynde would yell at the puppet, "Fuck you, Madame, ya' fag-hag bitch!" and she'd snap back, "Fuck me? No thank you, Pauline, I'll hold out for a better offer! I'm not into lesbians, dearie."

Paul drank nonstop, screaming, carrying on and laying everybody out. I loved watching his nightly knockdown drag-outs with a potty-talking hand puppet.

As a guzzler, Paul Lynde was one of the bitterest men on the planet. But sober, he was as decent a human being as you'd ever meet. But drunk or sober there was one topic that turned him ugly. Paul Lynde was a despicable anti-Semite. He hated Jews. For a long time he didn't know I was Jewish. He thought I was 100 percent Italian.

I'd tell him to stop being so rude and ignorant, but he just kept on with the same sick Jew-bashing, "Hollywood's run by the fucking hook- noses. The Jews own this town, Skippy. Everything's controlled by them."

One day, sick of his hateful ranting, I cornered him and made him listen, "Paul, I'm Jewish."

He refused to believe it, "Oh fuck you, Mary. You're no Jew! I can spot those big-nosed fucks a mile away."

"Oh, yes I am, Paul. My mother's Jewish. You're talking to a Jew, Paul. A real, live Jew!"

When I finally convinced him I was Jewish, he completely changed toward me. That sorry-ass bigot wouldn't even look in my direction after that.

Paul wanted to be a bigger star, and he blamed his career problems and alcoholism on the Jews. Everything was the Jew's fault.

A bitter, bitter man, Paul loved to cruise the masseur ads in the gay magazines, find hustlers, take them to his apartment and ply them with drugs. He'd give them $100 for the night, then they'd roll him and beat him up. Night after night, they took him for everything he was worth. He was always getting robbed and beaten, but miraculously managed to escape the headlines.

Once, taking off in a plane with Paul, he got drunk and started cursing the passengers and the stewardess. A child was sitting next to him, and he shouted, "Get that fucking rug rat away from me. Toss that miserable fucking kid off the plane."

Finally the stewardess called the captain, who flew back to the airport and ordered Paul off the plane.

I couldn't believe this was the same gifted man who'd left Ohio to star on Broadway in Leonard Sillman's New Faces of 1952, then went on to a smashing hit in Bye Bye Birdie, achieving every success in the world of theater and television.

This was the pathetic, tortured Paul Lynde that the world never knew. Maybe if he'd been caught by the media, he'd have had to do something about his liquor and drug problems.

Speaking of attitude, my good friend, Virginia Mayo, threw me for a loop. Once a big star, who played opposite on and off the screen, with many of the greats including James Cagney and Jack Warner, she promised to be an interesting interview. But no matter what I asked, her answer never changed, "Don't ask me about that. I don't want to talk about it!"

She wouldn't talk about Cagney or Warner, or anyone she knew. Married to actor Michael O'Shea for many years, her whole life changed when he died. Angry at the world since then, she was my toughest interview ever!

Sharks are everywhere, scouring the waters in search of fresh prey. You think you're being careful, and boom, the big sting socks you in the wallet, and suddenly you're flat-ass broke.

Mimi Hines had always been one of the most levelheaded, easygoing stars in the business, until she was pushed far beyond the brink...

Mimi had been a hit on Broadway in Funny Girl and I'd visit her all the time at her beautiful Malibu home, where we threw many wonderful parties. Since Mimi was constantly traveling, she hired someone to manage her finances while she was away.

She'd worked hard over the years, saved a lot and was careful to keep on top of her financial affairs. The money manager Mimi hired convinced her to give him power of attorney.

When Mimi returned home after a lengthy road engagement, she discovered that the manager was nowhere to be found, and that the bank had repossessed her house!

Mimi was left with nothing. She flipped out, and had a complete nervous breakdown.

Eventually she decided to let her lawyers do battle with the bastard in court. Who better to tear through a hungry shark than a team of bloodthirsty piranhas?

Unfortunately they were unsuccessful, and she was locked out forever from her beautiful Malibu home.

Virtually wiped out and homeless, Mimi had no choice but to move elsewhere and find a new lifestyle that she could afford. Her ex-husband, Phil Ford, owned a couple houses in Vegas, and he graciously invited her to stay in the one next door to him.

No one forced Phil. He just felt a moral obligation to help his former mate. So, destitute and without options, Mimi Hines moved to a quaint little house, side by side with her unselfish ex. Whenever she pops into Hollywood, she's my house guest.

Mimi's endured as many labors as Hercules, but she didn't let them defeat her. She's a trouper of the highest order.

In the early 1970s, I practically lived at the Hollywood Park race-track in Inglewood, a grubby sub-urb of Los Angeles. I loved playing the ponies and went to the track at least five times a week, often with Jean Wallace or my good friend Yvette Vikers, best known as the

George Raft

star of the 1958 B-movie classic, Attack of the 50 Foot Woman.

Yvette, a statuesque blonde, attracted the attention of men whenever we went out together. One of them was George Raft, the star who spe-cialized in playing gangsters on screen and socializing with real ones off. At the track one day, Yvette introduced me to the actor, who was in his 70s by then but still a ladies man.

I don't drive, so we went to Hollywood Park in Yvette's car. When we were ready to leave, her car wouldn't start. So I asked George if he'd give us a lift. He agreed immediately, but instead of taking us home, we ended up at his place in Beverly Hills.

George began to give Yvette a tour of his home, proudly pointing out memorabilia on the walls chronicling his Hollywood career. I was not invited to join them on the tour and waited patiently in the living room for George and Yvette to return. They didn't.

Instead, they disappeared for what seemed like an eternity. Eventually I got bored and decided to take my own tour of the place. As I wandered down a hallway, I saw an open door and looked inside.

There I witnessed a scene that topped anything in Hollywood Babylon or The Day of the Locust, books that deal with the underbelly of the movie capital. Yvette and George were in his bedroom but not in his bed. They were having wild sex in a coffin next to the bed. Yvette really got into it and started moaning and screaming, "Do it to me, big guy! Do it!"

George was kinky and not at all romantic. I think he had turned into all the tough guys he played on film. In response to Yvette's ecstatic outbursts, Raft would say, "Shut up, goddamnit, and just take it!"

Fascinated, appalled and embarrassed, I quickly left before they spotted me.

I went back to the living room and had a drink alone. About half an hour later, they emerged from the bedroom as though nothing had happened.

Out of bed, George remained the perfect gentlemen, and after his Dracula sex with Yvette, he gave us a ride home.

CB

Of the promising young people I've interviewed, Alexis Arquette is a standout. Like his equally loopy sister, Rosanna, he's a natural talent with no airs – what you see is what you get. A terrific dramatic actor, who isn't afraid to go campy or drag, there's not a trace of attitude in that sweet, decent kid.

My good friend Nan Robinson, the daughter-in-law of actor Edward J. Robinson, introduced me to a man who would become one of my best friends, Troy Donahue. Nan brought him to my talent showcase at the Continental Hyatt Hotel on the Sunset Strip one night. He must have loved the show because he came back several times, almost always drunk out of his mind. Another attraction was all the gorgeous women who appeared in my talent showcases, and Troy loved beautiful gals.

We started hanging out together and often had breakfast at the legendary Silver Spoon restaurant on Santa Monica Boulevard in West Hollywood.

Inside and out, Troy, born Merle Johnson, Jr., was a beautiful man.

Despite his blond good looks, Troy was no bimbo. An Ivy Leaguer who dropped out of journalism school at Columbia to try his luck at acting in Hollywood, he was discovered by the notorious talent agent, Henry Wilson.

Wilson, among other things, was also an alcoholic and a drug addict. His most prominent client was Rock Hudson. Wilson specialized in finding gorgeous men with little acting talent and lots of muscles and giving them ridiculous names like Tab Hunter, Rory Calhoun and Guy Madison. He was credited with creating the "beefcake craze" of the 1950s that reached its apogee with bodybuilders like Steve Reeves, who became an international star, mostly in kitschy movies based on Greek myths.

Although Troy was one of Wilson's discoveries, he didn't really fit the beefcake mold. In fact, he was so thin I used to tell him that if he closed one eye he'd look like a needle. His cadaverous physique wasn't due to drugs but alcohol. Instead of eating, he drank, and drank, and...

I unsuccessfully tried to fatten him up by making spaghetti dinners and tuna casseroles, but he still looked anorexic. I know, because I often saw him without his clothes on.

Everyone who arrived in Hollywood wanted to meet Wilson, who seemed like a nice fellow to me, because aspiring actors knew the agent could turn them into a Hollywood star – for a price. Wilson "auditioned" prospective clients by offering them two things: a blowjob and movie stardom. Wilson got the blowjob but only succeeded in making good on the second part of his offer in some cases. Other pretty boys were too hopeless to be taken seriously as an actor, and Wilson couldn't do anything for their careers.

I never brought up the subject of Henry Wilson with Troy because I didn't want to embarrass him by asking how he had auditioned for the agent, but I presume the then unknown actor got the same two-fer offer Wilson gave his other would-be clients.

Whatever actually happened between Troy and Wilson during the audition, the two men had a friendly working relationship. The same couldn't be said about Troy's boss, studio head Jack Warner, whom Troy loathed, and for good reason.

Warner signed Troy to a long-term contract at only $750 a week even after he became a major heartthrob, and the mogul wouldn't let him out of the contract or give him a raise.

One night Troy stayed over at my apartment. The more he drank, the more he cursed Jack Warner. As he repeatedly punched a pillow in my bedroom, Troy imagined it was Warner he was attacking. The punching was accompanied by a rant about the hated studio chief: "That son of a bitch Jew bastard," he screamed. "That motherfucker took all my money after I made all those great movies for him!"

Troy only insulted Warner at my apartment, never daring to repeat his nasty comments to the slave-driver who generated his rants or to anyone else in public for that matter. Loose lips sink acting careers.

While attacking my pillow, Troy somehow managed to take off all his clothes, then passed out in my bed. Later that night, he woke and resumed drinking heavily. All of a sudden his mouth was on my dick, sucking away like crazy. Other people might have been thrilled but not me. I just don't enjoy getting blowjobs although I've always loved giving them. I immediately asked Troy to stop. My philosophy has always been that it's better to give than receive. Sometimes, I'd say, "Troy, I've got to get some sleep. Why don't you go home?" And sometimes he'd reply, "I don't have any place to go." Short of rent money, he confided that he used to sleep in the park, but he never asked me for a handout.

Troy claimed he was straight and only interested in men when he was drunk. Since he was drunk so much of the time, he spent a lot of time around gay men. His favorite pastime was going to Santa Monica's Will Rogers State Beach, which was popular with gays. All the pretty boys gathered around Troy as he played volleyball. He was also an excellent tennis player and a talented equestrian. He had a wholesomeness about him despite his drinking problem that made him look like a farm boy who had just got off the bus from Nebraska although he actually came from an Ivy League college in the Big Apple.

He confided in me a lot, especially about his first wife, actress Suzanne Pleshette. He loved Suzanne because she was strong. Troy was not.

His wedding night with Suzanne at the Beverly Hills Hotel in 1964 was a disaster. If it was true that he only liked guys when he was drunk, he must have been very drunk that disastrous first night of a marriage that lasted less than a year.

After the wedding reception at the hotel's landmark Polo Lounge, Suzanne decided to do a little shopping at the pricy stores on the premises. Bored, Troy went down to the pool and returned to the bridal suite with the pool boy!

Finished shopping, Suzanne returned to their room and found her bridegroom in bed with a teenager! When I say Suzanne was one tough lady, I'm not exaggerating. She threw a hissy fit, called the hotel manager, and had the pool boy fired. She couldn't believe what had happened...and on their wedding night! She refused to talk to her husband for several days after that disaster. I was surprised by her surprise. Before their marriage, Suzanne had been warned that Troy was bisexual. I guess she fell for his line, "...but only when I'm drunk."

Troy had a bittersweet end to a life of triumphs and tragedies. Eventually, he sobered up at AA meetings. I went along for support although my "drug of choice" has always been the racetrack, not the bottle. When I got bored at those dreary, endless 12-Step meetings, I'd slip out and sneak a drink at a bar nearby.

Somehow, Troy managed to maintain his sobriety, which may explain why he fell in love with a beautiful Japanese opera singer from Tokyo.

Along with AA, she helped Troy put his life and career back together, although he only managed to land small roles during his "comeback."

The comeback didn't last long. In 2001, while driving on the freeway, Troy plowed into a car in front of his. His chest crashed into the steering wheel. I kept begging him to see a doctor, but he insisted he hadn't been injured and never sought medical attention. About three or four weeks after the accident, he died of a heart attack caused by his collision with the steering wheel.

He was only 65, but still quite the hunk, if a scrawny one.

People often think Hollywood is a big happy family. Not exactly. Do plumbers dig one another because they share an interest in drain reaming? There are terrific friendships in this town, but sadly some of the strongest bonds wither in the face of challenges.

Peter Lawford's wife, Patricia touched me with the story of her last years with the great English actor. When he lay dying at Cedars-Sinai hospital, his once closest friends, Sammy Davis, Jr. and Frank Sinatra, didn't come by for a single visit or even send a message. Peter waited in vain for a phone call or the merest hint that his pals might give a damn. Their silence broke his heart, though when he died, Sammy and Frank popped up at his funeral, playing the best friend bit for the press.

Some so-called friends in this fantasy land aren't worth the flimsy cocktail napkins their fax numbers are scribbled on.

Timothy Leary was one fascinating interview from outside the showbiz ilk. In the 1960s he was a professor at UC Berkeley, where he experimented with psychedelics such as LSD, and advocated their mind-expanding benefits.

J. Edgar Hoover, America's favorite gun-toting cross-dresser, had Leary arrested and thrown in prison, where he spent the endless hours reading and learning anything and everything.

In prison, books continued to be Leary's drug of choice. He also studied the prisoners and learned a great deal about human behavior and how the mind works. By continuing to stretch his mind, he transformed prison into a free wheeling experience.

Timothy Leary was a brilliant, insightful man. And what a life he had! When he got fed up with his jailhouse digs, he busted out, was recaptured, and served a few more years before being released. Timothy Leary did hard time, showing us how to put our downtime to excellent use.

CHAPTER FIFTEEN

Decline and Fall of the House of Brando

I was riding along Mulholland Drive with a friend early one evening in the 1980s. Just as the sun sank into the ocean, we turned onto Sunset Boulevard and were drawn to an old man, his head hanging on his barrel bell as he walked his dog. This roly-poly fellow seemed to be hiding inside the oversized straw hat that slid around on his head, concealing him from the world. He kept a wobbly grasp on his cane, which barely supported his tremendous girth.

Beautiful wildflowers surrounded him and, as he shakily bent down to pick some yellow ones, the sticky pollen painted his hands.

The old man seemed drunk from the flowers' lingering aroma. He squeezed the flowers with all his might, then inhaled deeply to get a good hearty whiff.

I nudged my friend to slow down. We were now both quite intrigued at this strange scene when I noticed the sad, empty face of this hulking shell of a man.

"Stella!" suddenly flashed through my brain, and I yelled to my friend, "That's him! Stella! You know!"

"Stella? That's an odd name for a guy! Some old drag queen?" "You know...Streetcar...Stella...Brando! That's Brando!"

My friend was skeptical. "Nah, can't be. That's just some wasted old derelict. I know Marlon Brando when I see him."

"Well, you're seeing him, Darling," I smart-assed back. Those intense eyes were unmistakably Marlon's, and we'd just passed his house. Outlined against the fading sunset, Marlon Brando cast a giant shadow. Oh, how my heart sank at the sight of this once-great actor, so despondent and withdrawn. I watched the melancholy figure as cars sped by. I wanted to reach out and help somehow, but we drove off and left Marlon to his private torments in that yellow field of dreams.

A few months after that particular moment, I met Christian Brando, Marlon's son. Whether my wish to help Marlon was coming true or not, I was diving head first into the House of Brando.

Edie Williams, Hollywood's sexy girl, who took Christian's virginity when he was just 14, introduced me to Christian at lunch at the Hard Rock Cafe. Edie got around, leaving a trail of pink panties in countless bedrooms, boardrooms and bar rooms throughout Hollywood. A blonde playmate, Edie traditionally showed up for the Academy Awards, only to find that she had no invitation...or clothing under her absurdly flimsy gown.

Over the course of many years, doing talent showcases and my cable interview show, I came to know some of the hottest up-and-coming young starlets. In the beginning, my friendship with Christian was more of a girl-getting franchise, but I didn't mind because he was such a nice young man, and it was my pleasure to help him fill his dance card.

Christian came to visit me quite often at my West Hollywood apartment. One day he brought over a lovely, dark-haired girl whom I'd never seen before, and introduced her as "my beautiful wife, Mary"!

"Wife? Well, Christian, congratulations! When did all this happen?"

I was happy for the two, but surprised, considering just the day before

I'd seen him with some blonde number.

They laughed and explained they'd been legally separated, but had remained good friends.

At first, I was furious with Christian for not telling me, and guilty about setting him up with girls. But when Mary told me they treated the separation like a divorce, I felt better. Like so many young married couples, these former childhood sweethearts discovered they could survive better as friends than spouses.

Whenever they came over, we'd listen to classical music or just sit and talk for hours. But when Christian came along, he'd grab a beer, shove a porno tape into the VCR, and watch it, like a little kid sneaking a peek at his father's girlie collection.

Once the stag film routine got stale and Christian felt comfortable talking with me one-on-one, he opened up about his father and mother, the difficulties in being a celebrity's kid, and everything he couldn't tell his own pop.

Christian had a difficult time being "Marlon Brando's son." He never knew whether people liked him or his princely position in Hollywood's hierarchy. Of course, he didn't want to give away the perks of his life, but somewhere in the morass of it all, he'd plead, "Skippy, remember, I'm Christian. Forget the Brando bit, okay?"

I'd never do anything to embarrass him, so I was careful to introduce him as simply Christian. Christian so desperately wanted to be liked for himself, and not because his padre was one of the greatest actors on the planet.

In time, Christian let me peer behind his tough, macho mask. Hiding under that thick skin was a lonely boy. I admit he brought out my paternal side, the person he could confide in freely, who'd be his friend without strings. Christian adored his father and looked up to him, but Marlon wasn't always around to give him the love and attention he craved.

It was more difficult for Christian to talk about his mother, Anna Kafshi. In the 1960s, Marlon and Anna's divorce and child custody battle grew into an all time war. Anna was a contract player at MGM in the fifties, usually cast as a sultry, exotic type. The news media had a field day and turned a serious, private matter into a sensational public circus. When it was over, Marlon had won full custody of Christian and trashed Anna Kafshi. The truth is, Anna is a loving women who deserved far better than the bum deal Marlon dealt her.

Long before I met Christian, I was friends with Anna. For years she lived in a mobile home, supplementing her paltry income by caring for seniors. I called her often, letting her know what a treat it would be to interview her, but she always refused. I tried to build her confidence, reminding her that she'd always be a star in the hearts of her many fans. Anna had been shy and modest, but after Marlon's treatment of her, she'd become terrified of people and going out in public altogether.

In the 1960s, men rarely received custody of children, but Marlon, one of the brightest stars of that era, had a lot of influence in the legal machinery. Money talks, and Marlon's attorney heard it screaming into his wallet.

So, Marlon got Christian, and Anna lost her child, her dignity and whatever remained of her good standing in the fickle Hollywood community. After the divorce, Marlon refused to have anything to do with Anna, and made it impossible for Christian to see his mother. He called Anna "the bitch" in front of Christian, and that was what he grew up learning about his mother.

Anna says that hired thugs entered her home and roughed her up to remind her to stay away from "Marlon's kid." She suffered bruises, black eyes, head injuries, but none of that could make her forget her son or her love for him.

I hated the thought of Anna's spirit being shot down so viciously. Common sense told me that this long-standing family dispute was none of my business, but since I had no sense anyway, I tried to help reunite mother and son.

Whenever I'd mention Anna to Christian, he'd just tell me, "Hunchy, mind you own business. This isn't Hunchy's business." (Hunchy was Christian's pet name for me, because of my scoliosis. I never minded it, because I knew he meant it lovingly.)

"Operation Anna" was always fresh on my mind and, as Christian grew to trust me more and was able to let down his guard, I pressed the Anna Kafshi issue in hopes of breaking through to the little boy who needed his mama's love and guidance.

"Don't you ever see your mother?" I innocently asked Christian, knowing the answer full well.

There was no response.

"You know, Christian, I talk to her often, and she asks me how you're doing. Anna Kafshi lives for you, Christian. This woman, who barely subsists on support checks from the government, lives only for you."

"Mind your own business, Hunchy. Brando business is not Hunchy business."

"Stop it, Christian. Don't be cute with me. Why don't you make an effort to see your mother?" I could churn up a good maternal nag when I had to.

Finally, my not-so-subtle tactics paid off – Christian, picked up the receiver and growled, "Okay, Hunch, gimme the number. Just give me the number."

Christian and Skip having fun

The white flag was up. I couldn't believe it. I had stepped in and landed a devastating upper cut right to the heart. Christian, the macho man of the world, stepped aside and let Christian, the lonely little kid, take center stage. I was ecstatic.

"Stand back, San Diego, there will be floodwaters tonight."

Of course we knew it would be a shocker for Anna, but I was positive this was one jolt she'd welcome. As Christian phoned his mother, I could almost see his heart surge through the phone lines, reaching down into Anna's heavy heart.

"Hi, Ma. How you doing?" His voice cracked and, as he spoke, tears nudged from his eyes. "Ma, what's going on out there. Ma?" I could only imagine what an effort it must have taken for Anna to speak through the tidal wave crashing within her. It was a short conversation, but I couldn't imagine a more heartfelt exchange. I told Christian how proud I was of him, and he was so embarrassed I'd witnessed that tender moment. Anna's words had touched Christian. I'd never seen him so vulnerable. That phone call kept me in a great mood for days. I figured if Anna and Christian could be reunited, maybe there was hope for the rest of humanity.

With the phone call out of the way, the next logical step was a reunion. I went out on a limb and pressed, "Chris, do you know how much your

DECLINE AND FALL OF THE HOUSE OF BRANDO

mother would love to see you? If you went to visit her-"

Chris cut me off. I was ready for the reprimand, I could feel it coming. "No, Skippy. I have a much better idea. I'll bring her here for a visit." What?!!!

I was knocked out, down for the count. How terrific! Well, it seemed like a great idea at the time...

The next day, Christian bought a bed, set up a guest room at his place and drove to Anna's place in San Diego.

Anna was overjoyed. This was a dream come true for her. She enjoyed that dream for about a day...until the wrath of Marlon came crashing down on the happy reunion. Somehow Marlon got wind of Anna's reentry into the sacred House of Brando, and he was furious.

He called Christian and screamed, "What the fuck are you doing? Get that bitch out of that house and give her a shopping cart. I don't need a goddamn bag lady down here."

Poor Christian didn't know what to do. He'd learned at an early age not to defy his father. So he told Anna she'd have to leave.

Anna was devastated. Perhaps she didn't realize just how deep the spite flowed. Perhaps we were all naive enough to think Anna could be allowed to spend more than just one day with her own son.

Marlon's cruelty to Anna sickened me. Christian arranged to have his heartsick mother taken back to her mobile home in San Diego, thus ending Anna Kafshi's reign as queen for nearly a day.

That brief visit meant the world to Anna, but she saw how ruthlessly Marlon behaved if Christian attempted even the slightest display of affection toward her.

Christian knew better, but he lit into me anyway. "Skippy, this is it with my mother. You're gonna have to mind your own business. My old

261

man's pissed. And that's not good, understand?"

He had a point. You don't fuck around with the Godfather. So, I became a closet Anna Kafshi fan after that. I'd have regular conversations with her, but I never said a word to Christian. I'd report to Anna on the goings-on in the Brando family and keep her up-to-date. It was the least I could do to return some dignity to the life of this shamelessly persecuted woman.

During one of our conversations, Christian approached his paralyzing fear, "Skippy, what should Marlon Brando's son do for a living?"

"Anything you want! You choose what you want to do with your life."

I reminded Christian that when he dropped out of high school, he'd moved to Alaska and become a fisherman. He loved hard work.

And then I remembered my friend, Bill Cable – an actor who was now in the tree surgery business – had mentioned he was ready to take on a partner. Knowing how much Christian enjoyed physical work, I arranged for him to meet Bill.

Bill Cable had given up on the heartache and endless merry-go-round of trying to become a star and instead went into business for himself. Beverly Hills already had an assortment of pool men and plumbers, so Bill set out to become tree surgeon to the stars.

He quickly became everyone's favorite tree stud, and all the ladies wanted to hook up to Bill's cable. His beefy build and smooth charm snared many a fresh Hollywood darling.

TV's Cassandra Peterson, a.k.a Elvira, Mistress of the Dark, cast a fleeting spell on Bill until he got the urge to twang his thang somewhere new. Roving Bill couldn't stay in one bedroom for long. He did a lot of the celebrities' trees...and a lot of the celebrities.

Bill and Christian made quite a team. Those two macho, free-spirited lady-killers had a lot in common, and became the best of pals. They even shared an apartment for awhile, until Bill fell hard for an enticing beauty named Shirley and decided to marry her.

When the guys formed their new business, Hollywood Tree Surgeons, their first and biggest client was already lined up...Marlon Brando. A typhoon had devastated Marlon's Tahitian paradise, leaving trees and branches strewn over the ravaged tropical landscape.

With the island in shambles, Marlon hired the guys to clean up the place and make room for an aircraft runway. This would require them to cut down the damaged trees and clear them away.

Cleaning a yard would be demanding for a first assignment, but clearing an island?

Marlon needed it done, and he wanted to give Christian first shot at it.

Before long the guys were in Tahiti, hacking away. Residents of neighboring islands pitched in, but Bill and Christian supervised the operation. It was taxing, muscle-stretching labor, but the guys loved it, and their friendship grew in the months that it took to clear the wind-swept paradise.

Bill and Christian were a regular pair of Robinson Crusoes, taming that isle with all that brawn and sweat they could muster, plus a little help from a friendly six pack.

Not wanting to sacrifice productive man hours, Marlon had natives keeping tabs on the guys. Every day, after the grueling task of tackling those trees, they'd throw down some beers, fish in the deep blue shark-infested waters, sail to nearby islands and run wild. With just the two of them so far from civilization, Bill and Christian could roam around as they pleased, buck naked and free. It was their own Garden of Eden.

When Bill's new wife, Shirley, arrived on the horny lagoon, Christian wasted no time. Every time Bill's handsome head was turned, tropical storms Christian and Shirley invaded one another. For the time being, "Eve" had her way with the two "Adams," and all was well in Eden.

After six long months of laboring hard over the trees and slamming down just as hard on Shirley, Christian and Bill returned stateside with all kinds of interesting Tahitian tales. I was so happy to see "the kid" again, who put his arm around Bill and gushed, "Skip, this nut save me from a shark."

It seems Christian and Bill were out fishing, when their small boat tipped over. Christian was in the direct path of a hungry saw tooth. Bill wrestled it into a death lock, saving Christian and becoming a hero in the process.

I was amazed, but couldn't help wondering if Bill would've spared Christian form the shark's menu if he'd known Christian was having Shirley for breakfast every day. Bill was modest, but Christian let everyone know Bill was his savior. Christian was indeed a lucky man. It's not everyday you get saved from Jaws by the man whose wife you're fucking.

I flashed on the idea that this sea-soaked saga – part of it at least – might play out well on my cable show. Ever since Christian and I became friends, I'd asked him to appear on the show.

Bill liked the idea, and I sensed a theme in the making – Kids of Hollywood Greats. I called my friend, Christina Crawford, who'd just topped the best-seller lists with Mommie Dearest.

Christina was hot to do the show, but Christian wasn't. "Hunchy just wants me on his show because Marlon's my dad." "Christian, you can talk about whatever you want. It'll be the Christian and Christina Show." Christian warmed to the idea, and insisted on having Bill join him. I was thrilled. That show was one of my most memorable. Christina had plenty of material to work with, Christian displayed his flair for showmanship, and Bill and Christian did dead-on imitations of Marlon Brando, the Godfather. It was an hysterical tribute.

After the show aired, Christian described how Marlon popped an artery seeing Christian publicly talk about his family and imitate his untouchable father. Christian loved imitating his father, not to make fun of him, but to show off his wonderful ol' man.

With the exception of Marlon's bad review, I received only accolades about the show. Everyone loved Christian and wanted to know where he'd been hiding. It was obvious he'd inherited the star quality and good looks that blessed the careers of both papa Marlon and mama Anna.

Along with the deluge of letters and phone calls from Christian's new fans, there were those particular fans who also wanted to get a hold of him...without any clothes weighing him down.

Lorene Landon (no relation to Heavenly Highwayer, Michael), a young classical pianist, appearing at Ye Little Club, was the most vocal – "Oh, Skippy, please, I just have to meet that major hunk, that Brando guy."

I teased her, "You mean Marlon? He'd go for you in a heartbeat, but you might want to get into Sumo wrestling. It'll come in handy if you ever hope to tackle his paunch."

Lorene wasn't amused, "Not the old Brando, Skippy! The young, good-looking one!"

Lorene was persistent and the match sparked – Christian and Lorene became an item. I had an uneasy feeling about the two of them, but I never said anything to spoil their steamy liaison.

Meanwhile Bill and Christian's enterprise pushed straight up to the stars – Jack Nicholson, Mimi Hines, Shelley Winters, every celebrity who cared about his yard started throwing bucks in Bill's and Christian's direction. The guys were climbing to the top, one golden twig at a time, until one day, without warning, while Christian was balancing high up on a narrow branch, he lost his footing and crashed.

Marlon checked him right into St. John's Hospital for emergency surgery. Although the procedure was a success, Christian had to swear off tree surgery for the time being, to mend properly.

With this impediment, Christian's spirits flagged. He'd worked hard most of his life, and his self esteem derived from a day's labor. This was a difficult adjustment for him.

Once Christian lost his grip on that branch, he lost his grip on what was important.

On his thirtieth birthday, Christian came into a handsome trust fund his mother had demanded of Marlon when they divorced. He had his eye on a Laurel Canyon house, so he took some of the trust money, added it to a generous loan from Marlon, and instantly the house was his.

The combination of having a great deal of money and time on your hands can be lethal when there's no plan, no direction and no goal.

Christian's new "down boys" (drug addicts and money leeches) swarmed to his new digs and a powder keg was primed to explode.

I noticed an unhealthy change in Christian. All he could talk about was his down boys and high times at Laurel Canyon. Although I never saw Christian take drugs at my place, he was out of it most of the time. I could feel Christian's life sliding into the toilet and, as a friend, I wanted to help him back out of that sewage trap.

Although Christian loved to swear he'd never be an actor and "get mixed up in that phony business," I listened to the yearning under his righteous words. People were drawn by his smoldering charismatic looks, and I knew about a low-budget film in Italy. Christian needed to get far away from his seedy friends, and the film might give him an opportunity to learn and expand.

The Assassination of Renata Fonte was to begin filming in Rome. It interested Christian who, still hot on the Shirley Cable trail, insisted Bill and Shirley accompany him. Unaware of the Shirley-Christian tryst, Bill was delighted at the invitation and the bit roles Christian got them in his movie debut.

Christian Brando

Bill teased, "You ought to get married again, Christian. Wouldn't you love a hot number like Shirley, waiting for you every night?"

Christian just smiled and deadpanned, "You bet I would, Billy. I sure as hell would."

After the film was completed and the happy threesome returned, Christian slipped right back into his sleazy crowd. I was hoping the trip would work a miracle, but that just didn't happen.

When Christian wasn't getting wasted, he and Shirley were getting bolder. Bill Cable walked into his bedroom one night and found them screwing each other to the wallpaper. Christian looked up into Bill's angry baby blues, but Bill didn't say a word. He grabbed Shirley's garter belt from the foot of the bed, threw it in her face and, without a glance at Christian, who lay naked and speechless, flipped them off and left muttering, "Thanks buddy. Thanks a whole fucking lot."

The next day, Christian came by my place – he and Shirley were scared to death of Bill. Plugging your best friend's wife has certainly been known to motivate murder, but I knew Bill Cable's level head, and wasting anyone at all, not to mention his wife and best friend, wasn't his style.

Nevertheless, if felt like a good time to throw Christian another life jacket. So I called up my friend Giovanni in Rome, to see what we could cook up in another part of the world. Meanwhile I took Christian to visit my old friend Shelley Winters.

Anxious to meet her friend Marlon's son, Shelley invited us to her class at the Actors' Studio. Christian picked me up in his big red truck. I loved riding in this wonderful rig as he took control of that four wheel monster. If only he'd had that kind of power over his own life.

Christian and Shelley hit if off right away. She invited him to come to her class anytime. No obligation, just watch and see if acting might be his thing.

Christian went once but it wasn't for him. High strung as a colt, he couldn't sit still in a classroom for any length of time.

So I got back in touch with Giovanni who'd arranged for Christian and Jacqueline Stallone to appear on a talk show in Barcelona, Spain.

Though he was no sainthood candidate, Christian had always been committed to work, and had never before roamed aimlessly as he'd been doing with his homeboys.

I was thrilled when Christian got excited and the ham in him started to surface. I sent them off and Christian and Jacqueline were a big hit on the show. When they returned, Christian was happier than he'd been in a long time and brought me a piece of the freshly bulldozed Berlin wall to show his gratitude.

When he hit town, Lorene called me up. She wanted to contact Christian, but since both his moods and drinking intensified when he was with her, I pleaded ignorance.

But then Christian disappeared. For ten days he couldn't be reached. And the parent in me had the strangest feeling of dread.

Six o'clock in the morning, I was jarred awake by a pounding on my door. I seldom went to sleep until early in the morning, so only a psycho would even try to drag my ass up at that hour.

Then came the wailing and shouting, "Skippy. Skip. Goddammit, open the door. SKIPPY!"

The frantic voice was Bill Cable's. I prepared myself for the worst as I pushed the covers off the bed. Bill banged harder and harder.

"My God, what in the-" I opened the door and Bill fell inside, paler than death.

"Bill!!! It's Christian, isn't it?! What's happened to the kid. Please, Bill, what?"

Bill stumbled frantically around the apartment. Finally, "Oh, Skippy, Christian did it. Finally did it, Goddammit. Can you believe it?" My heart was racing the Indy 500. Where were the brakes?

"What, Bill? For God sakes, what's happened to Christian?"

"Cheyenne's boyfriend's dead. He was k-killed!" Bill stammered, like he'd just been shot himself. (Cheyenne was Christian's sister, and I knew they'd never been close.)

"Dead? Oh my God! Holy Jesus! That's terrible. Just awful. But what's that go to do with Chris-"

"Christian did it. Goddammit, Skippy. Christian shot Dag Drollet in the head."

I couldn't stand up. We reached to each other...and then Bill collapsed. Time just froze, solid. My mind traveled back, years... Bill was going with a stripper named Baba. On the surface, Baba was not only beautiful and fun, she had a heavenly body. Sadly, unable to believe anyone actually loved her, she overloaded her veins with drugs, till she could no longer live inside her body. Finally, doped up and shaking, she sat with me. I tried to help her kick the habit, but I couldn't do it for her, and she wouldn't do it herself.

One terrible night, worried when she hadn't shown up at the club, Bill and I went to her apartment. After knocking and banging, we feared the worst and kicked down the door.

But it was worse than we imagined. The living room floor was painted in blood. And there lay Baba's naked body, with a bloody .45 resting on her outstretched hand and – Oh, Jesus! Her head was severed from her body. I'd blacked out.

When I came to, all I could hear was the police saying, "the decedent" this and "the decedent" that. Baba had come home the night before, depressed and strung out, shoved a gun in her mouth, and blasted herself into oblivion.

Bill and I tortured ourselves with, "Should we have seen it coming? Could we have prevented it?" but nothing could bring back our sweet friend.

Oddly, Bill and I grew closer after that. Our mutual loss, ironically, strengthened our friendship.

Now, here we were again, caught up in another senseless tragedy.

In a fog of disbelief, I attend the hearing. In the chilly rooms of the Santa Monica Courthouse, the judge demanded: "Christian Brando, how do you plead to the charge of murder in the first degree?"

"Guilty, Your Honor."

Christian saw that the only way was the honest way, and he took responsibility for his actions, to whatever degree that was possible.

It's terrible he hadn't thought rationally before proclaiming himself the great equalizer, and ending a man's life. Cheyenne eventually admitted she'd fabricated Dag's beating her, hoping Christian would intervene in their domestic problems by roughing Dag up a bit.

Skip and Bill Cable with Christian Brando 2 days before he went to jail

Since she and Christian were never close, she didn't know his unpredictable state of mind when she toyed with his sympathies.

As the judge took the floor and finalized the inevitable, Christian was cuffed and led away.

I looked over at Marlon, who'd been still through the whole trial, staring straight ahead. Now, at the end, Marlon looked around the courtroom, at all the faces focused on him – the press, friends, well- wishers, curiosity seekers. And once again, I saw the sad man wandering aimlessly though the wildflowers.

Marlon later called a press conference, reflecting, "A sad event has occurred in our family. Death has visited the house of Brando," and then quoted Shakespeare on death's untimeliness.

Christian was sentenced to seven years in prison and visitations were limited to his immediate family. He called often, and we had long conversations about his future plans. He told me he wanted to live in the Northwest, become a fisherman again or work with trees.

Christian has served his time. He knows he's been given a second chance and he prays for forgiveness for the terrible tragedy he brought to Dag Drollet and his family.

Cheyenne's eventual suicide straddled the Brando family with more heartache. Christian has often told me his deep remorse and regret he can never reclaim the souls that have been lost forever, but he vows to live a life free from the selfish vices he once let control him.

Christian often called me "Dad" because he badly needed a father-figure in his life. I'll always think of him as my son.

We had a very, very unusual father-son relationship. At first, our association was nothing more than a girl-getting franchise. Beautiful women performed at my various talent shows, which Christian went to regularly. I don't know if he liked the show much, but he certainly liked the women who appeared in my showcases.

I would introduce him to one of the performers he liked, and he'd take the woman back to my apartment because at the time Christian was living with his father on Mulholland Drive. He'd make love to them on my couch. In some ways, Christian and I were a perfect match. He, like his father, was an exhibitionist, and I am a voyeur.

Christian used to call me "Hunchy," short for hunchback and a cruel reference to my appearance caused by scoliosis or curvature of the spine. I didn't like the nickname, but I put up with it because I did like Christian and even more because I felt sorry for him. He was just one of the many kids I called "Hollywood's Lost Boys," the neglected children of famous parents who were working all the time and ignored their offspring. They needed an older person to mentor them, and I was happy to oblige.

I don't think I ever saw Christian when he wasn't drunk and stoned out of his mind. On more than one occasion, after returning to my apartment with a pick-up from my talent shows, he'd say to me, "Hunchy, c'mon? Want to watch?" Although I was a voyeur, I wasn't particularly interested in these private performances because Christian was emaciated with the body of a young boy.

Maybe he inherited his exhibitionism from his father, Marlon, who also didn't object when Samia invited me to watch as she penetrated the star with a cucumber.

Like George Raft, Christian was a sexual sadist only more so. But instead of using a coffin like Raft, Christian found my couch suitable for his purposes.

He liked to beat up women, really smack them around while making love, if that's the right term for what went on at my place. Really freaky sex that shocked even me! His behavior in bed surprised me because everywhere else he was shy and never even talked about sex.

Besides serving as a father-figure to my lost boys, I also acted as an armchair psychologist, listening to them tell stories about their past they were too ashamed to disclose to anyone else. I learned from our mutual friend, soft-porn starlet Edie Williams and former wife of porno king Russ Meyer, that she had deflowered Christian when he was 14. Maybe that's why he took out his anger on other women during sex. I don't know because he didn't talk about sex with me, he just had it with me.

Christian crashed at my place when he was alone as well. He would sit on the couch in my living room naked and masturbate while watching porn videos. His favorite porn star was John C. Holmes. In a rare instance of sexual candor, Christian said he liked Holmes's videos because he had the biggest cock in town.

One night, drunk and stoned as always, he apparently got tired of watching porn and wanted a live performance. Naked as usual, he said, "Come over here and put your mouth on it." I tried to accommodate him but his dick was too large to fit in my mouth, so I ended up just licking it like an ice cream cone. After a while, I said, "I give up!" and stopped licking, which made me feel like a baby.

During another booze-soaked encounter at my place, Christian told me about his many half-siblings. According to Christian, one day a new maid came over to clean his father's home. Marlon awoke from a deep sleep and nonchalantly made love to the young girl, Maria Christina Ruiz. Eventually, Marlon fathered three children by the maid, a delicate little-girl type.

Every afternoon after she cleaned, she would go into his bedroom and wait for him to join her. It was a form of relaxation, a siesta with benefits. Marlon left money in his will to take care of her and the kids.

Eventually, Marlon bought Christian a run-down shack off Laurel Canyon Boulevard above the Sunset Strip. Like most substance abusers, Christian didn't consider housekeeping a priority. His place was a mess with trash strewn all over the place – a typical junkie's crash pad in a very pricy neighborhood like Laurel Canyon, except for the place his cheap father bought him – probably to get the kid out of the house.

Alcoholics and drug addicts typically seek out people with similar interests regardless of their social status. Years ago, Johns Hopkins University created 20 questions to determine if a patient has a problem with alcohol. Question No. 7 is "Do you turn to lower companions and an inferior environment when drinking?" Christian would have answered yes, if asked. He would pick up bums he met at the local market or on

Hollywood Boulevard and bring them back to his place to drug and drink.

Because I was instrumental in reuniting Christian with his mother, actress Anna Kashfi, who was married to Marlon for two years in the late '50s, Marlon hated me. But he hated his ex- wife even more because she had told him she was descended from Indian royalty. Her birth name was Johanna O'Callaghan. Her father had been a steelworker in London, where Anna worked in a butcher's shop before becoming a model and a moderately successful actress who co-starred with Rock Hudson in 1957's Battle Hymn, in which she played a Korean woman!?

Inexplicably, Marlon never forgave Anna for lying about her pedigree. When they got divorced, he used his power and money to get sole custody of Christian, whom he forbade to have any contact with his mother. I never knew anyone who hated a woman as much as Marlon did. Just because she wasn't a princess!

When Marlon found about my setting up a lunch date with Christian and his mother, whom he hadn't talked to in years, Marlon became furious – with me! Several times after that, thugs showed up at my door unannounced because my apartment building didn't have a security gate or buzzer. I didn't let them in, but they looked terrifying through the peephole. The men were tall and huge, probably Tahitian since Marlon owned an island in Tahiti. Through the closed door, the thugs would shout, "Stay away from Christian."

I was so frightened I stayed away from my apartment for weeks. Maybe I was just being paranoid, but as Henry Kissinger quipped, "Even paranoid people have enemies." I was never physically harmed by Marlon's minions, just shaken up.

During his son's trial for murder, Marlon glared at me many times. If looks could kill...

I was good friends with Bob Shapiro, O.J. Simpson's and Marlon's lawyer during Christian's trial. Bob was always the gentleman and treated me with kindness and respect. I told Bob, "If you need me to testify on Christian's behalf, let me know. I'm available." He later got back to me and said Marlon had categorically refused my help.

After Christian pleaded guilty to manslaughter and received a five-year sentence, I walked over to console him, but his father physically put himself between me and his son so I couldn't get near him.

I was there to witness the finally tragedy in a life filled with them. In 2005, Christian looked very ill, and I kept begging him to see a doctor. He brushed off my concern by saying it was just a cold.

It wasn't. Christian died of pneumonia in January of that year at the Hollywood Presbyterian Medical Center in Los Angeles. He was only 49.

Beautiful Anna Kafshi phones me often. A proud, decent woman subsisting on Social Security, she gives her time and goods to charity. A photographer once spied her coming out of a thrift store where she'd donated some clothing, and jumped on the phony "homeless Anna" story. Lovely as ever, Anna's working part time and volunteering with the elderly.

Despite the awful way Marlon treated her after their breakup, Anna refuses to say anything derogatory about him. She has too much class.

CHAPTER SIXTEEN

Skip to the Future

As interview number 8,000+ draws near, I know I've found my niche coming to know each woman and man as my friend – stars every one of them, whether their stardom's realized yet or not.

I look into eyes, touch a hand, interview with my heart – and the interview falls into place.

Throughout my career, I've loved being a one-man band, creating an idea, drawing in people to put it together. My cable show is a prime example. I've produced every show, created the lighting effects and over-all staging, and then turned everything over to a crackerjack team of engineers, directors and camera people...so I can relax...and the result is polished and professional.

That way, when I get home and watch the show, the only person I scold is "Skippy, oh Skippy, you jerk, shut up and let somebody else get a word in edgewise."

After the success of our Los Angeles show, people told us they wanted to see it all over the country. So, we took it to New York, San Francisco, Chicago, Washington DC...and beyond!

Today, we're still looking at Hollywood, but through slightly blood-shot, hopefully wiser eyes...and it's all just as exciting as the first show back in 1972.

Many of the legends disappeared from the public eye, so it delights me when they pop up and tell us our show helped them dust off their fading star and start anew. We all get such satisfaction from knowing we helped rejuvenate a career.

People tell me I've opened the doors for gay entertainers. If that's true, I'm grateful. I've experienced a lot of cruelty because of my homosexuality and the way people perceive me, but I've done my best to triumph over this, and learn from it.

For the longest time, it hurt me deeply. Now I simply refuse to give cruelty power. No one and no one's actions are worth my unhappiness. I do the best I can, in every situation, forgiving myself and others along the way. In the face of malice, I send a compassionate prayer, asking the universe to support this person out of his pain. I figure, if a person feels love, he'll be loving – toward me and others. If he's not loving, he's in a disconnected place more painful than I'll ever be. I walk on, thanking God and the universe for teaching me the wisdom of forgiveness, the blessing of generosity and the grace of appreciation.

Looking back over the years, I see a lonely, mixed up little boy learning to be a man who could spread some cheer, and was blessed along the way. I've tasted life, from the best to the worst, traveling around in this great, confused, upside down world. Throughout, I've met the most wonderful, colorful people, who taught and guided me. I've been lucky, wandering everywhere, taking my talents with me, never worrying about where that next croissant or rice cake would come from. I've been my own person, struck out on my own and hit pay dirt most every time. Not because I'm a genius, but because I've opened the doors, worked hard and joyfully, and let lady luck or God put it together for me.

Sure, I've been ripped off, abused, raped, scorned, and belittled, but

I've never stopped pushing on, and doing what I love most.

My future? Wide open. I'm still the boy with the "Betty Grable legs," ready to circle the world again, to see it through fresh eyes, and embark on a one-man show of my crazy Lowe-down life.

Who knows when my grand finale will come? I don't fear the final curtain. Whenever it's time to pack my bags for that heavenly tour, that great camera in the sky will zoom in on my lifeless head, heart, body and Betty Grable legs and I'll say, "Mr. Director, I'm ready for my ultra-extreme tight shot now."

Fade to black...basic black – and pearls, of course.

End of *Hollywood Gommorah*
April 3, 2014